RICO

How Politicians, Prosecutors and the Mob Destroyed
One of the FBI's
Finest Special Agents

by

Joe Wolfinger and Chris Kerr
with Jerry Seper

TELEMACHUS PRESS

Cover designed by Telemachus Press, LLC

Cover art:
Copyright ©Thinkstock/101345253/Hemera
Copyright ©Thinkstock/76800422/Creatas
Copyright ©Thinkstock/137216906/iStockphoto

Images:
#1 With permission, Connie Rico
#2 With perssmission, Connie Rico
#3 Public domain, Mass. State Police
#4 Public domain, United States Department of Justice
#5 With perssmission, Connie Rico
#6 With perssmission, Connie Rico
#7 With perssmission, Connie Rico
#8 Public domain, Mass. State Police
#9 Public domain, United States Government
#10 Associated Press, Fair Use

Published by Telemachus Press, LLC
http://www.telemachuspress.com

Visit the author website
http://www.RICOBOOK.COM

ISBN: 978-1-938701-64-1 (eBook)
ISBN: 978-1-938701-65-8 (Paperback)
ISBN: 978-1-939337-19-1 (Hardback)

Version 2012.1.05

Printed in the United States of America
10 9 8 7 6 5 4 3 2 1

ENDORSEMENTS

A great read on how narrow minded prosecutors and the government ruined the life and reputation of an FBI legend and hero. Great insight into how investigators and prosecutors can twist an investigation and the law to suit their own agendas.

–**J. Pistone**, aka Donnie Brasco, a former FBI agent who worked undercover for six years infiltrating the Bonanno and Colombo crime families in New York. His book on the experience, *Donnie Brasco*, became a best-seller and a top Hollywood film starring Al Pacino and Johnny Depp.

Two retired FBI agents, with long and distinguished careers, began investigating accusations against a former colleague. What they discovered was shocking malfeasance of justice—fed by media distortions and incompetent local prosecutors. The result is a compelling book that exposes what can happen when the scales of justice are stacked against a good man.

–**Kenneth Tomlinson**, former editor-in-chief Reader's Digest

H. Paul Rico was a good man, an outstanding public servant and an unsung American hero. He was the FBI agent who destroyed the highly profitable Raymond Patriarca Mafia organization in New England by sending Patriarca to jail twice. In the process, he helped create both the Witness Protection Program and the FBI use of informant plea-bargained testimony. He retired from the bureau critically aware of the dangers inherent in using informant testimony. Ironically, he was killed 30 years later in the course of a Boston press vendetta against the FBI by self-righteous law enforcement people who used false plea-bargained testimony elicited from an informant.

–**Alan Trustman**, co-owner of World Jai Alai Inc. and author of screenplays for several successful movies, including *Bullitt* and *The Thomas Crown Affair.*

This book is dedicated To Connie Rico and her family, whose loss of a devoted husband and father was not just a tragedy but a terrible injustice. May you take solace in the fact that your faith in him was well deserved.

Table of Contents

Dramatis Personae

Joseph "The Animal" Barboza: A feared serial murderer considered by his colleagues to be crazy, but who has the greatest potential to provide information to the FBI about Raymond L.S. Patriarca Sr., leader of the New England La Cosa Nostra crime family. Reputed to have killed more than 23 people, he later became a top FBI informant.

James J. "Whitey" Bulger Jr: The clever, ruthless and murderous leader of the Winter Hill Gang in South Boston, who fled to avoid a pending indictment in 1994 and remained an FBI "Top Ten Most Wanted" fugitive until his June 2011 capture in Santa Monica, Calif. He is a loan shark, robber, extortionist and serial murderer. His brother, William "Billy" Bulger, was the former leader of the Massachusetts Senate. Whitey Bulger was recruited as an informant by his boyhood neighbor, FBI Agent John J. Connolly, Jr.

John B. Callahan: Brilliant certified public accountant who attended Yale University and was a former Arthur Anderson and Co. partner, he liked "hanging out" with mobsters. A muscle builder and Olympic weightlifter, Callahan was regarded as a financial genius and he served as president of World Jai Alai Inc. until he apparently lost interest and his performance deteriorated. When he was discovered to have mob associates, he was forced to resign. He was the victim of a mob hit, his body left in the trunk of a car at Miami International Airport.

Dennis M. Condon: An FBI agent regarded by his fellow agents as incorruptible and as a person of the highest integrity. He was a partner with FBI Agent H. Paul Rico on several big cases. After retirement from the FBI, he served as head of the Massachusetts State Police and Secretary for Public Safety. He was described by his then-boss, Massachusetts Gov. Michael Dukakis, "as fine a public servant" as he had ever known.

John J. Connolly Jr: FBI agent assigned to the Boston field office from 1973 until he retired in 1990. He operated Bulger and other top mobsters as informants. Later corrupted by his informants, his case set off a firestorm of negative news coverage and speculation about widespread corruption in the FBI's Boston office. Convicted in 2002 on charges of racketeering and obstruction of justice, he was sentenced to 10 years in prison.

Stephen "The Rifleman" Flemmi: The co-leader of the Winter Hill Gang in Boston who murdered over 20 people and was described by several who observed him in court to "reek evil." Invited to join La Cosa Nostra, he declined and retained his independence in the Winter Hill Gang. He worked as an informant for Rico until he was indicted for a car bombing, for which he was acquitted. He later became an informant for Connolly. He pleaded guilty in 1981 in the murder of Tulsa, Okla., businessman Roger Wheeler.

District Attorney Timothy Harris: The prosecutor in the Wheeler murder case, who signed off on charges against Rico after first demanding more evidence from investigators. He opposed a request by attorneys for the seriously ill Rico to be moved from jail to a hospital. Rico died in custody, still shackled to his gurney.

Sgt. Mike Huff: The Tulsa Police Department detective who arrived first at the scene of the Wheeler murder at an exclusive golf club. He stayed with the case for more than 20 years. Although liked by many of his fellow officers, Huff appeared to be naive and to believe many of the uncorroborated allegations he was told regarding the Wheeler killing. When testifying in Congress, he blamed the breakup of his marriage on his involvement in the Wheeler case.

John V. Martorano: A murderous thug known to his colleagues as "The Executioner." He provided muscle for the Winter Hill Gang and murdered over 20 people. He was the killer of both Wheeler and Callahan. He also was one of the accusers of Rico in the Wheeler murder conspiracy. In return for confessing his murders, he received a reduced prison sentence of

14 years. In 2007, he was released from prison and given $20,000 to start a new life.

Austin McGuigan: Connecticut lawyer who served as the Connecticut Chief State's Attorney. He was described by his colleagues in law enforcement as a "barracuda for publicity." For 30 years, he had been cited as an expert on organized crime's penetration of gambling. In spite of never convicting or even charging anyone at World Jai Alai Inc. with any crime relating to the gambling business, he repeatedly provides quotes to newspapers about the penetration of the business by "organized crime."

H. Paul Rico: A legendary FBI agent assigned to the Boston field office in the 1950s and 1960s. He was eccentric and Runyonesque in his manner and appearance and had a talent for persuading people, including hardened criminals, to provide information. He may be the most successful FBI agent of his time. In the 1960s, his informants and cooperating witnesses devastated the leadership of the New England Mafia. Following his retirement from the FBI, he became head of security and then general manager at World Jai Alai Inc.

Roger Wheeler: The chairman and chief executive officer at Telex Inc. A multimillionaire businessman regarded as hard-driven and tough with a reputation for being difficult, he was the classic entrepreneur—tenacious and aggressive—who drove himself and others to the limit. Even though he was religious and opposed legalized gambling, even saying once he would vote against it if it came up in an election, he explored other gambling opportunities and he bought World Jai Alai Inc. with financing arranged by Callahan. He was killed by Martorano in Tulsa in 1981.

Fred Wyshak: An assistant U.S. attorney assigned to Boston who relentlessly pursued cases against Rico and Connolly. He was regarded as zealous, driven and a competent prosecutor, who often was overbearing, obnoxious and insulting for no apparent purpose. He and his top assistant, Brian T. Kelly, were characterized in the courtroom by Boston Magazine as "Batman and Robin"—the physically imposing Wyshak considered by many who worked with him as a prickly and brash Batman.

RICO

How Politicians, Prosecutors and the Mob Destroyed
One of the FBI's
Finest Special Agents

Chapter 1: The Murder

WEDNESDAY WAS ALWAYS Roger Wheeler's day to play golf at Tulsa's exclusive Southern Hills Country Club and this May 27, 1981, spring day was no exception. A 12-handicapper, the free-wheeling Tulsa-based businessman and multimillionaire felt at home on the Perry Maxwell-designed championship course, the site of three U.S. opens and an unprecedented four PGA championships.

The sun had filled the clear-blue sky. The chilly spring morning had warmed up considerably. A light breeze had begun to push its way through the course's natural twists, tiered greens and man-made doglegs, rustling the leaves of its massive maple and pine trees. Southern Hills, with its 67,000 square foot clubhouse at the top of a tree-lined drive, its fully equipped fitness center, two swimming pools, and four indoor and eight outdoor tennis courts fit a man like Wheeler like a custom-tailored suit.

After what Bob Allen, Wheeler's golfing partner that May 1981 day, said was "an exceptionally good day of golf," Wheeler—as was his custom—showered, dressed and shared a scotch with friends before leaving the clubhouse's rear exit to return to his office at Tulsa's Telex Corp. Inc., a highly successful software company where he was both chairman and chief executive officer.

The 55-year-old entrepreneur, who just three years earlier had acquired the Miami-based World Jai Alai Inc. (WJA) for $50 million, carried his heavy golf bag with its expensive clubs to the parking lot, where he loaded it into the trunk of his black Cadillac—as he had done numerous times before. It was about 4:30 in the afternoon. Children innocently played in the nearby swimming pool.

The two men who sat in the golf club's busy west parking lot in their late model brown sedan next to the swimming pool seemed out of place but went unnoticed. Parking near Wheeler's Cadillac, the men waited for him to emerge from the clubhouse. They knew he'd be there. They had his description, his tee time and knew how long it would take him to finish 18 holes of golf, get dressed and have a quick drink with friends.

They were there to kill him and Wheeler—described by his friends and associates as very cautious, almost paranoid—never saw it coming. As he sat down in the driver's seat of his car, Wheeler was approached by one of the waiting hired assassins, a heavyset, black-bearded man with dark sunglasses—who, without warning, shot him once in the face with a .38 caliber revolver. The shooter then quietly returned to the waiting sedan, jumped in on the passenger side and the vehicle sped out of the Southern Hills parking lot, passing through the ultra-private club's 61st Street entrance entry gate without notice. Those in and near the parking lot told police only that they had heard what sounded like a firecracker.

Married and the father of five children, Wheeler was dead at the scene. He had been slain with a single gunshot to the head, in broad daylight, at a prestigious private country club, with no witnesses to the actual encounter—an extraordinary event for Tulsa and its police department. In a city of less than 400,000 with an annual homicide rate of about 50, the assassination of a prominent citizen just doesn't happen and Wheeler was, indeed, a prominent, well-connected citizen.

Tulsa homicide detectives said Wheeler's body was found lying across the front seat of his Cadillac with several live rounds on both the seat and the ground. There were flash burns on his left arm, indicating he had tried unsuccessfully to shield himself from the shooter. This led almost immediately to speculation by police that an armed robbery had been attempted and Wheeler, trying to defend himself, might have dislodged the cylinder of the murder weapon, allowing the bullets to fall.

But the "armed robbery gone bad" theory quickly fell out of favor when police discovered more than $900 in Wheeler's wallet. Nothing else had been taken.

As chairman and CEO of Telex, which made computer terminals, tape decks and other electronic equipment, Wheeler commanded a corporate empire worth millions of dollars. Telex was described in a 1973 lawsuit brought by IBM as having experienced "a phenomenal growth in revenues." Under Wheeler's 15-year leadership role, the company's annual income rose from $5 million in 1965 to $165 million by 1980. He also owned seven other companies that dealt in resources ranging from oil to magnesium.

Tulsa Police Department Major Stanley Glanz, chief of detectives at the time of the Wheeler killing, and his team of investigators were suddenly confronted with a capital crime that was not at all typical of the routine homicides that occurred in Tulsa. The team proceeded cautiously to develop a theory and, as customary forensics examinations were being conducted and concluded, it began to discuss possible motives for such an execution-style slaying.

After only a single day on the case, Glanz—who eventually would spend 23 years with the Tulsa Police Department before being elected sheriff of Tulsa County—told reporters that the 11-member task force he created to investigate the death had not discounted any theory of why Wheeler had been shot, but the "speculation now is that it was an assassination, and even a paid assassination."

Adding weight to that theory was the fact that police could not locate the getaway car, despite having a partial listing of its six-digit Oklahoma license plate from a witness and having been able to compile a detailed description of the vehicle from others who had been in the Southern Hills parking lot the day of the killing.

Two days after the murder, a Tulsa police spokesman told reporters the task force investigation had focused on three possible motives: an armed robbery attempt by assailants who may or may not have known their victim; an attempt to abduct Wheeler that went bad; and that Wheeler had been the victim of paid assassins.

At the time, no one knew, of course, that more than 20 years later, the Wheeler family would still be looking for justice in the case or what role World Jai Alai's supposed nefarious underbelly had played in the killing. Wheeler had sought a cash cow in his purchase of the jai alai operation and what he got was much more: revengeful mob bosses, contract killers, allegations of skimming, organized crime and, eventually, charges of corruption and conspiracy involving one of the FBI's most successful and respected agents.

It was Wheeler who died that May 1981 day but more than 20 years later, the fallout from that killing would claim yet another victim, H. Paul Rico, an FBI agent whose investigation and cultivation of organized crime figures in the Boston area as informants and cooperating witnesses had become legendary in the 1960s and 1970s.

One of the Tulsa task force members was a young police corporal, Mike Huff, who had responded to the original call of the country club shooting and was first to arrive on the scene. And while others left the task force, went on to other jobs or retired, Huff eventually would become the officer responsible for the investigation—his dogged pursuit of the case extending over the next 20 years. He was on the case of his career.

World Jai Alai was known as a cash-producing proposition. Wheeler told Florida gaming officials that when he was negotiating to buy the operation, the previous owners said "Jai Alai is a real money-making machine." Wheeler told friends he knew there were "shady characters" inside the organization but his business-savvy and hard-driven management style would prevail.

Glanz also was aware that World Jai Alai had its dark side; a long-standing public reputation of being a corrupt gambling enterprise with longtime ties to organized crime. He summed up the popular wisdom regarding the business when he said, "There's no doubt that organized crime is involved with jai alai."

The Tulsa media quickly came to the conclusion that Wheeler's holdings in World Jai Alai was a possible explanation for the brazen daylight killing. But while task force investigators also were focusing on the possible ties between World Jai Alai, organized crime and the Wheeler murder, Glanz was quick to note that gambling authorities in Connecticut—where jai alai had an established foothold—reported that Wheeler had no known connection to organized crime.

A week after the ruthless killing, Tulsa police also acknowledged that they had been unable to find the getaway vehicle, which had been a prime objective. Leads had dried up. The case was going nowhere. But Glanz sought to keep the investigation open and based on fact rather than newspaper-driven speculation. He characterized as erroneous claims by a Tulsa television station that police had begun to concentrate on a theory that Wheeler had been killed by organized crime.

Wheeler, whose life ended as part of a systemic and well-timed killing conspiracy, was born in Reading, Mass., the son of a Boston newspaper proofreader. Described as energetic and business-oriented from an early age, he published a neighborhood newspaper at 14, ran a vegetable stand and organized a stamp-collecting service. At 16, he started a second business—hauling wood from Vermont—using a truck he bought on credit.

He served in the U.S. Navy during World War II and attended Rice University on the G.I. Bill, graduating with a bachelor's degree in engineering. He met his wife, Patricia, at an ROTC dance and impressed her when he repaired the jukebox so they could dance.

Wheeler rarely granted interviews, once explaining to a reporter that the stories could draw the attention of kidnappers. He said he felt comfortable surrounded by "FBI types" and employed six former agents at World Jai Alai. He considered himself a religious man, a good Presbyterian, and went to church every Sunday. "It's good self-discipline," he said. Baptized into the church with his wife as adults, he was active in many charities. He once gave a party at his home for the patients of the local Children's Medical Center.

But Wheeler had a tough side as well. He was viewed as a hard-driving businessman with a reputation for being difficult. Many said he could be unpredictable and abrasive. While friends conceded that he stepped on toes, they also said he had a genuine Midas touch with regard to business.

The New York Times described Wheeler as a classic entrepreneur—tenacious and aggressive—who drove himself and others to the limit in building an eclectic business empire. Although his name was associated with gambling after he purchased the jai alai operations, The Times noted he bought the operation purely for its investment value.

He rarely visited the jai alai companies he owned and had little interest in the sport, which at the time operated four frontons, or arenas, in Florida and one in Hartford, Conn. In a June 1981 article, Sports Illustrated referred to Wheeler as "the largely absentee owner of Miami-based World Jai-Alai Inc." The magazine also noted that friends described Wheeler as a "churchgoing man who found gambling personally abhorrent," but that he nevertheless had become attracted to legalized gambling for investment purposes.

Tulsa detectives had sought the help of the FBI in the Wheeler investigation. The New York Times reported that the bureau had been asked to check on Wheeler's far-flung business activities, adding ominously "including the jai alai holdings." A Tulsa police spokesman acknowledged at the time that while the FBI didn't have jurisdiction to investigate a local murder, it could assist by following up on state leads.

Just four days after the Wheeler killing, The New York Times asked in a news story if his purchase of World Jai-Alai had "anything to do with his death at the hands of a stocky, bearded gunman, wearing sunglasses, who left him sprawled, dying, across the front seat of his parked car?" The newspaper said jai alai had frequently been the target of corruption investigations and had been suspected of having ties to organized crime. It said a professional "hit" did not seem out of the question.

The jai-alai connection, The Times said, had led Connecticut authorities to reopen a dormant grand jury investigation into suspected underworld involvement in that state's three jai alai frontons. The newspaper said Chief State's Attorney Austin McGuigan confirmed that he had been assured by Gov. William O'Neill that he would be given the resources needed to revive the investigation.

"There are other theories, too, and the Tulsa police say that they are treating all as equal possibilities," The Times reported. "Mr. Wheeler may have been killed, they say, when a robbery or kidnapping attempt went awry. Wealthy people always live with those potential dangers. Still, it is the jai-alai connection that continues to arouse the most speculation."

Lest anyone think Wheeler would have backed down from a challenge by external threats to his jai alai investments, they should have been forewarned. In fact, the difficulty of doing business with him was demonstrated in 1979 when a prominent San Francisco lawyer asked a federal appeals court to enforce a contingent fee arrangement that Wheeler found to be, after the fact, too generous.

In 1973, according to court records, Wheeler and Telex won a $259.5 million antitrust judgment against IBM, but two years later, the 10th Circuit U.S. Court of Appeals reversed this decision, deciding in favor of IBM. The court awarded the computer company $18.5 million damages, prompting Wheeler to hire one of the best appellate lawyers in the country to take the case to the U.S. Supreme Court.

In hiring Moses Lasky, senior managing partner at the well-known San Francisco law firm of Brobeck, Phleger & Harrison, Wheeler insisted on a contingent fee arrangement, resisting Lasky's normal hourly fee agreement. After some negotiation, Lasky reluctantly agreed with the stipulation that if he actually filed the case with the Supreme Court, a minimum $1 million dollar fee was due. After some substantial preliminary work, Lasky filed the case.

Meanwhile, Wheeler and his in-house counsel worked behind the scenes and obtained a "wash settlement" with IBM, in which each side walked away with nothing. Wheeler promptly reneged on his agreement to pay the $1 million dollar fee and Lasky took him to court—a dispute that resulted in a protracted legal fight and a loss for Wheeler, but a case that is now studied in law schools around the country.

Brobeck, Phleger & Harrison v. Telex Corp. often is cited in rulings showing that the courts have consistently upheld "creative fee agreements when they are not unconscionable, irrespective of the novelty of the payment scheme, or the absence of risk."

It is, of course, not difficult to imagine the outcome of that dispute if it had been with organized crime figures—who would not have used the courts to settle their differences but employed a more vigorous means.

Chapter 2: The Arrest

MORE THAN 22 years had passed since multimillionaire businessman and entrepreneur Roger Wheeler had been shot dead in the parking lot
of a prestigious, ultra-private Tulsa country club. That had not been lost on
the handful of homicide detectives who had spent much of their careers
investigating the case.

Certainly not Tulsa Police Detective Mike Huff, now a sergeant, who
found himself in the south Florida village of Miami Shores in the pre-dawn
hours of Oct. 10, 2003, leading a squad of seven police officers up the
walkway to the two-bedroom, two-bath ground-floor condominium of
retired FBI Agent H. Paul Rico.

Within sight of Biscayne Bay, the officers pounded loudly on the front
door in the 4 a.m. darkness and when the 78-year-old former agent and his
wife, Connie, opened it, they rushed inside.

"I'm Sergeant Mike Huff," announced the Tulsa detective, although he
hardly needed an introduction since he and Rico had met and talked before.
Then a 28-year veteran of the Tulsa Police Department whose dogged two-
decade pursuit of the Wheeler case had become legendary, Huff informed
Rico he was under arrest for conspiracy in the May 27, 1981, murder of the
Tulsa businessman—killed at the exclusive Southern Hills Country Club in
Tulsa with one shot in the head from close range in full view of children
playing in the country club's crowded swimming pool.

Some of the officers who took part in the raid said Huff's demeanor
was harsh and tough. One Miami police officer took note of Rico's feeble

condition, even suggesting to his wife that he should be dressed warmly, eat something before he was taken to jail and that she should prepare a package of his medications to take with him. Rico, who retired from the FBI in 1975, had long suffered from a cardiac condition and had a pacemaker.

At one point, Connie Rico berated the officers for not arranging to meet with her husband instead of storming their home, saying her elderly and sick spouse would have presented himself whenever and wherever they ordered. In a private note, she said her husband did not say one word during the time he dressed and ate, and that "only one Miami police officer had any semblance of kindness."

The officers said Huff seemed immensely pleased to finally be making an arrest in a case he once acknowledged in sworn testimony before a House committee that had both "consumed and obsessed" him and had "destroyed my family." He also told the House Committee on Government Reform in December 2002 that the Wheeler case may have been sabotaged by corrupt or indifferent FBI agents, adding that the Southern Hills club where Wheeler was killed had been picked as the murder site by organized crime figures "with an assumption that the Tulsa Police Department wouldn't solve the case."

"They were wrong," he boasted to the committee, continuing with a tirade against murderers and those law enforcement authorities like Rico whom he said had helped kill Wheeler: "I have spent nearly one-half of my life working murder cases, and I am sickened by the thought of law enforcement officials, or anyone else for that matter, protecting murderers. They are scumbags that should be locked up along with the killers."

The early-morning raid on Rico's home was the culmination of a two-decades long obsession. It was vindication for Huff.

But Rico's arrest surprised many within the FBI and the law enforcement community. A renowned and often-commended FBI agent whose work in the bureau's Boston field office in the 1950s and 1960s was legendary, he was known for the development of high-level government informants and cooperating witnesses whose use devastated organized crime in New England. One federal judge who also worked as an organized crime strike force prosecutor said Rico had dealt such serious blows to the New England crime syndicate that it had not fully recovered in over forty years.

Rico, who through his attorney "flat-out categorically" denied any involvement in the Wheeler killing, had been commended by FBI Director J. Edgar Hoover and other bureau officials for his role in a bank robbery case involving James J. "Whitey" Bulger Jr., boss of a crime syndicate in Boston known as the Winter Hill Gang. Following his capture, Bulger was sentenced to 20 years in prison for robbing banks in Massachusetts, Rhode Island and Indiana.

The Wheeler investigation spawned other surprises and concerns with regard to Rico. The circumstances surrounding the issuance of the arrest warrant for the retired FBI agent were, at best, unusual. The warrant itself was issued by a family court judge—selected, according to Huff, because he was trusted not to leak information in a sensitive case.

But it wasn't a secret to anyone involved in the Wheeler investigation that Rico was in line to be charged in the killing—certainly not Rico, who could have fled if he was so inclined. Tulsa County District Attorney Tim Harris had already brought charges in the Wheeler murder against Bulger and Winter Hill Gang members Stephen "The Rifleman" Flemmi and John V. Martorano. Huff had asked that Rico be included in that original charging information, but Harris refused, saying he needed more evidence.

The Tulsa newspapers also had alerted those connected to the case that prosecutors were considering charging Rico.

Several veteran law enforcement officials also described the Rico arrest in Miami Shores as unusual. Early morning, heavy-handed arrests are typically used against dangerous criminals who are likely to resist or with whom the element of surprise is important. Many law enforcement authorities said an arrest directed against an elderly man with an unblemished record who is not likely to flee was an indication that prosecutors or investigators were seeking to shock or even punish a defendant before trial.

Evidence presented in an affidavit filed in court by Huff on which the Rico arrest warrant was based was very strong concerning several career criminals involved in the Wheeler murder, according to an examination of the document. The affidavit said Martorano admitted to law enforcement officers that he was the bearded man who shot and killed Wheeler in 1981 in the parking lot at the Southern Hills golf club.

Martorano said a well-known Boston mobster, Joseph "Joe Mac" McDonald, then on the FBI's "Top Ten Most Wanted" fugitives list, was the getaway driver, and that two other career criminals, Flemmi and Bulger, were co-conspirators. McDonald, who always carried a one hundred dollar bill in one hand and a longshoreman's hook in the other, died of a stroke in 1997 after being released from prison.

In addition, Martorano said John B. Callahan, former president of World Jai Alai Inc. (WJA), the company Wheeler purchased in 1978 for $50 million, was a co-conspirator. Callahan, a Boston-based certified public accountant and financial wizard who attended both Boston College and Yale University, had helped arrange the sale of the WJA to Wheeler. The six-foot, 275-pound Callahan, a one-time Olympic weight lifter, was found dead on Aug. 2, 1982, his bullet-riddled body stuffed in the trunk of his Cadillac in a parking lot at Miami International Airport.

Regarded as a person with a quick wit and a warm, engaging personality, Callahan had left World Jai Alai in 1976 after two years as its president. His departure came after Connecticut law enforcement authorities began an investigation into his suspected ties to organized crime figures in Boston, particularly the Winter Hill Gang, with whom he had been seen fraternizing. The FBI also was looking for Callahan for questioning when his body was discovered.

A former partner at the Big Five accounting firm of Arthur Andersen and Co., Callahan was described by friends and associates as one of the best financial minds in the city. They said he worked hard but was criticized for having a short attention span. And despite his professional accomplishments, they said he had a penchant for hanging out with gangsters.

Court records show that Martorano told authorities that Callahan was part of a group trying to buy the WJA from Wheeler. According to an affidavit in the case, Callahan wanted Bulger, Flemmi and other members of the Winter Hill Gang to protect the company from other organized crime groups. In exchange, the affidavit said, Callahan offered to pay the Winter Hill mobsters $10,000 a week—to be skimmed from parking concessions.

But it's questionable whether World Jai Alai would have needed protection from other organized crime groups. At the time, Rico and at least five other retired FBI agents were employed by the company and it is unlikely they would have been intimidated by an organized crime threat or that they would have permitted a skim to occur. Callahan would have had to fire the former FBI agents and pay $500,000 annually in protection to the Winter Hill Gang.

While a review of the affidavit shows that it is strong on probable cause concerning Martorano, Flemmi, Callahan, McDonald and Bulger and their involvement in the Wheeler murder, it is conspicuously thin in linking Rico to the conspiracy. The accusations against the veteran FBI agent consist of allegations by convicted mobsters seeking to save themselves from lengthy prison sentences.

Flemmi, incarcerated at the time of his interview, told investigators that in 1965 he worked for Rico as an informant in Boston. He said Callahan told him that he and Rico wanted Wheeler killed. Martorano corroborated Flemmi's statements, saying Callahan delivered to him an envelope-sized piece of paper containing information that included Wheeler's description and location.

Martorano, who acknowledged in an arrest affidavit that he had not met with or spoken to Rico before the murder, said Callahan told him the source of the information on Wheeler was Rico. Martorano certainly had no concerns he would be contradicted on this point since he had killed Callahan a year after the Wheeler murder.

Bulger, Flemmi and Martorano were lifelong criminals, members of the Winter Hill Gang. Rico had known of them since his assignment to the Boston FBI field office in the 1950s. In fact, he had recruited and operated Flemmi as an informant and had arrested Bulger on bank robbery charges. The three mob members were involved in a variety of criminal activities including extortion and robberies. Bulger was the leader of the gang and was reputed to be a ruthless killer. His brother, William M. Bulger, was the president of the University of Massachusetts and former leader of the Massachusetts State Senate.

Court records show that Martorano described himself as the "chief executioner" for the Winter Hill Gang and admitted killing over 20 people. He told law enforcement authorities he never kept count of how many people he had killed, adding that "until in the end, I never realized it was that many."

Flemmi, who earned his nickname "The Rifleman" as a soldier during the Korean War, had close associations with both Irish and Italian mobsters in Boston. Court records show he had a close partnership with Bulger, for whom he served as a front man—collecting money and inspiring fear in those who didn't pay their debts on time. Flemmi admitted to authorities he took part in 10 murders and acknowledged that he probably committed twice that number.

On its face, the suggestion that Rico was needed to provide Wheeler's description and location is unsupported by the facts. While Rico had never been to Tulsa, Callahan had helped Wheeler acquire the WJA. He knew the Tulsa businessman's description, home address, office location and that he played golf on Wednesdays at the Southern Hills Country Club. Callahan certainly had no need to get that information from Rico.

Rico also was an experienced organized crime investigator who understood the vulnerability of discussing criminal plans over the telephone, when anyone could be listening in. But Flemmi told investigators that in May 1981, he had a telephone conversation with Rico in which the former FBI agent confirmed over the phone that he and the others wanted Wheeler killed. Unclear from the available documents is why Rico would have taken the risk in a developing criminal conspiracy of involving himself in a telephone conversation with a well-known criminal who the veteran agent would have known could be subject of electronic surveillance at any time.

Flemmi and Martorano had killed as many as 40 people and both were providing information to prosecutors to get themselves out of murder convictions in Oklahoma, a state that since reinstatement of capital punishment in 1976, has boasted the highest execution rate in the nation. One law enforcement officer assigned to transport Flemmi noted that when confronted in court, Flemmi "reeked evil like a real top shelf bad guy." Prosecutors knew it would have been difficult to obtain a conviction using mobsters such as Flemmi as witnesses against a former FBI agent who had an exceptional background fighting organized crime.

Rico once speculated during a conversation with his wife that Callahan may have told members of the Winter Hill Gang in Boston with whom he was associating that they were small-time criminals and if they could get into jai alai, they could break into the big-time. Rico thought they were "gullible" enough to think they could run the whole thing. Privately, Connie said, her husband questioned why he had been pursued so vigorously by the people working the Wheeler case.

On the afternoon of the day of the Rico arrest, Huff went unannounced to the WJA, where he interviewed Dan Lecciardi, general manager who had worked for Rico at the company for more than 20 years. In a 30-minute conversation, Huff discussed whether Rico could have been a part of the Wheeler murder plot and was assured by Lecciardi—who was unaware his former boss had already been arrested—that Rico could not have been involved. At the conclusion of the conversation, Lecciardi said Huff walked to the door, stopped, turned and dramatically announced, "Oh, by the way ... I just wanted to let you know that we just arrested Paul."

The Rico family, which had always been close, was shocked and dismayed by the arrest. Born in 1925 in Cambridge, Mass., into a distinctly middle class family, Rico was raised in Belmont, Mass., ironically less than 20 miles from Wheeler's birthplace in Reading, Mass. Rico's father was employed for 30 years at the local telephone company as a wire supervisor—a secure job that produced a quality middle class life.

Rico had begun dating Connie Sloan when she was 14 and they became, as she described, very good friends, hanging out together and occasionally cutting class and skipping school. She described their relationship as teenagers as all very innocent and typical for the time. She said she first met Rico after he transferred to Belmont High School from a private school so he could play football. When another girl pointed him out as the new boy in school, she told her, "He's very handsome."

At the time of his arrest, the two had been happily married for over 50 years. They have five children; Joyce, a medical doctor; Melissa, a nurse and a lawyer; Suzanne, an engineer; Christine, a social worker; and John, also a lawyer. The children had kept a scrapbook filled with news articles about his cases and accomplishments.

On the day police carted her husband off to jail, Connie Rico reached out for help to the group with whom she and her husband had always been close, the Society of Former Special Agents of the FBI. Joe Frechette, a former FBI agent who was a close friend, also accompanied her to the jail to visit her husband. She later described the visit as an "awful experience," saying everything that could have gone wrong did.

After "waiting and waiting" to see her husband, she said he appeared in a small room the size of a telephone booth with a glass window separating them. The light was out and the phone didn't work, making it impossible to communicate either by voice or even by sign language. Later, Rico discovered he could make collect calls so the couple "talked a lot" on the phone—almost every day.

As practicing attorneys, two of Rico's children, John and Melissa, got themselves placed on the list at the jail of Rico's lawyers. While the jailers knew John was Rico's son, they did not know Melissa Ferrari was his daughter. Melissa, also a former nurse, was able to assist her aging and ill father and also gave him haircuts, pedicures and manicures. The Miami jailers had assumed that Melissa, who was practicing law in Germany, was part of the Oklahoma law firm that had been engaged by Rico and at one point, when they asked her how an attorney based in Oklahoma could spend so much time in Florida, she explained that she was part of the "global division."

While in custody, Rico often was transferred to Jackson Memorial Hospital in Miami, where his medical condition was assessed and treated. Rico had earlier been diagnosed with serious medical problems. He had severe coronary disease. Ten years earlier, he had undergone bypass surgery. He had a heart pacemaker and, prior to his arrest, had developed atrial fibrillation, an abnormal heart rhythm. He also suffered from diabetes and was under a very complicated daily regime of medicines.

When a person is arrested in Florida on a felony warrant issued in another state, they are entitled to a probable cause hearing before they can be extradited. For first degree murder, no bail is set in Florida, however, until the defendant is returned to the state in which they were charged. Rico's attorney knew if the witnesses against him, Flemmi and Martorano, died before trial, their preliminary hearing testimony could be used against his client. He sought a delay in the preliminary hearing until he was prepared to cross examine them vigorously.

But the delay request was a serious mistake as Rico's health declined so precipitously that his survival in jail became doubtful. In December 2003, Rico waived extradition to get to Oklahoma where he could have a preliminary hearing and bail could be set. On Dec. 7, 2003, Rico was hospitalized again after suffering severe injuries his attorney said were the result of an attack and beating by other inmates.

Miami jail officials denied he had been beaten and attributed the bruising over most of his body to an incorrect dose of a blood thinner he was taking. Five days later, his attorney filed a motion in Oklahoma for bail or a medical furlough, noting he was not a threat to the community or a threat to flee. In the motion, the attorney described Rico as a 78 year-old retired FBI agent with severe medical problems who had always responded to subpoenas and requests for testimony.

The motion included 39 letters written on Rico's behalf by FBI agents who had served with him. The motion noted that even career criminals like Mafia bosses Raymond L.S. Patriarca, Peter Gotti and Thomas Gambino had sought and received pre-trial releases. The Rico motion was denied.

On Dec. 19, 2003, Rico's attorney filed a new motion requesting that his client be assessed for mental competence to stand trial, adding that as a result of the beating by inmates he had suffered delusions in which he saw snakes coming out of the walls. In early January, 2004, a gravely ill Rico was transported by the Tulsa County Sheriff's Office to Oklahoma—his first visit to the state.

Glanz, who had been chief of detectives for the Tulsa Police Department at the time of Wheeler's murder, was now Sheriff of Tulsa County and, although at the time he did not oversee the jail and corrections, his deputies transported prisoners. Glanz said he did not feel good about the charges against Rico and, in light of his weakened physical condition, ordered that he be transported by private plane and ambulance.

The Tulsa County sheriff's deputies who transported Rico said they found him to be a pleasant, upbeat person. Throughout the trip, they said they engaged the former FBI agent in small talk. Rico asked about the weather in Oklahoma, the jail and what would be happening to him when they arrived. When they got to the plane, he asked if they had a deck of cards so they could play on the trip. They said he did not seem threatened, threatening or particularly anxious.

One deputy remembered that Rico seemed to have an "air of innocence" about him. The same deputy transported Flemmi to court in Tulsa, noting that when he was around Flemmi, he knew he was in the presence of a bad guy. Things didn't seem to faze Flemmi at all, the deputy said, adding that he remembered commenting to a new sheriff's deputy that he should watch Flemmi closely.

Was Harris, the Tulsa prosecutor, also closely watching? Was he worried he was relying primarily on two witnesses in his case against Rico who were admitted murderous thugs and looked so much like what they were that a deputy sheriff could recognize it just by being around them? His coming showdown with Rico, speeding at him like the bullet that killed Wheeler, would be an interesting one.

Chapter 3: The Hearing

H. PAUL RICO'S defense attorney, Garvin Isaacs, passionately pleaded for medical treatment for his client, saying he was seriously ill with congestive heart failure. He asked Tulsa County District Court Judge Carlos Chappelle to grant an emergency medical furlough so the 78-year-old retired FBI agent could prepare for his day in court.

Isaacs said Rico, who had been named on conspiracy charges in a high-profile, 22-year-old Tulsa murder, was anxious to prove his innocence.

"I am telling you this man is sick, extremely sick," the Oklahoma City-based attorney told the judge during a Jan. 16, 2004, hearing called to determine whether Rico should be ordered to undergo a mental competency examination. Isaacs argued that Rico had recovered from a recent beating during his incarceration at the Miami-Dade County Jail, had regained his mental composure and now wanted to withdraw a Dec. 19, 2003, motion to determine competency.

He warned the court that in light of his client's rapidly failing physical condition, it should move quickly to a preliminary hearing and the setting of bail.

"He's in a weakened condition. Every day he gets weaker," Isaacs said, noting that Rico was in grave danger medically. He asked the judge to keep the much-decorated former agent alive so he could defend himself against the charges, and argued that Rico should be admitted to a private Tulsa hospital where he could be treated by specialists and get his strength back. He assured the judge that any further delay would make a trial moot.

The motions denied, Isaacs pleaded again for the court to at least order that the shackles be removed from Rico's legs. He said there was no reason for the prosecution to oppose such a request unless it wished to inflict further pain and suffering. A defendant normally is entitled to bail if he is not a threat to flee or a danger to the community. At 78 and infirm, Rico was neither.

Once again Judge Chappelle denied the motion. Rico died a few hours after the hearing, at about 11:45 p.m., still shackled to his bed. Tulsa police confirmed that Rico died alone with jail guards outside his room.

The death angered a number of retired FBI agents, including Samuel "Mike" McPheters of Moses Lake, Wash., who called it "an atrocity." The 30-year bureau veteran, who had investigated everything from organized crime figures in South Florida to homicides on Indian reservations in the Northwest, said he had last seen Rico just days before his arrest in Florida and "he was doing fine. This whole thing just precipitated his death."

McPheters, a bishop in The Church of Jesus Christ of Latter-day Saints, the Mormons, said Rico "had to die for something that no one knows he ever did." Two dozen other agents wrote letters to the Tulsa court to register their displeasure with the case, only to be dismissed as blind loyalists.

John F. Kehoe, former Massachusetts Public Safety commissioner and an FBI agent in Boston for 29 years, also defended Rico as a "very capable and tremendous agent" who was very adept at developing informants. "I don't think he ever did anything that went over the line," Kehoe said. "He stayed within the bounds of the bureau and the regulations that we all lived by."

A different eulogy was being offered by Tulsa County District Attorney Timothy Harris, who told The Boston Globe on learning of Rico's death, "I believe all parties wanted a trial and a verdict rendered by a jury. It's not the closure desired or expected by law enforcement. But life holds different turns and I don't think anyone could have expected this."

Later Harris, a graduate of Oral Roberts Law School, spoke more candidly to another Oklahoma lawyer, saying, "We did our part and God took care of the rest."

Tulsa Detective Sgt. Mike Huff, who had doggedly pursued Rico for more than two decades and ultimately arrested the retired FBI agent at his

Miami Shores condo in October 2003, told The Boston Herald, "We wanted our day in court, too. This wasn't a guy that had one bad day that he made a slip up and somebody wound up dead. This was something much more complicated." The conspiracy was much deeper.

"It's unfortunate for people to not get to hear this story and come to their own decisions and conclusions about what happened," Huff said. "We did our job and we'd do it all over again."

During his pre-trial arguments, Isaacs had questioned Harris' adamant and unrelenting opposition to a medical furlough, pointedly asking whether the prosecution hoped the former FBI agent's health would deteriorate to the point that his guilt or innocence would not have to be addressed. Isaacs said Rico, who had a pacemaker and had undergone three bypass surgeries, was disoriented after being beaten by unknown assailants in the Miami-Dade County Jail, but had recovered his mental competency since being moved to the Tulsa jail and "wants a jury trial to clear his name."

Making note that Rico had lost 53 pounds during the three months since his Florida arrest, Isaac told the court the accused agent had his own medical insurance and, as a result, his treatment wouldn't cost the State of Oklahoma anything; it would, in fact, save the state the expense of dealing with his many medical issues. He also noted that all of the witnesses who testified during the pre-trial hearing, including the sole prosecution witness, had agreed that Rico was mentally alert.

Rico was not in the courtroom during the hearing, but on a video feed. He sat in a wheelchair and said nothing. Isaacs offered to take the proceedings to the hospital room where Rico was being held but Harris opposed the motion and Judge Chappelle once again ruled in favor of the prosecution. Ultimately, Judge Chappelle delayed the preliminary hearing in the case for three weeks, saying he wanted a psychological evaluation by the court to see whether Rico was fit to stand trial.

Veteran courtroom observers viewed the order as unusual, almost unprecedented, noting that while defense attorney Isaacs wanted to withdraw his Dec. 19, 2003, motion to determine competency because of the beating at the Miami-Dade County jail, prosecutors were looking to proceed to a competency hearing.

Typically, defendants try to prove their mental incompetence in order to avoid trial; it is extremely rare in a pending criminal case that the prosecution does not accept a defendant's claim that he is mentally competent and ready to stand trial. Surprisingly, Judge Chappelle didn't just rule that the prosecutors should proceed to the preliminary hearing, he also wanted to hear testimony about Rico's mental competence.

Dr. John Richard Smith, board-certified psychiatrist who had assessed mental competence in as many as 150 prosecutions and civil trials, was the first witness. He described visiting Rico the day before and finding him shackled to a bed with an oxygen tube around his neck that had been left unplugged. He said Rico's hands and feet were cyanotic, meaning they were bluish in color from a lack of oxygen. He said Rico was so weak his water cup kept falling out of his hand. He advised the on-duty staff that Rico needed oxygen and a nurse started the oxygen machine.

In a two-hour interview, Dr. Smith said Rico demonstrated that in spite of his weakened physical condition, he was clearly mentally competent. The doctor said the former FBI agent knew court procedures, the judge's role, the prosecutor's role and the jury's role. "He was very able to very quickly and easily explain all of those things," the doctor testified.

Dr. Smith also said Rico spoke of his family; noting that he was devoted to them and missed them. He said Rico also displayed a sense of humor despite his difficult circumstances. He said he was not surprised Rico had been unable to fully recall the incident in which he was beaten and bruised and couldn't say precisely what had set off the deliriums he had suffered. But Dr. Smith told the court he was confident Rico was now fully fit and competent to stand trial.

Rico's wife, Connie, testified that they were a close family after 52 years of marriage. A registered nurse in her own right, she confirmed that her husband had lost more than 50 pounds since his Miami arrest, that he had congestive heart failure, that he developed pneumonia after he was incarcerated, and that he was in an extremely weakened condition.

She said that despite his declining physical condition, he was mentally alert and competent. The day before, when she visited him, she said he told her he was eager to prove his innocence and that the man she had known for almost all of her life said "let's get this going ... get me to trial."

Melissa Rico Ferrari, a practicing attorney and registered nurse, proved that she was her father's daughter during her testimony at the pre-trial hearing. In an obvious fight for her father's life, she wasn't about to back down. And even as the system faltered, court records show she never failed him.

Now living in Germany, she had traveled to the United States on three occasions to visit her father following his October 2003 arrest, once at Thanksgiving, three days in late December and the day before the court hearing. When she saw him in December 2003, he was in a Miami hospital after he had been assaulted by the jail inmates. He was suffering from pneumonia as a result of being shackled to a bed with four-point restraints. He had been immobilized for several weeks and, as a result, had developed pneumonia.

Ferrari argued that while her father was mentally competent during her December visit, his physical health had declined dramatically. She told Judge Chappelle that her father appeared to have aged over a decade in the month he had been held, that his health had continued to spiral downward and the day before, when she visited him in Tulsa, he couldn't raise his head from his pillow. She told the judge, "My father's real goal is to survive ... to prove that he is innocent."

But the prosecution sought to show that Rico was manipulating the system, with Harris' arguing that Miami-Dade jailers had attributed Rico's bruising to an incorrect dose of blood thinner. He rejected the idea that an aging former FBI agent would be attacked by inmates in a jail. That animosity between the prosecutor and Rico's daughter was evidenced during a cross examination of Ferrari by Harris, during which the following exchange occurred:

Harris: Since he suffered from delirium of which no one knows the cause, it's certainly a possibility that he can suffer delirium at any time, it seems to come and go. Would you agree with that?

Ferrari: No. Because ...

Harris: Okay.

Ferrari: ... he had ...

Harris: Thank you.

Ferrari: … delirium …

Harris: Thank you, Ma'am.

Ferrari: … only on one occasion that I am aware of at this point.

Finally, Isaacs objected that the prosecutor was trying to cut the witness off and, according to court records, Judge Chappelle agreed. Courtroom observers said it was obvious that Harris was eager to suppress any information that conflicted with the state's view of Rico, but that Ferrari would and could not be bullied by him.

A day earlier, Harris had noted that Rico had been transferred to a Tulsa hospital from the jail and asked Ferrari if she thought her father was now receiving good medical care. She applauded the decision to move him, but said it should have been made sooner. She characterized the Corrections Corporation of America, which operated the Tulsa County jail, as having taken "terrible medical care of my father in order for him to be in the situation he is in now."

She testified that the corrections management provider, which houses more than 80,000 inmates in 60 separate facilities, didn't have a listing of her father's medications, noting that he had been on a very complicated medical calendar for years, during which medications were given at specific times and on different days.

Dr. Joyce Rico, a doctor, also confirmed her father's health decline, but said he was mentally competent and most anxious to have an opportunity to clear his name. When Harris read to her on the stand portions of Isaac's motion for a mental competency examination that characterized Rico as "delusional, paranoid, anxious and confused," she testified that the words related to a specific time and event—adding that at the present time, her father's mental competency was not at issue.

Just before ending his case, Isaacs offered again to take the court to the hospital to interview Rico, a motion that once again was declined by Judge Chappelle.

Prosecution witness Kathleen Eckenrode, health administrator for Corrections Corporation, testified that she observed Rico for less than a week but was confident she had documented several examples of his "manipulative behavior." She said during his video arraignment when the camera came on, he began making grunting noises that stopped when she inquired if he was okay.

Eckenrode, a registered nurse with 25 years experience including 13 in correctional administration, firmly rejected the idea that Rico could be seriously ill and in a dangerously weakened condition. She said when he came into the institution, he was uncooperative and feigned weakness. She said at other times, she observed him sit up on his own. She said, "What concerned me was he was acting so weak and feeble."

She also complained on the stand that Rico had manipulated another nurse accompanying him to get an x-ray into leaning over to expose her "awesomely endowed" cleavage. She said she immediately took charge, telling Rico and the nurse, "We're not going to do that here."

Asked under cross examination if she though Rico could think rationally, Eckenrode said, "like a 70-year old geezer, yes." She also acknowledged under questioning by Isaacs that she had met with Harris, the prosecutor, earlier in the week to discuss the Rico case, but denied violating the Health Insurance Portability and Accountability Act's medical privacy regulations by discussing Rico's personal health information. She said she only discussed his behavior. Eckenrode also testified that she never talked with defense lawyers or family members of inmates.

Isaacs then asked Eckenrode to describe the policy of the Corrections Corporation about meeting with lawyers who represent an inmate. Since she had admitted that earlier in the week she met with Harris and his assistant, Isaacs followed up by asking if she met with them because they are prosecutors. She explained that the prosecutors had followed procedures, to which Isaacs argued that there seemed to be no such procedures for defense attorneys.

In summing up, Isaacs advised that the defense had withdrawn its request for an evaluation of Rico's mental competency and that the former agent wanted a jury trial to clear his name. He said he was gravely concerned about Rico's health, adding "He's in a weakened condition. Every day he gets weaker."

Several healthcare experts have questioned the circumstances of Rico's death and the medical treatment he received at the hands of the Corrections

Corporation. They noted that when Rico left the hospital in Miami for Tulsa on Jan. 8, 2004, he was stable. Records show his condition deteriorated with his treatment in Tulsa, culminating in a fatal renal hemorrhage caused by excessive anti-coagulants.

The Corrections Corporation's medical staff at Tulsa, responsible for treating him, permitted Rico to become dehydrated, which, according to the autopsy report, caused his body to accumulate blood thinners that resulted in the hemorrhage that led to his death.

After his death, Rico's body was sent to a funeral home rather than the medical examiner's office. It is highly unusual that his body would not have been released directly to the medical examiner when it is common knowledge among health care professionals that any death of a person in custody is automatically a medical examiner case.

It was the opinion of one medical professional who reviewed Rico's autopsy report that his medical care was apparently so poor as to warrant a re-examination of the nursing licenses of those responsible for it. It was almost as if someone said "make sure this guy doesn't make it out of here alive."

Veteran law enforcement authorities familiar with the case said a passionate prosecutor and a zealous detective, both convinced that two murderous thugs were telling the truth and a former FBI agent was not, caused Rico to be arrested, held in deplorable conditions for three months and subjected to questionable medical care. From the moment he was taken into custody until the time of his death, they described the ordeal as an arrest and punishment without a trial. They said Rico's death may have saved prosecutors and investigators from the embarrassment of a trial.

In the end, Tulsa County officials attempted to bill Rico's health insurance for his medical treatment and hospital stay. Connie Rico declined to authorize the insurance payment.

More than 400 FBI agents, along with former agents and friends, attended Rico's funeral Mass at Saint Rose of Lima Catholic Church in Miami Shores.

Chapter 4: Getting Started

H. PAUL RICO'S career as an FBI agent began in February 1951 and, in four short years, his work in the field prompted a supervisor to note that he had done "perhaps the most outstanding job of any agent in the office on the informant program." Rico was handling five approved informants, three of them described by the bureau as "better than average," and had come up with information that led to key arrests in major bank robberies in Massachusetts, Rhode Island and Indiana.

In one performance appraisal, a senior FBI supervisor in the bureau's Boston field office said Rico "has demonstrated unusual talent in developing new informants and directing these informants so they will be productive." While it usually takes a few years of work before an agent can master the unique job of being an FBI investigator, Rico—in short order—had become one of the most productive agents in one of the largest FBI offices in the country.

FBI agents, like other law enforcement professionals, know that the most important attribute of a first-rate investigator is the ability to persuade criminals, would-be witnesses, suspects and others to provide information and that a surprisingly large number of people can be persuaded to talk if they are handled carefully and skillfully.

Rico learned that lesson quickly and his efforts did not go unnoticed, certainly not by the FBI and other law enforcement officials. He was commended six times in letters from FBI Director J. Edgar Hoover for contributions he made to various criminal investigations. Those investigations included significant bank robberies, a Brinks armored truck robbery, a variety of thefts from interstate shipments and the capture of important fugitives.

He was promoted early to grade 12—just below the top of the bureau's general pay schedule for agents assigned to investigate cases. The promotion came in recognition of sustained quality performance, significant informant development and his contribution to locating and arresting Boston-area organized crime boss James J. "Whitey" Bulger for bank robbery. His work in developing informants and cooperating witnesses who solved still another bank robbery was recognized with a $300 award. Two Boston-area police chiefs and the Cambridge, Mass., District Attorney also commended Rico's work in separate letters in 1955 and 1956.

Rico's successful FBI career surprised no one, certainly not his family and friends. He had always been an overachiever, a competitor, tough-minded and determined. As a teenager, he transferred from a private school to Belmont High School, just outside Boston, so he could play sports. A popular student, he became one of the school's football stars, even though the team suffered its share of losses. One local newspaper account of a Belmont loss to another school described Rico's play at guard as "sensational."

In the fall of 1943, after football season ended, Rico dropped out of high school and joined the U.S. Army, determined to get into the fight. Even his enlistment showed the true measure of his character. While in his senior year at Belmont, Rico suddenly began to avoid his longtime girlfriend, Connie Sloan. The two of them had been nearly inseparable, spending much of their time together both at school and after. But suddenly he stopped asking her to be with him and dropping by her desk to talk as he had done in the past. He seemed to be distant and aloof.

Finally off to join the Army, Connie was left wondering why he had avoided her for several months and worried about whether he would return, what he thought of her and whether they would ever be together again.

But the behavior of the then-18-year-old Rico was meant to protect Connie in case something happened to him—revealing a pattern of conduct that would dominate his life, one in which he repeatedly took problems on himself, not burdening his worries and concerns on his family.

During World War II, Rico served in Italy in the Army Air Corps as a radioman and gunner in a Consolidated B-24 Liberator heavy bomber. He fought in the battles of the Po Valley, North Apennines and Rhineland and was awarded several medals, including three Bronze Stars. His service ended in December 1945, when he was honorably discharged as a staff sergeant.

Rico rarely talked about the war and his family didn't know that he had been awarded the Bronze Stars, the fourth-highest combat award of the U.S. Armed Forces. His service record shows only one small imperfection; he was reduced from corporal to private for being AWOL the day after Christmas in 1944. He explained he was 29 hours late in returning from a three-day pass due to transportation snags. He earned the rank back fighting in Italy.

When Rico returned from the war, Connie was working in York, Maine, for the summer as a waitress. He asked around to find out where she was and one day, she said, he simply arrived unannounced at her restaurant. Connie thought it was wonderful to see him again and they immediately resumed their relationship. Only after he returned safely did she learn the reason he had avoided her before he left for the war.

Connie graduated from Simmons College in Boston where she studied nursing. Rico completed high school and then attended Boston College on the G.I. Bill, also benefiting from the federal government's "52/20 Program" in which GIs received $20 a week for 52 weeks to attend college. At Boston College, he played on the chess team that won the national championship of Jesuit schools. He also found time to raise $1,400 among the merchants of the Town of Belmont for a semi-professional football team to represent the community. He played for three years on the team.

While at Boston College, he majored in history and graduated in 1950. He worked as a wine steward in his uncle's restaurant but disliked the work. When Rico and Connie went out on Fridays, they often would see a show and she would be home by 10 p.m. Since he always got her home so early, her parents loved him and thought he was the perfect boyfriend. In fact, Rico, who loved all sorts of games, would drop her off to go to a Friday night poker game. He loved games and competitions of every sort: football, poker, horse racing, chess and board games. Once, when he learned that some of the guys in the neighborhood who arranged hunting trips actually did very little hunting but played poker, he joined their "hunts."

A gambler by nature, he had a facility for numbers and odds and often was a winner, but never gambled enough to affect his family negatively.

In 1950, Rico applied for the FBI, a career move Connie thought might be difficult. She remembered the days they skipped school and thought the bureau would not take him—after all, she thought he wasn't the straightest kid in high school. But she was wrong; he had an unblemished record, had served honorably in WWII, and had graduated from a first rate university. He had shown considerable initiative for a young man in raising money for a Belmont semi-pro football team and finding time to practice and play while he was at Boston College.

The only thing negative on his FBI application was his response to a question that asked if any disciplinary action had ever been taken against him during the course of his scholastic career. He admitted being detained after school on occasion for being late to class, for talking in class and for cutting school. Hoover had high standards but these were hardly the sort of infractions that would bar one from an FBI career.

A background investigation generated favorable results and Rico, then 25, was hired by the FBI as a special agent on Feb. 26, 1951. The bureau discovered what everyone already knew: Rico had the attributes necessary to succeed as an agent; he was smart, socially adept and had a strong sense of humor. He knew how to deal with people and had the ability to gain the confidence of those he met. His colleagues described him as having a helpful nature and an easy conversationalist.

Rico met Hoover when he attended new agents training; at the time, all trainees were introduced to the director and shook his hand. There is no indication in Rico's official personnel file that the two ever met again. FBI legend says the introductions of new agents were designed to allow Hoover to weed out the ones he viewed as undesirable. Hoover's influence was so great that lore has it that at one session the director identified one of the new agents as "the pinhead" without further identifying who he meant. The class counselors were puzzled but were afraid to ask the director for clarification, so—setting out to solve the dilemma—the counselors reviewed the hat sizes for each member of the class to identify the person about whom Hoover was talking. Apparently, no such event occurred in Rico's class meeting with Hoover.

Rico completed the eight-week new agents training course on April 21, 1951, and was assigned to Chicago, his first FBI field office. He married Connie on the same day he graduated and they moved to Chicago six days later. The couple honeymooned in Niagara Falls on the way and once they arrived in Chicago, Connie found employment as a nurse.

At the time, a new FBI agent would typically be assigned to his first office for one year where he would handle applicant investigations and relatively uncomplicated criminal cases. Rico's initial assignment was no different and in March 1952, he was routinely transferred to Pittsburgh where he would expect to stay for several years. But shortly after he arrived in Pittsburgh, doctors determined that his father had inoperable chest cancer and had about six months to live. Rico requested a hardship transfer to Boston, saying his wife was a trained nurse and could help his mother and since his only sibling, his brother, was still a minor, he would have to assist his mother and father financially.

While the FBI under Hoover was efficient, it could be harsh, but sometimes it functioned compassionately. Rico's request was granted at FBI headquarters in Washington just two days after it was made and his office of assignment was changed to Boston—a move he would, under government policy, make at his expense rather than the bureau.

He arrived in Boston before the end of April and was assigned to Criminal Squad #2 where he handled a variety of criminal cases particularly investigations dealing with thefts from interstate shipments. Most agents at the time wanted this type of assignment since working criminal cases was where the action was and an agent could see the results of his work. The goal was to build a case, make arrests and go to trial.

Rico's first Boston performance appraisal was unremarkable except for the fact it noted he was aware of the importance of informants and was in the process of developing five potential criminal informants. Informant development and handling are difficult and many experienced agents never develop good informants, considering that the effort requires an agent to persuade a person to give information about the criminal activities of their friends or associates who might kill them if they find out.

An agent with that ability has a gift and Rico's expertise in developing good informants, particularly early in his career, was a rarity in any group of investigators and was prized by astute supervisors who understood the importance of informants and cooperating witnesses to building a first rate criminal investigative program. Five potential criminal informants were excellent production for a relatively new agent.

When Hoover took over a relatively unimportant and corrupt national law enforcement organization known as the Bureau of Investigation in 1924, he had 440 agents. He moved quickly to professionalize the agency and enhance its capabilities and reputation. He didn't get an increase in the number of agents for ten years, actually dropping to 400 agents in 1934.

By the time Rico joined the bureau, Hoover had renamed the agency the "Federal Bureau of Investigation" and had built it into one of the most powerful and respected law enforcement organizations in the world. Since 1934, the FBI has grown steadily, with more than 4,000 agents on board during WWII to address war-related national security investigations and intelligence operations. Today, the FBI has 13,847 agents and 21,678 support professionals, including intelligence analysts, language specialists, scientists and information technology specialists. They are assigned at FBI headquarters in Washington, D.C., 56 field offices in major cities throughout the U.S., 400 smaller resident agencies in cities and towns across the nation, and more than 60 international offices in U.S. embassies worldwide.

By the time Rico began to work for the FBI, Hoover had been the director for 27 years and was in total control of the bureau. Over the years, Hoover made countless rules and regulations that prescribed every aspect of FBI work. For everything that went wrong, Hoover's system ensured that someone was held accountable. Lack of success and failures were almost always found to be attributable to a personal failure of an FBI employee; the system could produce someone who was responsible for everything that went wrong. For serious infractions, an agent could be fired or subjected to reduction in grade or a disciplinary transfer, where he and his family were uprooted and transferred sometimes to an office thousands of miles away.

Minor infractions not perceived by most agents as serious were usually handled by a letter of censure from Hoover admonishing the culprit. There were so many minor infractions and consequent letters of censure that street agents interpreted them differently than Hoover might have expected. Most agents agreed that if you didn't get an occasional letter of censure, you probably weren't working very hard and everyone in the system understood that the more you did, the more you were exposed to the possibility that things could go wrong.

Bad things could happen to an agent who was working hard. Accidents, Acts of God and harmless mistakes did not happen in Hoover's FBI and such things certainly didn't excuse failures. Communications between the field offices and FBI headquarters were prepared by agents in the field but all were captioned as between the special agent in charge (SAC) of the field office and the director. A routine report prepared by an agent in the Boston field office to FBI headquarters would be from "SAC Boston" to "Director FBI" and every day thousands of documents addressed to "The Director" from the SACs throughout the country flowed into FBI headquarters.

Hoover, a voracious reader of FBI communications, frequently made notes in FBI files but could personally review only a small fraction of these communications. The headquarters staff would select items they thought should be brought to the director's attention and summarize them for him. Hoover read summary memorandums; he did not often read raw file material. Similarly, field SACs actually saw very few of the communications that were captioned as coming from them; subordinates approved them and SACs relied on their subordinates to call the important ones to their attention.

Rico was not immune from the onslaught, occasionally responsible for one infraction or another among the myriad of the bureau's sacred rules. In 1953, around the time his father died, Rico placed his revolver in a desk at the Boston field office and could not find it again for several months. FBI furniture was Spartan; agents used look-alike, grey metal desks. Apparently, while he was out of the office, the furniture was rearranged and Rico's desk was moved.

Rather than promptly bringing the loss to the attention of FBI head-quarters and turn himself in as the rules required, Rico did what most agents of the time would have done—he searched for the revolver believing he would find it. After two months, finally convinced he would not find it, he reported the loss. The details of the incident were summarized for the director, who wrote of the delay reporting it in the headquarters file:

"This looks like a rather gross lack of a sense of responsibility in the Boston office. Get all facts promptly. H." And when the director weighed in on such a matter, there was simply no chance a street agent could escape. But after reporting himself, Rico found the gun located in a desk in the office where it had been since he put it there. Its finding did not save any-one who had touched the case. He received a letter of censure for not promptly reporting the misplaced gun.

Several other agents who had assisted him in searching for the gun each received letters of censure for not reporting him and his loss. Rico's supervisor, who did not immediately call it to the attention of the SAC, was censured even though the SAC described him as the "most capable supervi-sor in the Boston office." The assistant special agent in charge (ASAC) was censured for lax administration of the office that allowed a service revolver to be lost and not reported immediately to the SAC. The fact that the gun was finally located in a desk in the office and was never really out of FBI control made no difference.

In the FBI culture of the day, everyone knew that a misplaced piece of equipment, even a gun that was finally located in an FBI office, was not a cardinal sin. Further, a good supervisor would never turn in a successful subordinate agent until he had a chance to find his missing equipment. An agent's fellow agents would always pitch in to help in such a situation. Let-ters of censure under such circumstances had little sting.

Rico's favorable performance appraisal in 1954 noting his work in dealing with informants also made note of the censure for the missing gun. It was less than a parking ticket in an otherwise laudable FBI career that spanned 24 years.

Chapter 5: Demonstrating Success

THE TWO MEN entered the bank shortly before noon, both wearing masks. One pointed a pistol at the customers inside and forced them up against a wall. The other kept them at bay with a sawed-off shotgun while his partner vaulted over a counter and scooped up about $13,000. As quickly as it had begun, it ended—the men fleeing to a black Packard waiting outside with a young woman as the getaway driver.

The November 1956 robbery at the Baltimore National Bank and Trust Company offered little in the way of clues for the law enforcement authorities who responded. Little, that is, until FBI Agent H. Paul Rico demonstrated his unique investigative skills to solve not only his own cases but those of his fellow agents.

One of the robbers was a recent escapee from a Massachusetts state prison after a running gun battle with guards. Another was an escaped federal prisoner and an armed robber sought by Massachusetts authorities. Rico produced an informant who identified the men, giving the information to FBI agents in Baltimore. Using Rico´s information, the Baltimore agents located the getaway car and tracked it to a motel where they learned the two gunmen and the driver had made a number of telephone calls to a Boston phone used by a known criminal associate.

Newspapers reported at the time that a teenage girl and two men among "the most dangerous criminals at large" had been apprehended. A snub-nosed .38 caliber revolver, a sawed-off shotgun and a large supply of ammunition were found in the motel. The two men previously had told authorities they would shoot any police officer or FBI agent trying to arrest them. In the end, they were, as so many blustery criminals are, taken without resistance.

For his work, Rico was presented a $300 Incentive Award and a letter of commendation from FBI Director J. Edgar Hoover. While in today's terms such an award seems small, at the time it was a substantial cash award and acknowledgement of a remarkable contribution to an important case. Compared to an agent's salary in the 1950s, the award in today's currency represents about $4,000.

Although identifying the suspects in a bank robbery case is, of course, the most important step in bringing such an investigation to a successful conclusion, it wasn't enough for Rico. Following the investigation that ranged between Baltimore and Boston, he developed one of the gang's Boston associates as a second informant. In January 1957, he had persuaded his new informant to travel with him to Chicago and Minneapolis where the informant located the three bank robbery subjects who were arrested in a mass raid by police and FBI agents.

By the end of the decade, Rico—who used his remarkable street skills to develop high-quality informants—was regarded as one of the best agents assigned to the Boston field office. He was frequently called on to work high-profile, complex cases. He often contributed significantly to solving many of the cases assigned to agents throughout the office and was often the subject of official commendations.

In his first ten years with the bureau, he had developed and refined the ability to deal with all sorts of people: from the most ruthless criminals to the top echelons of society. He talked with everyone and was smart enough to listen to what they had to say. He never talked "down" to people, particularly the criminals he assessed as potential informants.

Rico's method of developing informants was simple: he went to the places where criminals hung out and engaged them in conversations. He spent time visiting bars and restaurants and the horse and dog tracks often frequented by criminals. He kept informed on the activities of the criminals in Boston and would let them know he knew what was going on. At some point, he would look for an opportunity to break a potential informant away from the others so he could pitch him. His whole persona contributed positively to the good results he achieved. He was from Massachusetts and had the right accent and manner of dealing with people. He appeared to criminals to be tough, smart and knowledgeable. They respected him.

Probably the most important of his attributes was the fact that he believed inherently he would succeed in persuading criminals to cooperate with him. Many agents and detectives just don't believe they can succeed in persuading hardened criminals to become informants. Rico understood that under the right circumstances, an agent can persuade almost anyone to be an informant.

Rico was an intelligent, skillful interviewer with very unique abilities to spot people who would be likely to cooperate, to understand their motivations and then to persuade them to assist him in his investigations. He would prepare carefully for an important interview and would master the facts of whatever crime he planned to discuss with a potential suspect or witness. He would occasionally purposely misstate the facts to see if the person would correct him. He was interested in the truth.

Over the years, naive critics of law enforcement's handling of informants have commented negatively on the fact that agents have often used bad people as informants. Experienced investigators know that almost all good informants are themselves bad people. Obviously, this is because to gain information about crime an informant must be trusted by criminals and in order to be truly trusted he must be one of them. Boy Scouts can't tell you much about crime, murder or the Mafia; you have to deal with people who have done terrible things themselves to develop good information about crime, murder and the Mafia.

Under the FBI system, the highest level criminal informants were graded as "Top Echelon," or TE informants. To be a TE informant, the person must have provided high quality information and must be in the center of an ongoing criminal enterprise. Such persons are invaluable but difficult to control and handle. Experienced agents like Rico understood and appreciated the difficulties inherent in handling good informants and they carefully weighed and evaluated what they were told.

Rico knew informants are motivated to cooperate for many reasons, but they almost always cooperate for their own benefit. They tell you what they want to tell you. An informant may be motivated by the desire for revenge, to save himself from prosecution, to save himself from other criminals, to reduce competition, for the simple excitement of providing information to the FBI or just to make some money for the information provided.

Informants tell what they want, no more, and they put their spin on what they say. Informants lie, tell the truth, tell half-truths, exaggerate and embellish. Experienced agents understand this and evaluate what they're told carefully. Everything an informant tells an agent must be verified. Good agents know that in spite of the difficulties that informants present, they can solve the most important cases and no first-rate law enforcement agency succeeds without good informants.

The FBI system under Hoover placed the primary responsibility on field agents and supervisors to make the right judgments in handling informants and their information. The squad supervisor had the responsibility to know about all the pending cases and the identities of all the informants. The supervisor would be able to evaluate what the informants said and balance how far they were allowed to go with their continuing criminal activity. When agents seemed to be getting too close to their informants, the supervisor was responsible for dealing with the situation.

Most informants actively involved in crime don't tell the agents handling them about those crimes or ones they are about to commit. It is understood that a very quick turnoff would occur if the agent began to interrogate the informant about his activities. So while Rico and his fellow agents and their supervisors understood that their informants were involved in crime, often they did not have the facts to know precisely what crimes they had committed unless another source provided that information. And it was understood that snitches were "on their own" if they got caught.

The Hoover system required agents to document their contacts with informants and to record what they were told. Information about planned crimes and violence was particularly difficult to handle. When an informant provided this kind of information, supervisors and agents would develop a strategy to warn or somehow protect the intended victim while also protecting the identity of the informant. There was no standard answer—there really couldn't be since every case is different. A potential murder victim might receive an anonymous call warning of the hit, the police might be notified of the crime or the victim might be contacted by an agent and warned directly.

Since he entered the FBI, Rico demonstrated that he had an interest and facility for developing informants. He had an appreciation for the complexity of dealing with informants and he clearly understood the nuances of dealing with informants and their information. He knew an agent had to verify what they said—an agent didn't just take information provided by an informant and act on it without corroboration. Rico was smart and he excelled in this complex, often dangerous but critical area of FBI work.

While Rico was successful and received recognition and reward for his hard work, he was still subject to the FBI system under Hoover, which subjected agents to a system of inspections, oversight and countless rules and regulations. Particularly vulnerable were agents who displayed strong initiative and who were active in sensitive and difficult cases. Often the people who were the best at developing informants and solving the big cases were the worst at doing the little administrative things required by the system.

In 1957, Rico stumbled twice and, in spite of his rising status as one of the better Boston agents, he was not shown any partiality. He was treated just as any other agent would have been.

The first incident came after he was assigned to handle the robbery of the National Shawmut Bank of Boston in September 1956. Rico asked the bank manager to provide a list of "bait bills," which are those bills that have been recorded by the bank and often are useful in proving the money recovered from a robber was stolen from the bank. The banker didn't provide just a list of bills stolen, but without describing it as such, he provided a master list of bait bills, including money that had not been taken in the robbery. In the trial, the list caused some minor confusion but it was sorted out by the jury. The convictions were attained and the judge commented that the jury "seemed to have done a better job than the district attorney or the FBI." The judge's remark appeared in the newspaper and Hoover, who was very protective of the FBI's reputation, read about it and ordered an inquiry.

The subsequent inquiry led to a memorandum analyzing the situation and recommending that Rico be censured. Hoover, himself, approved the recommendation and in June 1957, Rico received a letter admonishing him "to carry out your assignments with greater care and closer attention to detail."

At the time of the recommendation letter, the Boston field office was undergoing an inspection during which case files were examined and another Rico error was discovered. Inspectors found that although all information that was required had been collected and recorded in one of Rico's informant files, a master checklist had not been completed. Failure to complete a checklist was an extremely minor thing but in July 1957, Rico was censured again in a second letter from Hoover calling on him to "afford closer attention to pertinent detail ..."

It seemed that everyone but Hoover understood that such letters addressed minor issues and mistakes. While the letters were surely annoying to the agents who received them, a letter of censure over such an insignificant oversight really did not carry much weight within FBI field operations. It is common knowledge that the agents handling the most significant cases and contributing the most to their investigative results were also the most vulnerable to such minor oversights and errors. So, while Rico continued to be held in high regard by his supervisor in Boston and, most importantly, his fellow agents, he was, at the time, as vulnerable to the FBI system as anyone else.

One story that circulated among Boston agents who worked with Rico in the late 1960s says that he was at the top of his game as a successful agent when an inspector asked why he had failed to sign out one evening when he worked late. Rico authored a memorandum of explanation that he entitled, "I FORGOT WHY I FORGOT TO SIGN OUT." Apparently, the inspector had a sense of humor and nothing came of it.

In 1957, Rico got a sample of what an agent could expect from Hoover during an active career. By the year's end, he had received one letter from Hoover that lavished praise for his investigative accomplishments and conveyed what was then a sizable cash incentive award, two letters that censured him for administrative errors, and a fourth offering sympathy on the death of his mother.

By the end of the decade, however, Rico's supervisors gave him their highest rating, "Outstanding," for his participation in the informant program. At the time, he was handling three approved informants and had three more under development. According to one supervisor, Rico demonstrated outstanding ability at identifying, developing and utilizing informants and his informants were regularly providing good information on criminal matters.

It was typical in the FBI in the 1950s and 1960s that agents initially were assigned to their first field office, where they would remain for about a year—where it was expected that they would make mistakes while going through the initial process that is critical in learning a complex job like that of an FBI agent. Agents would then be transferred to a second office, leaving all their rookie mistakes behind. In that regard, Rico stood tall among his peer group of agents.

Considered young enough to be enthusiastic and experienced enough to have acquired the skills essential to success, Rico was admired and thought of as one of the most productive agents in the Boston field office.

Chapter 6: The Boston Office

JOHN F. "JACK" Kehoe joined the FBI on Dec. 8, 1941, the day after the bombing of Pearl Harbor. A graduate of Boston College, he knew the bureau would be looking for agents to counter the growing threat of espionage. After assignments in field offices in New York, Los Angeles and Phoenix, he landed in at the bureau's Boston field office, where in 1962 he took over as head of the Organized Crime Squad.

Agents who worked for Kehoe were sure of two things: He knew exactly what he was doing and, more importantly, he knew what the agents on his squad were up to. Energetic, experienced, smart and capable, Kehoe was one of the major reasons the Boston field office became so effective in the 1960s in combating organized crime, where a loose confederation of organized crime figures had become one of the most successful crime syndicates in American history.

As the squad supervisor, Kehoe had the responsibility for ensuring that the Boston field office's organized crime investigations were producing results and that the right cases were being worked by the right agents. He also oversaw the recruitment and handling of the squad's informants. Unlike his successors, Kehoe had an uncanny knack for understanding the capabilities and needs of the agents on his squad and he matched those agents with assignments to ensure they had the right developmental experiences.

It was well-known within the Boston field office that Kehoe understood there were limits on how far the FBI could go in approving the activities of its informants and that some sensitive situations required the involvement and approval of the federal prosecutors who took the cases to court. He was not hesitant to direct agents to take sensitive issues to the prosecutors for approval before they proceeded. Exceptional supervisors tend to encourage and mentor the development of exceptional agents.

One of the agents on Kehoe's Organized Crime Squad was H. Paul Rico, who had worked on various squads in the Boston field office supervised by the special-agent-in-charge and the assistant-special-agent-in-charge. In the late 1960s, his well-established reputation as an outstanding investigator in an office filled with young agents destined to move ahead to senior positions in law enforcement and elsewhere was put to the test as a member of Kehoe's squad. It was a test he would not fail.

Rico and his frequent FBI partner, Dennis M. Condon, were two of the squad's most senior agents and they soon became its most successful. They handled important and often critical interviews and developed informants, witnesses and cooperating persons who helped solve big cases. The hard-charging and dedicated two-man crew would become the driving force enabling the squad to dismantle New England's infamous organized crime empires.

Condon was regarded by his fellow FBI agents as talented, capable, helpful, hardworking and a man of impeccable integrity. According to fellow agents, he was a "choir boy." By contrast, Rico was much more flamboyant and much less conscious of the minor rules that plagued agents.

After his retirement from the FBI after 26 years, during which he received more than 30 commendations including 10 Meritorious Awards, Condon went on to serve with the Massachusetts State Police as Commissioner of Public Safety and later as Undersecretary of Public Safety in the Executive Office of Public Safety under then-Gov. Michael M. Dukakis. During his FBI career, he personally located and arrested five criminals on the bureau's 10 Most Wanted List, an achievement which has not been equaled by any past or present agent.

Rico and Condon's impact on FBI Agent Sean McWeeney, who later would rise to become head of the FBI's Organized Crime and Drug program where he was responsible for more than 1,700 agents, was deep. McWeeney had about four years experience as an agent when in 1969 he was transferred to the Boston field office. He immediately was assigned to handle organized crime investigations in the Providence, R.I., resident agency, which reported to Boston.

At the time, Rico, Condon and Kehoe were based in Boston, but were required to be highly active in Providence because Raymond L.S. Patriarca, boss of the New England Mafia, resided in that city. Rico and Condon developed great informants and cooperating subjects who provided information that had a major impact on the investigation of Patriarca and his mob family. McWeeney quickly became the "go between" for Rico, Condon and Kehoe and Providence.

McWeeney, whose 24-year FBI career also included a stint as head of the bureau's Office of International Affairs, which manages all of the FBI's international investigations, thought that while Rico and Condon were very different personalities, they complemented each other. Rico was a flashy dresser who looked more like a mobster than an agent. Condon was a salt of the earth kind of guy who wore dark suits and white shirts. In spite of their differences, they worked successfully together as a team.

McWeeney regarded Rico, Condon and Kehoe as "cream of the crop" guys who worked hard, were successful, made a huge impact on serious crime and had fun doing their job. It was an environment that many agents found invigorating: hard work, challenging cases and great accomplishments. McWeeney and most of the other Boston agents looked forward to going to work every day; it was an exciting place.

At the time, the Boston informant system was highly protective of individual identities. Agents did not reveal to each other the identities of their informants and, as a general rule, they didn't protect their informants from other agents' investigations. Kehoe knew who the informants were and if someone were to develop a case on a productive informant, Kehoe was expected to evaluate the quality of the case against the quality of the information being provided. If the cases weren't important enough, he used them as a motivator to gain additional cooperation.

Typically, Rico followed the other agents' cases and, when they needed information, he tasked his informants to produce it. Rico was careful to fully and accurately document the information his informants produced.

In 1970, one former FBI agent assigned to the Boston field office described Rico and Condon as "giants of the bureau on a different plane" than the newer agents. They set the example for the young agents—working big cases for long hours and obviously enjoying the job. They were enormously successful and their work was legendary, credited by one informed observer as dealing such serious blows to the New England Mafia that it had not fully recovered in over forty years.

Kehoe made work assignments to ensure that the newer agents worked alongside the more experienced Boston agents so they would learn "what's going on." An assignment to work with Rico or Condon also provided the new agents an opportunity to also learn how to skillfully conduct a penetrating interview or handle an often elusive and sometimes dangerous informant.

William C. (Bill) Ervin, who later served as the special-agent-in-charge of the FBI's Indianapolis field office, also was assigned to the Organized Crime Squad in Boston in the 1960s. Ervin remembered Rico as being tremendously successful in developing informants who produced quality information. Rico's principal method of recruiting informants was to be where they were and to get to know them. In spite of his tough veneer, Ervin said he found Rico to be gracious and humble, with a helpful nature. He said Rico did not "socialize" with his informants but he did believe you had "to be in their face" to be successful at developing information. He said Rico learned an agent had to be where the criminals and would-be informants hung out and it was important to let them know that you knew things about them.

Ervin, who also served as special-agent-in-charge of the FBI's Honolulu field office, recalled that Rico and Condon served as mentors to the newer agents, adding that Rico was approachable and a "nice quiet guy" who didn't like petty bureaucracy. When Ervin brought a case against Peter Limone, a Boston-area Mafia boss, to a successful conviction, he said Condon led the applause by presenting him with a bottle of wine. Ervin said he thought it was an exceptionally nice gesture from a senior, well respected agent to make for a younger agent. He said praise from Condon or Rico meant a lot.

It was well known in Boston that Rico, who eventually did not work cases but only handled informants, marched to his own beat. Although normal working hours were from 8:15 a.m. to 5 p.m., he would show up in the office at 10 or 11 in the morning and he might not sign in. He often worked late into the evening. He wore suede shoes, a bow tie and a sport coat at a time when the FBI was all about blue suits, white shirts and dark red ties. His relationship with informants was close but, as far as anyone knew, he never compromised investigations. As his informants provided information, Rico would pass information to others in the office about crimes that had happened or were going to happen.

David L. Divan, who later became head of the FBI's Public Affairs Unit at the bureau's Washington, D.C., headquarters, served on the Boston Organized Crime Squad in the late 1960s. He remembered Condon and Rico as stars, although he thought Rico's dress habits made him appear more like a character out of a Damon Runyon Broadway play than an agent of the period. He said Rico was short, stocky, a bit overweight and constantly smoked cigars. Divan said Rico presented quite a picture, noting that while Rico was on the "cutting edge," Condon was very responsible, even tempered and kept the team in balance.

But Divan noted that underneath the facade, Rico was regarded by his fellow agents as a warm and nice person. He said Rico took time to mentor him and other new agents on how to deal successfully with criminals and informants. Divan also recalled meeting Rico's family and said the veteran agent was devoted to his wife and children.

Rico spent much of his off duty time with his extended family often pursuing his interests in horse and dog racing. During the 1950s, when one of his children was born and it was customary for new mothers to remain in the hospital for several days, Rico and his 17-year-old cousin went to the horse track, then visited his wife, Connie, and his new baby in the hospital. They went to the dog track that evening.

At the time, since his cousin was only 17 and too young to get into the Suffolk Downs track, Rico wasn't timid about breaking what he must have thought a silly rule—he acquired a pass from one of the track employees and let his cousin use it to get in. Even though his cousin was rather obviously of Irish descent and the name on the pass was "Redondo," Rico didn't hesitate. But he did instruct his young cousin "to tell the truth" if he was challenged about the pass.

Rico's oldest daughter, Joyce, remembered that for about a dozen years, her father stopped playing golf so he could spend more time with his children. He also stopped going to the horse track and on Saturdays, often took his girls shopping and to lunch.

In raising his children, Rico held as a fundamental principle the idea that a person was honest and kept his commitments—"If you said you would do something, you did it," was his mantra. Once, one of the Rico daughters promised a young girlfriend to exchange visits after the friend moved out of state. The girlfriend did visit the Rico home but when it came time for the Rico daughter to reciprocate, she balked. Rico insisted his daughter live up to her promise and put his sobbing daughter on the train, disregarding her protests as a lesson in fulfilling one's obligations.

The Rico family often spent summers at Cape Cod. The "Wellfleet Trip" is family legend and occurred one summer day when they were at the cape. Rico took two of his pre-teen daughters, Christine and Joy, on what was to be a great sailing adventure. The plan was to sail from Brewster, Mass., to Wellfleet, Mass., a trip of about ten miles. Connie packed sandwiches and cookies for them and they sailed with no problems to Wellfleet, taking advantage of the high tide.

After enjoying some hot dogs and ice cream and knocking about Wellfleet, a city of about 3,000 at the outer end of Cape Cod, they began their journey back to Brewster. Unfortunately, they discovered the tide had gone out and the water in the bay was only a few inches deep. They promptly ran aground. Rico got out and pushed the sailboat across the mud flats. The going was slow and it was dark as they approached land near Orleans, Mass., about half way back to Brewster.

Connie was so worried she called the U.S. Coast Guard, saying her family had failed to return from their sailing trip. The Coast Guard officer who took her call asked where her husband worked and if he panicked easily. When Connie responded that he was an FBI agent and was very calm, he told her not to worry, "He will find his way back."

Rico finally dragged the boat ashore in Orleans where he saw a light from a house. As they approached the house, Christine heard a dog barking and Rico said it was OK, "It's only a German Shepherd." Christine immediately began to cry. The dog was friendly and the woman in the house let them call Connie who picked them up. Rico and the other children retrieved the boat the next day. His family was the main thing to him but it was Rico's work in the FBI that distinguished him to his fellow agents.

Neil Welch is the outspoken maverick and highly competent former Boston Organized Crime Squad member who later became special-agent-in-charge at the Buffalo, Detroit and Philadelphia field offices before moving on to the New York office, where he was assistant director in charge and oversaw more than 850 agents. He recalled that Rico was one of the stand-out agents on the Boston squad of about 30 young energetic and talented agents. He said he was a preferred "go to guy" if you needed a partner on some of your work, having both the necessary skills and being easy to work with. Welch, an early member of the squad, thought Rico was a person who would someday be a top agent.

Welch and many of the young agents were single and had no deep connection with Boston. They roomed together in group lodgings, socialized together, had fun working extraordinarily long hours and learned how to do the interesting and important work of the FBI. Rico was married and had roots in the area, although he worked closely with his fellow agents but wasn't part of the single agent social scene. After he was transferred, Welch, who once was listed by a special blue-ribbon commission in Washington as one of five finalists to succeed FBI Director Clarence M. Kelly, recalled hearing Rico mentioned from time to time as someone doing great organized crime work in Boston.

Like Welch, many of the agents who worked in the Boston field office moved on to bigger assignments and more senior positions in the FBI or, after retirement, to significant law enforcement positions or private industry jobs. Many of Welch's ideas as a senior FBI official became the core of the restructuring of the bureau following the death of FBI Director J. Edgar Hoover.

Kehoe, who retired in 1970, became executive director of the New England Organized Crime Intelligence System, a Wellesley-based agency developed to foster information-sharing among law enforcement branches. Later, he was offered the job of Massachusetts Commissioner of Public Safety and led the Massachusetts State Police for seven years. When he died in 2004, the Boston Globe reported that Kehoe had "won the respect and admiration of his troopers, often standing with them in dangerous situations."

Kehoe would be missed by the FBI; years later his supervisory position at Boston's Organized Crime Squad would be filled by an agent of much less quality and serious trouble would ensue.

Condon, following his retirement from the FBI, served as Massachusetts State Police Commissioner and then as the State Undersecretary for Public Safety. He was described by Dukakis as "as fine a public servant" he ever worked with.

Floyd I. Clarke, who later served as the FBI's deputy director and, for a period, as acting director, also was assigned to the Boston field office in the mid-1960s, where he handled bank robbery investigations. While deputy director, the bureau's No. 2 post, Clarke dealt effectively with an extremely sensitive internal affairs investigation that led to the firing by President Clinton of FBI Director William S. Sessions.

James D. McKenzie, who later served as an FBI assistant director and headed the FBI Academy, was assigned to the Boston field office in the 1960s and assisted both Rico and Condon in their interviews. He described Rico as a great interviewer, saying he was always fully prepared. McKenzie said Rico believed it was important to engage criminals and other would-be witnesses in conversation. He said when he was trying to develop his first Mafia informant, Rico knew the person had been mistreated by one of the Mafia lieutenants and suggested getting his guy to talk about the mob underboss he hated. He said the approach worked and while the information he obtained wasn't earth shaking, it was something the man shouldn't have revealed to him. The agent/informant secret relationship had begun.

By the mid-1960s, the Boston field office had Rico, Condon, a complement of other capable and enthusiastic agents and a first rate organized crime supervisor in Kehoe, all poised to make an impact on organized crime. It was early in the battle against the Mafia but the office had a unique collection of talent and experience ready to confront the organized crime syndicates that had swamped Boston and the East Coast.

No matter what would come in the future, Boston was an effective FBI office in the 1950s and 1960s, at a time it needed to be—manned by some of the bureau's best people.

Chapter 7: Organized Crime

AS THE NATION'S top prosecutor, Attorney General Robert F. Kennedy was the first to focus the forces of the FBI on the Mafia, making it the top organized crime priority of both the bureau and the Justice Department. His call to arms was in direct contrast to the long-held and often-stated public pronouncements of FBI Director J. Edgar Hoover, who denied for years the existence of either a tightly-bound Mafia organization or even a loosely-connected federation of organized crime syndicates.

And while Irish mobsters had begun a murderous and bloody campaign against each other in the early 1960s, particularly in the nation's Northeast, Kennedy's FBI-led war against organized crime and the Mafia focused exclusively on the Italians. With the attorney general's encouragement and backing, the FBI gained additional funding and resources, and shifted its focus from bank robberies, hijackings and other violent crimes to organized crime. Over the next 30 years, FBI agents would make significant inroads into a multitude of powerful and often deadly crime families scattered across the country.

Overall, the changes at first took hold slowly. But a few FBI field offices moved quickly, and Boston, New York and Buffalo took the lead in the 1960s and Detroit in the 1970s in fighting the Mafia.

Veteran FBI Agent H. Paul Rico and an active organized crime squad would lead the way in Boston and that field office would achieve success earlier than the rest.

In April 1961, FBI Headquarters in Washington, D.C. sent a letter to each of the special-agents-in-charge of bureau field offices throughout the country emphasizing the importance of criminal intelligence in their organized crime programs. The letter said that to complete the FBI's picture of organized crime, it was "urgently necessary to develop particularly qualified, live sources within the upper echelon of the organized hoodlum element who will be capable of furnishing the quality information required."

The letter, for the first time, showed that the government was acknowledging the existence of the national Mafia Commission, or governing body, and noted the need to develop live sources, or informants, to provide information about it.

At about the same time, Joe Valachi, a member of the Genovese Crime Family—one of the "Five Families" that dominated organized crime activities in New York City—began to cooperate with federal authorities and revealed the intimate details of the Mafia and the workings of the commission. Facing the death penalty for killing a fellow inmate at the federal prison in Atlanta, Valachi testified in Congress and both the interest and the awareness of the Italian Mafia came to the forefront of Americans' consciousness.

The commission, whose existence had long been denied by Hoover, was created in 1931 and included the bosses of the five New York families at its core. Later, the crime bosses in Chicago, Buffalo, Philadelphia and Detroit became involved. Today, it remains active but law enforcement authorities say its power, influence and activities have diminished.

In its 1961 letter, FBI headquarters said the penetration and infiltration of organized criminal activity was a prime objective of the FBI and the bureau's field offices were urged to give a renewed impetus to the development of quality criminal informants.

In Boston, Rico knew the long history of that city's organized crime gangs, particularly among the Irish and Italians. Somehow, the two groups coexisted by cooperating more than fighting with each other. Court records and law enforcement documents show that both groups committed many vicious crimes and murders, but most often murdered only other mobsters or people deeply involved with them.

The so-called Winter Hill Gang was one of the more successful Irish gangs in Boston, and Rico knew it well. Its primary criminal pursuits included murder, bribery, extortion, loansharking, gambling and, eventually, drugs. The gang also was involved in the collection of "tribute" from persons involved in a variety of criminal activities—ranging from illegal gambling to narcotics distribution. The murderous reputation of the Winter Hill Gang members was critical to its success, with gang members frequently and unabashedly turning to kidnapping, force, violence and murder to achieve their goals.

Although many believe the gang's name came from its one time leader, Howie Winter, it actually was derived from the Winter Hill neighborhood where it was based. The gang's roll call of members and associates varied over time and included more than a hundred. The Boston Herald is generally credited with coining the gang's name.

Howie Winter, born on Saint Patrick's Day in 1929 in Roxbury, Mass., became the gang's leader after James "Buddy" McLean was killed in 1966 in the Irish Gang Wars. By the late 1970's, the Winter Hill Gang's leadership passed to James J. "Whitey" Bulger after Winter was convicted of federal charges in connection with fixing horse races. In 1994, Bulger fled when he was charged with 19 counts of murder, conspiracy to commit murder, extortion, narcotics distribution and money laundering. He remained a fugitive for 17 years in spite of being listed among the FBI's Ten Most Wanted fugitives.

The Irish Gang War began with a fight at a Salisbury Beach, Mass., party on Labor Day Weekend in 1961 after several men had viciously beaten George McLaughlin. McLaughlin's brothers were Bernard "Bernie" McLaughlin and Edward "Punchy" McLaughlin, bosses of the nearby Charlestown Mob. Since George, Bernie and Edward were tough guys who hired themselves out as muscle, the beating was unacceptable. They demanded that McLean, then the Winter Hill Gang leader, give up the men who had beaten George. McLean refused. Several nights later, Bernie McLaughlin and others tried to plant dynamite in McLean's car, but fled after McLean's wife heard them and McLean opened fire on them. The next day, McLean shot and killed Bernie McLaughlin in a cafe in City Square, Charlestown.

The war raged for almost a decade. It was into this dangerous atmosphere that the FBI's Boston field office sent Rico, one of its best and most experienced agents. At the time, Rico was operating in all the places where gangsters and criminals could be found and actively recruiting them as informants. It was his style in turning a gang member into a snitch to get to know them first and then develop a personal relationship, always treating them with respect. He was the most recognizable FBI agent known to the mobsters and hoodlums. They knew him and he knew them.

While Rico developed close relationships with many of the Boston-area gang members, he clearly understood that the testimony they offered often was inherently unbelievable. If there was anything in it for them, many would say whatever they wanted the agent to believe or whatever they thought the agent wanted to hear. An agent had to be careful in developing relationships with their informants and in assessing the information they provided—knowing they were dealing with inherently devious, often dishonest people. The work was not only dangerous, but complex.

Alan Trustman, a Boston native who served on the executive board of World Jai Alai Inc. in Florida and was a Rico friend and confidant, said the veteran agent's informant recruitment efforts were immeasurably complicated by the Irish Gang War, during which dozens of gangsters were murdered. Trustman described Boston as a "sports-mad town" in which the Irish Gang Wars were widely regarded as sport; people knew who was going to get whacked next and, at least in the early years, found themselves rooting for one side or the other—the McLaughlins or the McLeans. Some of those killed were known to Rico and most likely were actual or potential informants.

Over the years, the war accounted for more than 60 brutal murders and despite the carnage, the Irish criminals in Boston were regarded by the FBI and most of law enforcement as second-fiddle lackeys. They primarily killed other mobsters, tough guys and hangers on. The Irish hoodlums had few contacts outside of the greater Boston area and, at the time, did not seem to have seriously corrupted local law enforcement. The full extent of their activities just wasn't known. While a victim in the Irish Gang War would be understood to have died at the hands of Irish gangsters, the actual murderers probably would not be known.

The Italians usually kept their distance from the Irish. They had active regimes in Worcester and Springfield, Mass., and New England was controlled by the Italians. It was clear that the Mafia, known to the Italians as La Cosa Nostra—loosely translated as "this thing of ours"—had engaged in large scale police and political corruption and that, combined with their nationwide contacts, made them part of a national problem while the Irish were considered to be a local problem.

James Ring, the FBI's organized crime squad supervisor in Boston in the 1980s and 1990s who was known to his agents as "Pipe," said the Irish were no different than a Los Angeles street gang and were probably less well organized. Irish, Middle Eastern, Russian, Chinese, Latino and other groups received FBI attention but weren't considered nearly as high a threat as the Italian Mafia. In Boston, the focus was on the New England Mafia.

While many organized criminal groups that operate in the United States are structured around ethnic or national identities, in the 1960s the Italian Mafia families were the clear Number One target of the FBI's organized crime program. Rico and his colleagues knew that Irish mobsters in Boston were engaged in criminal activity in the 1960s, but they considered them to be rather crude and low on the FBI's priority list. The Irish were seen as tough muscle guys into gambling, loan sharking, armed robbery and bank robbery among other things.

In March 1962, under the authority and the encouragement of the Kennedy Justice Department, the FBI's Boston field office surreptitiously planted microphones at several Mafia offices and hangouts. The information gained from the secret listening devices and from the informants cultivated by the Boston office would be the two principal tools used in the collection of dramatic and often critical information over the next several years in identifying members and associates of La Cosa Nostra, and their criminal activities.

The bugging, telephone taps and informant reports ultimately made clear that Raymond L.S. Patriarca was the La Cosa Nostra boss in New England and the Number One target for Rico and his FBI colleagues. Patriarca firmly held the reins of the New England Mafia family.

Born in 1908 to Italian immigrants in Worcester, Mass., Patriarca and his family moved to Providence, R.I., in 1911, where he was raised and began a life of crime. During his lifetime, Patriarca was arrested or indicted 28 times, convicted seven times and imprisoned four times, serving a total of 11 years. More than half of his prison time was for a murder conspiracy charge during the 1960s.

Patriarca began as a made member of the New York Mafia, but in the 1950s he took over the combined New England Mafia organization. He centered his operations in Providence and aligned himself with the then-small Colombo family in New York. He had displayed his criminal appetite early, arrested between his 17th and his 21st birthdays on charges of violation of prohibition laws, failure to stop for a police officer, breaking and entering, conspiracy to murder, armed robbery and auto theft. In December 1930, he was sentenced to a year and a day in federal prison in Atlanta and he was paroled in October 1931.

In 1938, Patriarca, who by then had earned the title "public enemy" by the local police, was convicted and sentenced in Norfolk, Mass., to three to five years in prison for carrying a gun without a permit, possession of burglary tools and armed robbery of a jewelry company. The conviction provided the opportunity to demonstrate his power and influence. After serving only 84 days of his minimum three-year sentence, Patriarca was able to use his influence to get himself out of prison. He made a pardon petition through Daniel Coakley, a disbarred lawyer on the Massachusetts Executive Council, who presented it to then-Gov. Charles F. Hurley just before it was presented to the council. The governor acted favorably on the petition. When questioned later by the press, Coakley praised Patriarca's mother and said "this boy comes from a wonderful family."

Hurley explained that he had been influenced by the statements of three clergymen in the pardon petition. Later inquiry determined that one of the priests did not exist; another said his name had been used without his permission; and the third said his name had been used by fraud.

Patriarca promised that if released, he would live with his mother in Providence and work as a carpenter. In fact, once released, he got married, went to Miami on a four-month honeymoon and promptly resumed his criminal activities. His benefactor, Coakley, was impeached and removed as councilor from Massachusetts' fourth councilor district. The fact that La Cosa Nostra had so thoroughly corrupted the government was one of the factors that made it a higher target for the FBI and Rico than the Irish mobsters.

Patriarca continued his involvement in various criminal activities through the 1940s when he was charged with burglaries, carrying burglary tools, armed robberies and murder. In 1941, he pled guilty in a 1937 holdup and was sentenced to 2 to 3 years. In 1944, he was paroled and returned to live in Johnston, R.I., where he said he would make a living pruning, spraying and fertilizing in the apple orchards of his brother-in-law. Somehow he did not apply himself to gardening; he quickly returned to his criminal business.

In 1950, Patriarca was named by the Senate Special Committee to Investigate Crime in Interstate Commerce, better known as the Kefauver Committee after its chairman, Sen. Estes Kefauver, Tennessee Democrat, as "king of the rackets in New England." In 1957, the Massachusetts Crime Commission described Patriarca as the "most powerful influence" in an interstate gambling network, accusing the mob boss of doing an estimated $2-billion business annually in the Bay State.

In 1958, Patriarca was called before the Senate Select Committee on Improper Activities in Labor and Management, also known as the McClellan Committee after its chairman, Sen. Senator John L. McClellan, Arkansas Democrat, in its investigation of strong-arm distribution tactics. The panel, later known as the Senate Rackets Committee, had targeted Patriarca's National Cigarette Service, a vending machine company. The mob boss explained that he was able to start the business with $80,000 in capital that his late mother left him in a box in the cellar. When then-Committee Counsel Robert Kennedy asked why, if he had $80,000 sitting in the basement, he had committed the burglaries, Patriarca responded, "Why do a lot of young fellows do a lot of things when they haven't (got) a father."

A year later, when the rackets committee subpoenaed crime leaders from around the country, only Patriarca refused to take the Fifth Amendment. Questioned by committee counsel Kennedy, Patriarca described himself as an honest businessman and said the police and press were hounding him unfairly. Patriarca explained his employment record over the years, claiming his first job was as a bellboy in 1923 or 1924, then a salesman who "bought stuff" and would go out and sell it in cars. He couldn't remember doing anything from 1932 to 1944 when he began to work as a counterman and manager in a restaurant. He said after working there for a year, he played the horses until 1950.

By the end of the decade of the 50's, Patriarca was indeed a big deal in criminal circles and had a long record of involvement in serious crime. Now in charge of the New England Mafia Family, he had demonstrated his corrupt influence on the government and had been named as one of the top leaders of organized crime in the United States. Patriarca was overheard on one bug telling an associate, "in this thing of ours, your love for your mother and father is one thing, your love for The Family is a different kind of love."

When in August 1961 Patriarca was called to appear before a Senate McClellan subcommittee, he displayed his combative nature by paying for a large advertisement in the Providence Journal-Bulletin to criticize what he described as the newspaper's "unwarranted and unjustifiable characterizations" of him.

The ad said: "Since my release from prison in 1944 after completion of a sentence for a crime committed in 1938 when I was thirty years of age, my time has been continuously and assiduously employed in honest endeavors ... This is the result of my firm resolution made while I was imprisoned to amend my life. This resolution has been conscientiously and strictly maintained. I challenge you to prove by competent evidence that I have since, in any degree, deviated from that resolution by my engagement in any illegal or criminal enterprise or activity."

It continued: "The tranquility of my family has many times and oft been rudely disturbed by the rehashing of my criminal record in your news columns. I, more than you, deplore that record. How bitterly I realize the truth of a great poet's words 'The evil that men do lives after them; the good is often interred with their bones.' Your newspapers seem to take a fiendish delight in their unwarranted and unjustifiable characterizations of me which slyly infer (sic) that I am now and have always been engaged in illegal activities ... What can I, with my criminal record, expect from a newspaper which often has paraded in its obituary columns the peccadilloes of many former decent Rhode Island citizens."

That claimed tranquility was short-lived as secretly-placed microphones installed by the FBI in 1962 discovered. The bugs covered Patriarca at his office; Jerry Angiulo, described as the "overall boss of rackets in the Boston area" and Patriarca's "chief lieutenant," at Jay's Lounge in Boston; and Joseph Modica, a Patriarca associate, at his business. While these electronic sources were extremely productive, particularly those in Patriarca's business, the prevailing legal view within the Department of Justice at the time was that the information they produced could only be used for intelligence and not direct testimony since the devices had been placed as a result of illegal trespasses without a court order. Nevertheless, they provided rich intelligence about Patriarca's crime family.

Those bugs and others detected a number of murder plots from 1962 to 1965, according to FBI records, also putting the spotlight on political payoffs to the governor's office, legislators and judges in both Rhode Island and Massachusetts. In addition, informants recruited and maintained by Rico and his partner, Dennis Condon, along with various electronic surveillance, produced information that painted an exacting picture of organized crime in Boston.

Rico, operating in the midst of the Irish Gang War, kept his focus on the Italian crime syndicate run by Patriarca, who officially became "king" of the New England Crime Family in 1952 when Philip Buccola, who had been head of the family, retired to Italy. It also was the year Rico joined the FBI.

Chapter 8: "The Animal"

IT WAS 1966 and Joseph "The Animal" Barboza, a Mafia hitman, was living up to his nickname. Easily one of the most feared killers in the country, Barboza was a serial murderer, reputed to have killed more than two dozen people in his lifetime. He was so unpredictable that many of his mob associates believed he was crazy.

It was this loose cannon that FBI Agents H. Paul Rico and his partner, Dennis Condon, targeted as an potential informant—setting their sights on a man they were convinced had the greatest potential to provide insider information against Raymond L.S. Patriarca, boss of the La Cosa Nostra crime family in New England.

Rico and Condon knew it would be a daunting challenge, but the two veteran agents, working out of the bureau's Boston field office, were confident they could turn Barboza. They just needed a little time and a little help.

The recruitment of a high-level hoodlum who could and would give-up information about La Cosa Nostra and even agree to testify in open court against their former mob bosses was the ultimate achievement for any FBI agent in the investigation of organized crime. Many attempted it, few were successful.

And when the opportunity arose, Rico and Condon moved quickly to add Barboza to their growing and productive list of informants and cooperating subjects. Word on the street was that Barboza was beginning to feel the pressure of a pending hit—having been told that Romeo Gallo, a shooter for the Brooklyn Gallo Mob, was in town with a contract to kill him. At the same time, he had to come up with bail money in connection with a pending stabbing case.

Rico and Condon didn't hesitate. They encouraged the Boston Police Department to turn up the heat on Barboza and, in short order, he was arrested in the city's "Combat Zone," the name given by the Boston Record-American newspaper to the adult entertainment district in the city's downtown area. Arrested along with three associates, including Arthur C. Bratsos, police found an Army M–1 semi-automatic rifle, a loaded .45-caliber automatic pistol and a knife. Because of pending court action and a new charge of illegal possession of firearms, Barboza's bail was set high at $100,000.

Bratsos and another Barboza criminal associate, Thomas J. DePrisco, were both small-time burglars and thieves who were part of Barboza's "crew." In attempting to raise bail money for Barboza, they started shaking down the wrong people who complained to Gennaro "Jerry" Angiulo, an underboss in the Patriarca crime family. Angiulo authorized a hit on the two men and on Nov. 1, 1966, Bratsos and DePrisco were found dead in a black Cadillac in South Boston. The $72,000 they had already collected for Barboza's bail was gone.

The Angiulo group had promised Bratsos and DePrisco the final $28,000 they needed to make the bail demand. But when Bratsos and DePrisco went to the Nite Lite Lounge, a mob-owned bar in Boston's North End, to pick up the money, a dozen mob associates, murdered them and stole the cash. They beat and shot Bratsos and DePrisco and dumped their bodies. Barboza believed that Joseph Salvati was one of the ones who participated in the murder of his friends and the theft of his bail money.

In a 1976 report by a Massachusetts Board of Pardons investigator, Salvati was described as a mob "runner, hanger around, coffee man and driver." The report, by Investigator Joseph Williams, Jr., also identified Salvati as one of Barboza's known associates.

Rico, who had distinguished himself in the FBI as an agent who knew how to bring an informant to the table, used the killing, among other things, as leverage to begin working on Barboza. Developing a person of his stature in the mob as an informant or cooperating subject would be a huge accomplishment. To be successful, Rico knew he had to develop a personal relationship with the killer, along with gaining his trust and some-how persuading him that although cooperating with the FBI would surely cause the Mafia to make a serious effort to kill him, it was the best course of action for him.

Few agents or police officers have the ability to persuade such a per-son to defect from his criminal family. It's a select group of agents, indeed, whoever hit homeruns in the business of cooperating witnesses—like get-ting Sammy "The Bull" Gravano to testify against Gambino Crime Family boss John Gotti. Gravano, a Gambino underboss, was the highest-ranking member of organized crime ever to roll over on his bosses.

Likewise, Barboza's defection offered the FBI the possibility of gain-ing much-needed information against the Patriarca Crime Family—a La Cosa Nostra enclave considered one of the most active mob families out-side of New York City.

To achieve their goal, Rico and Condon were relentless but cautious. They knew Barboza was a significant threat, a former light heavyweight boxer, a man who had killed several people and wouldn't hesitate to kill them.

The son of immigrants from Portugal who settled in New Bedford, Mass, Barboza was first arrested in 1945 at the age of 13 on charges of breaking and entering. Later, when he was 17, his gang broke into 16 houses in New Bedford in the space of a few days and stole money, watches, liquor and guns. He was sentenced to prison the first time at age 17, but escaped. At 21, Barboza was convicted of robbery by force and violence, assault and battery with a dangerous weapon, kidnapping, larceny of autos and escape from prison. In 1958, a state psychiatric report deter-mined that Barboza had a "sociopathic personality disturbance, anti social reaction." Over the next decade, Barboza would live up to that assessment—repeatedly demonstrating a sociopathic personality disturbance.

While Barboza was of Portuguese descent, he had hoped to become the first non-Italian member of Patriarca's crime family. He committed a number of murders and crimes, including assault and battery, loan sharking and burglary, on behalf of the Mafia to help his cause. But he had little chance to become a member of the Patriarca family; behind his back, Patriarca referred to him as the "nigger."

Just how crazy Barboza was may best be illustrated by an incident in 1965 when he personally approached Patriarca and requested permission to murder a man who lived in a three-story house but who Barboza had never been able to line up to kill. Barboza told Patriarca he planned to pour gasoline in the basement of the house, set it afire and either kill the person by smoke and fire or, in the event he started to climb out, he would have two or three gunmen there with rifles to kill him as he stepped out a window or door.

Barboza told a quizzical Patriarca he planned to cut the telephone wires so a call for assistance could not be made and also to ring false alarms in other sections of the city so the fire engines could not respond quickly. He also explained that the first floor apartment was apparently occupied by the intended victim's mother, but that the murder of this innocent person was of no concern to him. Barboza told Patriarca it wasn't his fault the mother would be present and he did not care whether she died or not.

Patriarca, whose reign as boss of the New England crime syndicate was both brutal and ruthless, nonetheless understood the limits of what a person could and should do. He told Barboza he did not think it was a good idea.

While Barboza initially declined to cooperate with Rico and Condon, the agents had a fall back plan that involved mobster Stephen "The Rifleman" Flemmi, the brother of Barboza's best friend and partner Jimmy Flemmi. A few months earlier, Rico had recruited Stephen Flemmi as an informant and it was that connection that kept the lines of communication open between Barboza and the agents.

Flemmi told Barboza that the Boston police had a bugging tape in which Angiulo swore he would have Barboza killed and that he was giving the contract to Maurice "Pro" Lerner, a particularly dangerous assassin for the Patriarca family and the one person who Barboza feared. In March 1967, Rico and Condon interviewed Barboza at the Walpole Massachusetts State Prison, where they were told by the mob hit man that his crime family associates and friends had double crossed him—an obvious reference to Flemmi's information about Angiulo.

It was at that point that Barboza decided to cooperate with the agents, agreeing that they had a common enemy—the Italian Mafia. But there was a condition. He said he would talk to them if they wouldn't use what he said against him and, at first, he said he wouldn't testify in court. It was the job of the agents, however, not only to learn what he knew but also to get him to tell the truth in court and Barboza's information was proving to be so important that neither Rico or Condon hesitated in pushing him further. This particularly rang true after Barboza told them that, as a matter of fact, he use "to see Raymond Patriarca and get his 'OK' before he made most of his moves" and he claimed he knew what had happened in practically every mob murder that had been committed in the Boston area.

Barboza, like most cooperating subjects, put some limits on the information he was willing to share, telling Rico and Condon he wouldn't provide any information that could be used to let his best friend, Jimmy Flemmi, "fry". But he was up-front with the fact that Jimmy Flemmi also was a murderous thug and aspired to be the "Number One Hit Man" in the Boston area.

Technically, Barboza would not be an informant but would become what is known at the FBI as a "cooperating subject"—a person who has committed a crime or crimes, and could be prosecuted, but who has decided to cooperate with authorities. Barboza was a cooperating subject on the level of Joseph Valachi, who introduced the American public to the existence of the Mafia, or Gravano, who brought down Gotti and the Gambino Crime Family. Cooperating subjects of this magnitude generally get a pass on most, if not all, of the crimes they have committed. It is the obligation of those dealing with them, particularly FBI agents and prosecutors who prepare them for trail, to be comfortable they are telling the truth—and to independently verify what they are saying.

Barboza was such an important cooperating subject that the federal government took extraordinary steps to protect him. He became one of the stepping stones that led to the creation of the federal Witness Protection Program. Barboza's protection and that of his wife, Janice, and daughter, Terri, became the responsibility of the U.S. Marshals Service, which devoted significant resources to ensuring he would live to testify.

Barboza's importance as a government witness is described in a Sept. 17, 1975, memo by Gerard T. McGuire, deputy chief of the FBI's Organized Crime and Racketeering Section in Boston, who said Barboza was "the key witness in one of the most important cases this section has ever won, and his survival, or lack thereof, has current importance in the development of witnesses in the New England area."

When the jails where Barboza was being held were regarded as unsafe, he was moved to Thatcher's Island, a half mile long craggy clump of rocks off the coast of Gloucester, Mass. The island had two lighthouses and two unoccupied Cape Cod style homes that hadn't been used since the lighthouses were modernized. Sixteen marshals were assigned to guard the Barboza. The marshals occupied one of the houses and the Barboza the other.

Rico and Condon, who visited the island on several occasions to check on the "physical wellbeing" of Barboza and his family, prepared carefully to interview the Mafia killer. They studied and mastered the known facts for each session, but conducted themselves during the interview as if they didn't know all the facts. Occasionally, Rico would even misstate a fact or two, in a manner calculated to test Barboza's knowledge. Both agents worked hard to conduct an interview that would produce the truth, but Rico was the key in gaining Barboza's cooperation. As dangerous as Barboza was, he had respect for Rico and trusted that the agent would do what he said he would do.

According to Rico's March 1966 FBI personnel appraisal, he was rated excellent with comments that he had been assigned exclusively "to the development of Top Echelon informants and had worked primarily on this important program." The records also said Rico had "exceptional talent in his ability to develop informants and his participating was considered outstanding."

In his March 1967 FBI performance appraisal, Condon also received an excellent rating, with a note saying he handled "complicated matters in an able and capable fashion." It was further noted that Condon was "dependable, enthusiastic and showed a great interest in the bureau's work" and that he had "an outstanding knowledge" of the hoodlum and gambling element in the Boston area. The appraisal also said he was considered to be "an outstanding investigator" and that his participation in the informant program "is considered outstanding."

On June 20, 1967, both agents are recommended for salary increases, noting their handling of Top Echelon Criminal Informants in the Boston field office. A FBI memo notes that Rico and Condon were assigned to develop a prosecutable case against La Cosa Nostra members in the Boston area and did so "via highest devotion to duty, requiring personal sacrifice in time on a continuing basis." Three days later, J.H. Gale, special agent in charge of the Boston field office, recommended incentive awards for Rico and Condon, saying their "shrewd guidance" of a confidential information had led to the reasons for numerous gangland slayings in the Boston area and the identities of those involved in them.

Rico and Condon interviewed Barboza for over a year. FBI Agent James D. McKenzie, then a relatively new agent in the Boston field office, assisted Rico and Condon in some of their interviews. Whenever Condon couldn't be there, McKenzie took notes as Rico conducted the interview.

McKenzie remembered an incident on Thatcher Island that revealed Barboza's cruel and out of control nature. Barboza said he wanted a dog to protect him so Rico went to the pound and found the "biggest, stupidest dog" he could find. He gave the dog to Barboza. Rico returned to the island and found that Barboza was trying to teach the dog to attack using hand signals. McKenzie and Rico thought it unlikely that Barboza could successfully teach the dog to respond. But after a couple of weeks of what they suspected was a harsh training regime, Barboza appeared to have succeeded. He was able to direct the dog to attack the Marshals who were on the island protecting him. Rico and McKenzie secretly snatched the dog one evening and took him back to the pound.

Rico and Condon occasionally were joined in the Barboza interviews by his attorney, John E. Fitzgerald, and often by local police detectives. Captain Joseph Fallon, former chief of the Boston homicide squad, participated in a number of the interviews. At the time, Fallon was assigned to Boston District Attorney Garrett Byrne's office.

FBI and court records show that Barboza provided information that devastated the crime families in New England, including intelligence about the activities of the Mafia and specific information that enabled the government to charge several of the mob's leaders with serious crimes. It was Barboza who first outlined for law enforcement authorities as a mob insider the fact that there was one crime family that controlled the Boston underworld and that it allowed lesser groups to operate in parts of the city.

While the Irish Gang War was of interest to the FBI, the Italian Mafia remained its primary focus. Barboza would testify against the Italians.

FBI transcripts from its bug in Patriarca's office showed that the organization was broken into groups called families and that each family was headed by a boss and underbosses. The families were staffed by lieutenants and soldiers, who were ordinary members. The New England Family was headed by Patriarca. At one point, Patriarca was overheard telling an associate that he would deny any knowledge of the Mafia or La Cosa Nostra if asked about it.

Once Rico and Condon had pushed the right buttons, Barboza testified in three major cases; two Boston area murders and a federal organized crime conspiracy case.

But the first case to go to trial in which Barboza was a key witness proved to be a disappointment. It involved the prosecution of Angiulo, the Boston head of La Cosa Nostra, for conspiracy and accessory before the fact for the murder of former boxer Rocco Diseglia. Three other hoodlums were charged with the murder itself. The case was handled by Suffolk County District Attorney Garrett H. Byrne. At the time, the FBI had strict rules about field agents becoming involved in local prosecutions. Agents were under rigid orders to provide actionable evidence and intelligence to local authorities, but FBI Headquarters in Washington, D.C., had to give its approval for an agent to sit at the prosecution table to assist prosecutors. Such approvals were rare. Rico and Condon turned Barboza over to the district attorney's office and its detectives and sat on the sidelines as they prepared the case for prosecution.

Barboza testified that the murder of Diseglia was ordered by Angiulo. He said he saw the victim being driven away by the three men charged with the murder. Later, one of the men told Barboza that Angiulo had discovered they robbed gambling games in which he had an interest. Angiulo told them to kill Diseglia or they themselves would be killed for robbing his games.

All four defense attorneys focused their attack on Barboza's credibility. Angiulo's attorney asked Barboza if he expected to make money from his testimony and evidence was introduced that he had explored a book deal. After just two hours of deliberation, the jury acquitted all four defendants.

Angiulo's attorney said, "This trial has showed that Joseph [Barboza] is not only one of the real killers in the Commonwealth, but also one of the real liars." The prosecution had not met its burden of proof. The judge told the jury it could not find the defendants guilty unless the prosecution had proved its case beyond a reasonable doubt. The government had failed to prove its case, but there would be other cases and different verdicts.

Barboza himself was the victim of a mob hit, gunned down in February 1976 in San Francisco as he was getting into his car after visiting a friend. The weapon used to kill him was described in a June 1976 FBI report as a shotgun, noting that the longtime mobster "died instantaneously."

Although Barboza was armed with a .38-caliber revolver at the time of the shooting, he never had a chance to draw it—hit by three shotgun blasts at close range. His attorney, F. Lee Bailey, was quoted as having said his client's death was "no great loss to society."

Chapter 9: Success

IT WAS JAN. 30, 1968, just prior to the start of the much-anticipated trial of Mafia boss Raymond L. S. Patriarca. Defense attorney John E. Fitzgerald Jr., who represented one of the government's key witnesses in the case, had just turned on the ignition key to his car when, suddenly, he and the vehicle were consumed by an explosion. The dynamite-caused blast blew him out of the car and into the street. A second explosion thrust the steering wheel and what was left of his mangled vehicle into the sky. The explosions broke the windows on nearby houses in Everett, Mass., a Boston suburb.

When the bomb exploded, Fitzgerald, who had expected an attack with guns, remembered thinking, "Oh my God, they put a bomb in my car." The massive blast ripped off part of one of Fitzgerald's legs and caused other extensive injuries. As he laid suffering in the street, he called out for FBI Agent H. Paul Rico.

At the agent's home, his wife, Connie, first received an urgent call from her husband's supervisor. Where's Rico, he wanted to know. The phone rang again; it was a call from the special-agent-in-charge of the FBI Boston field office. He also wanted to talk to Rico. Finally, a call from the U.S. attorney's office in Boston. They also needed to talk to the veteran agent.

Rico was on the job and, at the time, there were no cell phones and no quick way to reach him. No one told Connie Rico what was going on.

Fitzgerald had survived, losing most of one leg and requiring major reconstruction on the other.

Fitzgerald was regarded as a competent lawyer who defended a group of clients known generally as lesser hoodlums. He had placed himself between Joseph "The Animal" Barboza and the Mafia and when he told the FBI that Barboza would cooperate with the bureau, they concluded he was doing so as a result of Fitzgerald's direction. Barboza, a professional light heavyweight boxer and member of the United States Boxing Association, was key to the government's pending case against Patriarca.

Rico was angry about the bombing since the lawyer had been assisting him in his interviews of Barboza. Rico had pulled Fitzgerald aside in late 1967, just three months before the bombing, telling the veteran defense lawyer there was a contract out on him. Fitzgerald told Rico he had armed himself and would get them first. Rico told him, "This is serious, these guys will take you out." Fitzgerald said he was not afraid.

Fitzgerald was placed under heavy security in the hospital. The Boston Globe found him remarkably upbeat, reporting at the time that he was in a hospital room with get well cards plastered all over the walls. He was encouraged by the fact that the doctors had been able to save one leg and that he would be able to walk again with an artificial limb. The Globe reporter noted that before the interview was completed, Rico and his partner, Dennis Condon, entered the room. The two FBI agents were frequent visitors to Fitzgerald as he recovered.

During one visit, Fitzgerald told Rico he was going to write a letter to Barboza telling him he should regard the Mafia as his enemies and provide the testimony that would send them all to prison. But Rico responded by telling the lawyer he did not want Barboza to be pressured to testify against specific targets, preferring that he be allowed to testify to whatever he could—as long as it was the truth.

Barboza had talked with Rico about the 1966 murder of bookmaker William "Willie" Marfeo, a small time hoodlum who operated a dice game in a social club near Patriarca's office in Providence. He said that at the bidding of Henry Tameleo, a Patriarca lieutenant, he and Ronald Cassesso, a soldier in the New England Mafia, met with Patriarca in his office around June 1965 to discuss Marfeo's murder. The Providence Police Department had approached Patriarca and told him they wanted the dice game closed down. When Tameleo asked Marfeo to close the game, Marfeo angrily rejected the request and called Patriarca a "bum." Tameleo was furious and told Marfeo to pay up his insurance because he was a dead man.

Barboza quoted Patriarca as saying, "I want him whacked out and I want it done right away." Barboza and Cassesso agreed to do the murder for nothing, rejecting Patriarca's offer to pay them. Patriarca told Barboza, "I won't forget you for this." The information about the conversation with Patriarca in which Barboza and Cassesso agreed to murder Marfeo was confirmed by an FBI microphone secretly placed in Patriarca's office. The facts were clear.

But Barboza's role in the murder plot was interrupted when he was arrested and incarcerated a short time later for an unrelated crime. Patriarca then called on New Jersey mobsters to make the hit on Marfeo and on July 13, 1966, a gunman entered the Korner Kitchen restaurant where Marfeo was eating pizza and killed him with four blasts from a shotgun. The restaurant, located in the Federal Hill section of Providence, was a block from Patriarca's office.

In June 1967, three months after Rico gained Barboza's cooperation, Patriarca and two associates, Enrico "Henry" Tameleo and Ronald "Ronnie the Pig" Cassesso, were indicted by a federal grand jury in Boston for conspiring to murder Marfeo. The indictment was based on information provided by Barboza.

A month later, as the FBI interviews of Barboza were being conducted, Fitzgerald was approached by Tameleo, then a Patriarca lieutenant, and another hoodlum, Luigi "Lewis" Greco, a mob drug dealer and bank robber, who inquired on why Barboza was cooperating with the FBI. Fitzgerald explained that two of Barboza's friends had been killed while collecting money for his bail in an unrelated case, that his bail money had been stolen and that his wife and child had been threatened. Tameleo told Fitzgerald that Greco was "his man" and that any future deals should be made through him.

In August 1967, Greco told Fitzgerald the mob was willing to pay Barboza $25,000 not to testify in the Patriarca case. They discussed "whacking out" the victim of a stabbing for which Barboza had been indicted. Fitzgerald talked with Barboza and then told Greco that $25,000 was not enough. Greco raised the offer to $50,000. Fitzgerald conferred with Barboza the next day and then rejected the offer. Fitzgerald told Greco that Barboza would cooperate with the prosecutors—difficult news for the Mafia to swallow.

The trial of Patriarca, Tameleo and Cassesso was concluded in March 1968, and Barboza proved to be a credible witness. All three were found guilty by a federal district court of (interstate travel to facilitate) a murder conspiracy. Patriarca was sentenced to five years in federal prison. U.S. Attorney Paul Markham said at the time, "The case in the main depended on his [Barboza's] credibility. The jury obviously believed him, believed him 100 percent. It was a significant victory."

Rico received high praise for his work with Barboza. U.S. Attorney General Ramsey Clark wrote FBI Director J. Edgar Hoover saying, "The recent conviction of New England Cosa Nostra leader, Raymond Patriarca, and two of his cohorts is one of the major accomplishments in the Organized Crime Program. I have been advised by the Organized Crime and Racketeering Section and Mr. Paul Markham, the United States attorney in Boston, that without the outstanding work performed by Special Agents Dennis Condon and H. Paul Rico, these convictions could not have been obtained."

In June 1969, Police Sgt. Ray Peek and Captain James Kilmartin were returning to the Somerville, Mass., police station when they heard the holdup alarm at the County Bank and Trust Company. They sped to the scene and as they jumped from their vehicle, a man in a panel truck opened fire—wounding Peek in the leg. The gunman fled but when other officers arrived they captured four men inside the bank including Robert Daddieco. A conviction for bank robbery was serious enough but one for shooting a police officer during a bank robbery would mean many years of prison time.

At the time Daddieco was arrested, Floyd Clarke was a young agent with about five years of FBI experience. He was assigned to the Boston Bank Robbery Squad. Rico approached Clarke in the Boston FBI field office and suggested he take a shot at "flipping" Daddieco. Rico told Clarke that Francis P. "Cadillac Frank" Salemme and Stephen "The Rifleman"

Flemmi were responsible for the Fitzgerald bombing and Daddieco knew the whole story; that he was a witness to the planning of that bombing. He told Clarke that Daddieco did not like Salemme and Flemmi and the agent should play on that angle to get his cooperation. Rico said Daddieco distrusted both Flemmi and Salemme because he saw them as hit men for Patriarca who would do anything including turning on their friends.

Rico gave Clarke pictures of Salemme and Flemmi. Since Clarke was on the Bank Robbery Squad, he knew that if he was successful in getting Daddieco to cooperate, someone from the Organized Crime squad would be needed to help. So he asked FBI Agent James D. McKenzie, who had been assisting in the interviews of Barboza, to go with him.

Interviewing Daddieco in a jail holding area, the two agents were unsuccessful at first in getting Daddieco to talk with them. As they were about to leave, Clarke took one last chance and threw the pictures of Salemme and Flemmi on the table: "You tell me who the smart guys are—you or these two guys? You are caught inside a bank and facing years in prison and these two guys are still out on the street laughing their asses off that you are the one behind bars."

Clarke could see the animosity Daddieco had for the two. He told Daddieco the only way he could get even with them was to cooperate with the FBI. Daddieco thought it over and, eventually, agreed to cooperate.

During the many days McKenzie and Clarke spent with Daddieco, they learned details of the Fitzgerald bombing and the Mafia's ties to it. But Daddieco made it clear he would not testify against Howie Winter, the mobster identified as the second leader of the infamous Winter Hill Gang in Boston. It was clear to the agents that he was protecting a friend.

But Clarke and McKenzie learned they could rely on Daddieco's accuracy, and the bottom line to the Fitzgerald bombing was clear; Rico had been correct—Salemme and Flemmi were responsible for the bombing. They had practiced how to wire the bomb and actually tested its mechanism a couple of times in Winters' garage when Daddieco was present. In fact, they wanted Daddieco to go with them but he decided not to participate in the actual bombing. Daddieco was adamant that Salemme and Flemmi were the two that put the bomb in Fitzgerald's car. Daddieco also was upset that they would do it near a school.

This episode is confirmation that even though Flemmi was a valuable informant, Rico understood his responsibilities. He knew an agent couldn't continue to operate an informant who had committed such a serious offense and he moved to have him charged with the crime. Rico clearly knew Flemmi was an informant, not a friend. Clarke later went on to serve as the FBI's deputy director, the bureau's No. 2 position. He also was acting director for three months in 1993 while the new director, Louis J. Freeh, was being nominated, confirmed and sworn in.

On Sept. 11, 1969, Flemmi and Salemme were indicted in Middlesex County, Mass., for the Fitzgerald bombing. The two men managed to evade arrest and Flemmi spent the next few years as a fugitive in New York and Canada. He was closed as an FBI informant and a federal fugitive warrant was issued for his arrest.

In a June 17, 1970, letter, Fitzgerald wrote, "In all my dealings with [Paul Rico] I have never found him making unethical promises or deals or undertaking commitments [sic] which he could not fulfill ... although I lost a leg in the so called 'war against organized crime,' if I had to do it over again I would follow the same road, and my motivations would largely be the result of the integrity, professionalism and the high traditions of your organization as exemplified in my eyes by Paul Rico."

Chapter 10: Teddy Deegan

WELL BEFORE THE trial of mob boss Raymond L.S. Patriarca
had concluded, FBI Agents H. Paul Rico and Dennis Condon already had
been exploring other crimes about which a key informant in the case,
Joseph "The Animal" Barboza, could testify. The murder of Edward
"Teddy" Deegan was one of them. Deegan's body had been discovered on
March 13, 1965, in the rear doorway of Lincoln National Bank in Chelsea,
Mass., shot twice in the head and several times in the body.

Chelsea police described the killing as having all the earmarks of a
typical underworld "setup." Detectives theorized that Deegan and a couple
of other men planned to break into the building and as Deegan entered, his
companions and several others were lying in wait to kill him.

Five months earlier, Rico had learned from his informants that
Vincent "Jimmy The Bear" Flemmi—brother of Stephen "The Rifleman"
Flemmi—wanted to kill Deegan. Rico detailed what he had learned in a
memorandum and passed it to his supervisor at the FBI's Boston field
office. When agents obtain information from a sensitive FBI informant that
a person is to be attacked or murdered, the bureau takes steps to pass it to
the appropriate police authorities or to warn the intended victim in a manner that does not compromise the identity of the source. The goal, of
course, is to protect the intended victim while not identifying the informant.

Four days before the Deegan killing, the FBI had learned through its
covert microphone coverage that Patriarca and Henry Tameleo, a Patriarca
lieutenant, had talked about killing Deegan and that Jimmy Flemmi and

Barboza had requested authority to take down the mob gambler, book-maker and burglar. In one conversation, Flemmi described Deegan as an arrogant, nasty sneak who should be killed. The bureau also knew that Patriarca had given his approval.

While such conversations certainly are confirmation of a Mafia murder conspiracy, they cannot be used in court as evidence. The prevailing inter-pretation of Supreme Court rulings within the Department of Justice was that electronic coverage of a conversation was legal but if the recording device had been planted by trespass, as most such devices were, then law enforcement could use the information for background and intelligence but could not introduce the tape as evidence in a trial.

On the day after Deegan was killed, one of Rico's informants provided details on the murder, telling the veteran agent that Romeo "Scarface" Martin, Wilfred Roy French and Ronald "Ronnie the Pig" Cassesso were the killers and that Barboza and Jimmy Flemmi also were in on it. The informant said Deegan had been lured to a finance company where the door had been left open by an employee. Deegan thought they were going to burglarize the firm but when they got to the door, French shot Deegan. Martin and Cassesso came out of the door and one of them also fired into Deegan's body.

Murder is a local crime and when the FBI develops information on such cases, it generally is turned over to city, county or state police authori-ties to handle. The informant information on the Deegan killing was recorded by Rico and sent to Capt. Robert Renfrew of the Chelsea Police Department. Renfrew, a graduate of the FBI National Academy police training program, was the logical person to receive such sensitive information.

A few days after the Deegan murder, FBI Headquarters in Washington, D.C., ordered that the information provided by the Patriarca microphone that identified possible perpetrators in the murder be sent to local authorities. Notations in FBI Boston field office files indicate that this was done and the information was passed to Renfrew and to Inspector Henry Doherty of the Everett Police Department.

At this point, Boston police had a pretty good idea who had commit-ted the crime. A Boston police report quoted a reliable informant as advising that the murder was the work of Barboza, Martin, French, Cassesso, Freddie Chiampi, Anthony "Tony Stats" Stathopolous and Joseph W. "Chico" Amico. The Massachusetts State Police also generated a report showing that it had received information three weeks earlier indicating that Deegan had pulled a gun on Barboza at the Ebb Tide Restaurant in Revere, Mass., forcing Barboza to back down. The report noted that "unconfirmed information" showed that Martin and Cassesso had entered the Lincoln National Bank building and were waiting just inside the rear door. Stathopolous was positioned in a car on Fourth Street and French and Deegan entered the alley. When Deegan opened the rear door, he was shot twice in the back of the head and also in the body.

While informants had provided the police with a good start on their murder investigation, they needed hard evidence to charge and try the suspected killers.

At the time, Rico was busy himself with his informants and was trying to recruit others. On the same day Deegan was killed, Rico opened a file on Jimmy Flemmi to assess and possibly recruit him as a "Top Echelon" informant. Rico worked on recruiting Flemmi without much success. He contacted the veteran criminal four times and closed the informant file in September 1965. In March 1966, Flemmi was convicted of armed assault with intent to commit murder and sentenced to four to six years in prison.

In March 1967, Barboza began to cooperate with Rico and his first area of discussion was the Deegan murder. Barboza told Rico and Condon that Deegan had been causing some problems and had been "out of order" at the Ebb Tide Restaurant. He said Peter Limone, a Mafia lieutenant to Gennaro Angiulo, underboss of the Providence-based Patriarca crime family, offered him $7,500 to kill Deegan. Barboza said when he learned that Stathopolous would be with Deegan, Limone offered to pay him an additional $2,500 if he would kill both men.

Barboza said he spoke to Tameleo and told him that Limone said it would be all right to "whack out" Deegan and Stathopolous and that he was sure the "office" would okay it. Tameleo replied, "[H]e has ... as many sins as Deegan has and he goes too." Barboza explained that the "office" was what "people termed as the Cosa Nostra." Barboza said if Tameleo had not given his approval, he would have done nothing further about killing Deegan and Stathopolous.

When an FBI cooperating subject has important information about a crime that could be prosecuted in state court, the local district attorney and police have to be brought in to interview the would-be witness and prepare the case. The responsibility for prosecutive decisions, deciding what witnesses to use and how to present the case lays with the local district attorney. While the FBI took pride in the fact that its agents contributed to important local cases, the bureau was very cautious about allowing those same agents to play too prominent a role in local prosecutions.

In September 1967, Detective Sergeant Frank Walsh and Detective John Doyle, both assigned to the Suffolk County, Mass., District Attorney's Office, interviewed Barboza about the Deegan killing in the presence of Rico and Condon at the Barnstable County Jail. The detectives produced a six-page statement, the first of many such interviews. They and Jack Zalkind, the prosecutor assigned to the case, interviewed Barboza four or five days a week for six months to ensure he was ready for trial. Zalkind worried that Barboza might not be inclined to tell the whole truth so he repeatedly cautioned him to be truthful and if he didn't, he warned him "… that's perjury in a murder case; and I'll put you in."

In December 2002 testimony before the House Committee on Government Reform, Zalkind said that while he never liked Barboza and never really trusted him, there was "a lot of corroboration of his testimony"—enough for prosecutors to go forward with the case. For example, he testified, Barboza told prosecutors there were three guys involved in the shooting "and sure enough, there were three different types of bullets that were found in the body."

The Deegan murder trial was a tough battle. It began on May 27, 1968. The trial judge examined 1,183 potential jurors; a jury of 16 was finally selected. The proceedings of the trial consumed 2,749 transcript pages and the trial continued until July 31, 1968. The stenographic record occupies 7,555 pages plus 614 pages of pre-trial hearings.

Several people who may have participated in the crime died before the trial began: Martin was shot and killed on July 9, 1965; Arthur Bratsos and

Thomas DePrisco, Barboza's friends who were trying to raise his bail, died Nov. 15, 1966; and Amico was killed Dec. 7, 1966.

Rico and Condon were responsible for recruiting and bringing Barboza forward, while the local district attorney's office and detectives prepared him for trial. The two FBI agents also passed along to local detectives any information they received that was in conflict with that provided by Barboza.

Trial testimony was dramatic. It showed that Stathopolous waited in an automobile on Fourth Street near the back entrance of the Lincoln National Bank building in Chelsea, while his two companions, French and Deegan, entered an adjoining alley. The purpose of the trip was to break into the bank and a door to the building had been left open by a co-conspirator. Stathopolous heard a volley of shots. French and a heavy set man with a gun in his hand appeared and Stathopolous heard a voice say, "get him too." Stathopolous took off.

Barboza acknowledged that before the murder, he had met with Limone to give him weekly payments on loans and Limone asked to talk to him about "something important." He said they met and Limone offered him a contract to kill Deegan for $7,500, which he said had been approved by the "office." Barboza said he told Limone he would ask Tameleo about whether the murder had been approved. When he met with Tameleo, the Patriarca underboss confirmed that the murder had been approved. He said he told Tameleo, "If you don't okay it … I won't do it."

During his testimony, French admitted being in the alley with Deegan, saying he had gone with him and Stathopolous to the area. He said heard five to seven shots and left the alley.

Robert Glavin, who was serving a sentence at the time at the Massachusetts Correctional Institution at Norfolk, Mass., for first degree murder, testified that an inmate approached him on behalf of Cassesso about making a false confession to the Deegan murder. Glavin testified that Arthur Ventola, owner of Arthur's Farm, a giant fencing operation in Revere, Mass., told him the "office" wanted him "to cop out" to the murder. Glavin was offered $50,000, told that his kids would be taken care of and that "they" would do something for him at the parole board. Glavin said he thought he was being told, not asked, and he wanted help.

Glavin met with FBI agent John Hanlon, who told him to go along with it. Glavin later met with Cassesso and again was offered $50,000. That conversation also was reported to Hanlon and Rico, who told him that the bureau would do what it could to protect him. Glavin later was stabbed by another inmate in what was seen as an unrelated incident. But he was then moved to a special custody situation so he could be protected.

After Fitzgerald, the lawyer wounded in the car bombing, was released by Barboza and Stathopolous from the attorney-client privilege, he testified that he had known Greco, French, and Deegan since 1964, and that he also was acquainted with Tameleo, Stathopolous and Limone. He also testified that he saw French at the Chelsea police station on the night of the Deegan murder, and observed blood spots on French's sleeve and on his shoe.

Fitzgerald also spoke about the efforts to persuade Barboza not to talk. He described the offers of $25,000 and $50,000 for his silence, and the proposal that Greco would "straighten out," or even "whack out" the victim of the stabbing for which Barboza had been indicted. Limone testified that he knew Barboza only for a month or so before the Deegan murder. He offered no alibi for the day of the murder.

Joseph Salvati, who Barboza believed was one of the men who murdered his friends and stole his bail money, testified in his own defense, saying he did not recall his whereabouts on the date of the Deegan murder. He admitted knowing Cassesso and Limone but denied knowing Barboza, Greco and Tameleo before the killing. Salvati's attorney pointed out that the only information introduced in the trial against his client was Barboza's testimony.

Four of those charged in the case took the stand and were available for cross-examination by the defense attorneys in the case, who knew the conversations had been recorded and would implicate Patriarca. The judge asked the attorneys if they wished to cross examine each one, but there were no takers. The FBI took hits from Congress, the judge and the media for not disclosing the bug, although the bureau was never in a position to do so.

Barboza's testimony was critical. His direct examination took two days and his cross examination nearly six and a half days. His long criminal record was exposed to the jury. Barboza entered a plea of guilty to two conspiracy indictments on the opening day of the trial. In the end, the jury believed Barboza and deliberated for over seven hours to find all the defendants guilty. French was convicted of first degree murder and conspiracy and Salvati of conspiracy and being an accessory—each with a recommendation that the death penalty not be imposed. Greco was found guilty of first degree murder and conspiracy and Cassesso, Tameleo and Limone were found guilty on charges of conspiracy and being accessories in the killing. They were sentenced to death.

Barboza's testimony had had a shocking impact on the New England crime syndicate.

Senior Judge Edward F. Harrington, a former federal prosecutor who headed the Justice Department's Organized Crime Strike Force in New England, described the impact of Barboza's testimony on organized crime as huge. Harrington himself had earned a reputation as an aggressive prosecutor with the ability to convince mobsters to testify against their former bosses.

The government's current Witness Protection Program (WITSEC), administered by the Justice Department and operated by the U.S. Marshals Service, was established, in part, under Title V of the Organized Crime Control Act of 1970 as a result of Barboza's cooperation. His example of testifying against the Mafia encouraged others to do the same and had a long term devastating impact on organized crime in New England—from which it has yet to recover.

Chapter 11: The Mastermind

JOHN J. "RED" Kelley was quite a character in the New England underworld. Known as "The Great One," "The Great Planner" and "The Mastermind," he used whatever moniker described him best. He used them all as aliases, and used them well. Kelley was deemed to be so smart and such a skilled criminal planner that although he was Irish, the Italians—who controlled the New England crime syndicate—also employed his services. He was the brains behind more than a dozen major armed robberies and a number of mob killings.

His "modus operandi" was simple: Make a plan, develop a schedule, acquire the necessary equipment and execute a practice run to ensure that everything worked. He would then either participate in the plan or turn it and the needed equipment over to someone else to carry out. Often sporting short-brim hats with colorful bands, Kelley was the "contractor" for the Italian mob.

It was Kelley who, in August 1962, planned and executed the robbery of a U.S. Postal Service truck that netted what at the time was the largest cash haul in U.S. history—more than $1.5 million, all in small bills. The money was being taken from Cape Cod to the Federal Reserve Bank in Boston. Dubbed "The Great Plymouth Mail Truck Robbery," the heist went like clockwork. A robber wearing a police uniform flagged the mail truck to a stop on a remote area of a highway outside of Plymouth, Mass. A detour had been placed on the highway a mile before in order to limit the traffic in the area.

Once the truck was stopped, eight men armed with submachine guns suddenly appeared and held up the two hapless mail guards who were then bound, gagged and tied up in the back of the truck. The robbers then drove the truck 25 miles making periodic stops and off loading 15 bags of cash to their accomplices. All the robbers wore white gloves. Four cars were used, including two that had been stolen.

Boston-area newspapers described the caper as a professional job executed with cool efficiency.

Despite an intensive manhunt and investigation that included the non-stop surveillance and unabashed harassment of every known armed robber in the Boston area and the offer of a $100,000 cash reward, the case went unsolved for years. But in 1967, just two weeks before the statute of limitations ran out, Kelley and two others were indicted by a federal grand jury for the robbery. A few months later, Kelley, who was defended by famed defense attorney F. Lee Bailey, and another defendant were found not guilty. The third suspect in the case had fled before the trial and was a fugitive. Kelley had beaten the rap completely. And the $1.5 million was never recovered.

Soon after the acquittals, Kelley planned another major robbery. Just three days after Christmas 1968, two bandits wearing black ski masks, black gloves and carrying a machine gun held up a Brinks truck in the North End section of Boston. The robbery took place at 6:30 p.m. while the driver and one guard were on a coffee break.

A second guard was in the truck when the door was opened from the outside with a key and the two masked men scrambled inside. They waved the machine gun and disarmed the guard, putting a hat on his head and pulling it down over his eyes. One of the bandits drove the truck to a parking lot where they off loaded the loot to an awaiting station wagon and left the guard manacled in the truck. Over $524,000 was taken.

Unfortunately for Kelley, that robbery was quickly solved. FBI agents assigned to the Boston field office, along with Boston police detectives, determined that a Brinks guard was involved in the theft and when he was confronted, he quickly confessed and the detectives arrested Kelley and two other men, charging them with the crime.

Enter FBI Agent H. Paul Rico, flush from his recruitment of Joseph "The Animal" Barboza as a top level informant, whose information and testimony had wreaked havoc on the New England crime family. With Kelley looking at hard time, Rico was poised and ready to do it again.

The veteran agent had spent so much of his time hanging around the Boston-area places where mobsters gather, he knew and was known by them. As a consequence, when Kelley was in trouble and needed a deal, he was sure he could reach out to Rico as someone he trusted. Kelley had his wife contact Rico to tell him he wanted to talk.

FBI agents and other police authorities know that the initial interview with a person like Kelley in such a situation is critical. The detective or agent must know what to say and how to say it in order to communicate effectively with a hardened criminal like Kelley. A bond must be established between the agent and criminal who is contemplating cooperating or can be encouraged to do so. Rico and the agent who was assigned to the Brinks robbery case interviewed Kelley in the Charles Street Jail in Boston.

After an initial meeting on June 5, 1969, and a bit of persuasion during follow-up meetings over the next two months, Kelley told the agents he wanted to go the way Barboza had gone. He had been persuaded that it was in his interest to cooperate and Rico was the person he trusted to get him through the process. As a result, Kelley, the hardened criminal mastermind, submitted to a number of interviews about his crimes and his connections to the Italian mob. Like others, he was to be another major success for the FBI in general and Rico in particular.

At the time, a cooperating subject like Kelley would be debriefed in many interviews by an FBI team and by police detectives and prosecutors who would be responsible for developing a prosecutable case wherever one was appropriate. In this situation, Rico and his partner, Dennis Condon, formed the primary interview team and were occasionally assisted by a younger agent, Dave Divan, who generally took notes and recorded the results in the form of interview reports.

Typically when an important cooperating subject is developed, the FBI agents promise not to use whatever he said against him and assure him that he and his family would be protected. Working out whether or not such a witness would be granted immunity, or some kind of deal to minimize his prosecution and entry into the witness protection program, was beyond their authority.

The agents would certainly offer their opinions on any potential deal, but the decision was the responsibility of the prosecutors. In fact, if both local and federal crimes were involved, everyone who could prosecute had to agree. Since protection for the long term was the responsibility of the Justice Department and the U.S. Marshals Service, the circumstances in which a person would be afforded protection would be worked out by the Marshals Service, not by FBI agents. Deciding the extent and details of how the witness was protected, particularly within the Witness Protection Program, was the province of the Marshals.

Usually a firm deal would be made with a cooperator for his prosecution. The witness would plead guilty or be granted immunity. If he was required to plead, the prosecutor would agree to recommend a light sentence, no sentence or whatever sentence he thought was reasonable. A cooperating subject would be told to tell the truth and would be made to understand that if he lied, the deal was off and whatever he had said could—and would—be used to prosecute him. It was in his interest to tell the truth.

A cooperating witness would be assured that he and his family would receive protection but the precise details of his long term protection usually wouldn't be decided until after the person testified.

Once the details of the Kelley deal were decided, there was much to talk about. Rico formed a bond with Kelley in the sense that both were at the top of their game. Rico was a top FBI agent and Kelley was the master career criminal. They both understood and respected each other. Both were smart. Rico treated Kelley with respect, as he did all the criminals he worked with.

Divan found Kelley a fascinating person. He was very bright and, in Divan's opinion, probably could have made a fortune in business if he had been honest. Kelley was an institution in the criminal world and told them about the $524,000 holdup of the Brinks truck, the robbery of armored trucks of the Skelly Detective Agency that netted $177,000 and more than a dozen other significant robberies.

But what caught Rico's eye was the murder of Rudy Marfeo, the brother of Willy Marfeo who had been killed at the direction of New England mob boss Raymond L.S. Patriarca. Like his brother Willy, Rudy

Marfeo had angered Patriarca. Like his brother, he had failed to pay a tithe to Patriarca for his small-time gambling business. Like his brother, he was warned, and, like his brother, he ignored the warnings and was killed.

Kelley told the agents that Patriarca had tasked three men, led by Maurice "Pro" Lerner, to commit the actual murder but had Kelley plan the escape route and provide the guns. Lerner was a murderous thug known to his associates as "Pro" because he had played minor league baseball where he was said to be better with a bat than a glove. He carried his skills with the bat into his employment with Patriarca as an assassin and strong arm enforcer. One time he had to kill a person who had been cheating the Mafia. Lerner knew the guy would answer the door and for a few minutes before he knocked he practiced a swing with a baseball bat. When he knocked and the guy opened the door, Lerner hit him in face with the bat so hard that the blow killed him on the spot.

Kelley told Rico that Lerner was the most dangerous man he had known in his 25 years of criminal activities. Kelley said Lerner was extremely bright, unafraid and that he appeared to relish killing. He identified a grocery shopping trip that Marfeo took regularly and made a plan around killing him there. Kelley cut down the shotgun that was to be used in the murder in his basement and equipped it with a sling so that it could be carried under a coat.

Lerner and two other hoodlums entered the grocery store where Rudy Marfeo, Mary Baccarie and Anthony Melei were shopping. Baccarie said a man wearing a Halloween mask and golfing hat entered the grocery and pushed Baccarie to the floor and out of the way. As she fell, she heard someone yell, "Rudy watch out." Marfeo and his associate were both shot and left to bleed to death on the floor as Lerner and the other two thugs fled the scene. They followed Kelley's escape route as they got away.

Kelley provided Rico and Rhode Island prosecutors the details of the Marfeo murder and identified the gunmen, along with Patriarca and an associate as planning and directing the murder. Most importantly, he provided detailed information about his many meetings with Patriarca and the murderers and of his role in ordering them. He said that at one point, as the planning dragged on, Patriarca became impatient and said, "I don't want stories, I just want him killed."

A House committee that later investigated the FBI's use of murderers as informants concluded in a report that by the time Rico turned over Kelley to prosecutors to testify in the case, "Kelley was a fully prepared witness." The report said that one prosecutor, Assistant Rhode Island Attorney General Richard Israel, reported that the FBI had handed him "a major crime on a silver platter—hell a gold platter and we were going to break down the major element of Patriarca's unit."

In August 1969, Kelley testified before a federal grand jury in the Marfeo and Melei murders under a grant of immunity.

Patriarca was charged in Rhode Island and tried in the Superior Court in Providence. The newspapers reported that Kelley stood in the witness box with his head down with a stone-faced look that never varied and ranged from sadness to displeasure. His voice was soft and responded to questions politely. He talked about the patience required to make the big robberies succeed. Kelley was cooperative throughout his testimony providing the minimum amount of information without appearing to be evasive. He answered "possibly" to limit many responses. When asked how long he had been planning robberies, he answered, "possibly 20 years." He responded to a question about how many he had planned by saying, "possibly 12 or 15."

On the stand, Kelley admitted the $524,000 Brinks holdup, described the two Skelly armored truck robberies and talked about some robberies that were planned but never carried out because the circumstances weren't right. He testified that he had meticulously studied the grocery store and the surrounding area and that he had developed a suitable plan for the killers. He admitted providing them with a sawed-off shotgun; a carbine, Halloween masks and buckshot shells which he said were most effective for killing at a short range.

Kelley admitted being protected by various federal agencies and living in a hotel, having his laundry done and eating well. When asked why he had sought protection, he said that because if he testified "our lives would be in danger." When asked "From whom?" he nodded in the direction of Patriarca and the other defendants and said, "From this group."

In the end, Kelley was an effective witness and Lerner was convicted of murdering Rudy Marfeo and Anthony Melei and of conspiracy to commit murder. He was sentenced to life in prison. In spite of the fact that Patriarca swore on his "dead wife and children" that he was innocent and had been framed, he was convicted of conspiracy. Patriarca was sentenced to ten years to run concurrently with his five year sentence for ordering Willy Marfeo's murder. Three other defendants were also convicted of the conspiracy charge and sentenced to ten years each.

Kelley wasn't finished. Rico was able to get him to talk about Carlo Gambino, the head of the Gambino Crime Family in New York—or better known as the national Boss of Bosses of La Cosa Nostra. Kelley provided information about stolen property that had been given as tribute to Gambino by various mob figures. The property was taken in a number of robberies, truck hijackings and thefts and in a variety of different crimes. Once in Gambino's control, some of this property had been moved out of New York to other states. Kelley knew the details and also provided the names of several people who could confirm his story.

FBI Agent Sean McWeeney, who had been transferred to New York and was assigned the Carlo Gambino case, became the recipient of this information. McWeeney interviewed the people on Kelley's list and he finally found one who confirmed the story. Gambino was indicted for Interstate Transportation of Stolen Property but died of a heart attack before he could be tried.

Kelley had provided significant and damaging testimony against the Mafia. Patriarca had been convicted a second time and Gambino was indicted.

Very few FBI agents or police detectives have even a small part in developing or handling a cooperating subject like Barboza or Kelley. Rico had developed and handled two with devastating impact on the Mafia.

Screenwriter and author Alan Trustman said the convictions confirmed that Rico "was an FBI hero, the man who brought down the most profitable Mafia satrapy in the country, that of criminal genius Raymond Patriarca in Providence." In the process, Trustman said "Rico invented the Witness Protection Program" when he turned Barboza into a government witness against Patriarca. Barboza was the first person who entered the program, closely followed by Kelley.

Chapter 12: The Plot

THE NEW ENGLAND Mafia, one of the most active and feared in the country, was in disarray. At a time when organized crime was asserting itself all across the country, moving into positions of dominance or bolstering its controlling influence over an army of criminals, and law enforcement authorities were being confronted with Omerta, the apparently unbreakable "code of silence," it seemed as if everybody in the New England mob—once an unshakable branch of La Cosa Nostra—was talking to the FBI.

Even worse, everyone in the New England crime family was being convicted and going to prison. By the summer of 1969, Raymond L.S. Patriarca, one of the most powerful crime bosses in the United States, had been convicted of conspiracy to commit murder, along with his top lieutenants, Henry Tameleo and Gennaro Anguilo. Also convicted and sentenced to death or long prison terms in a variety of crimes were top New England mobsters Peter Limone, Louis Greco, Wilfred Roy French and Ronald Cassesso.

Everything was going wrong for the New England family. The FBI had bugged Patriarca's office and, while under current law it couldn't use what it discovered as evidence in court, agents had collected a wealth of information about his suspected criminal activities and those who carried them out.

A number of top mobsters also had turned against the family, including John J. "Red" Kelley, the consummate criminal planner on whom

Patriarca had relied to arrange and organize several high-profile murders and armed robberies. Kelley provided testimony to the government that would lead to another Patriarca conviction and to the indictment of Carlo Gambino, the so-called "Boss of Bosses."

Joseph "The Animal" Barboza, one of the mob's most feared hit men who was reputed to have killed 26 men, had turned on Patriarca, who had used the assassin for a number of killings and various criminal assignments. As a result of Barboza's testimony, four of Patriarca's subordinates were on death row.

As members of the Patriarca family began to fall, those who helped in their demise, mainly Barboza and Kelley, were being protected by the government and the Witness Security Program with its own acronym, WITSEC, was being created for them. Things weren't going well at all.

Barboza's unexpected cooperation had sent shock waves throughout the Mafia. He was the first major figure to testify against the New England mob and his success and example led directly to others doing the same. Kelley had come forward because of Barboza—arranging to testify on what he knew after sending his wife to meet with FBI Agent H. Paul Rico in Boston. His message was simple: he wanted to do the same as Barboza had done.

Even the local newspapers were carrying articles about the demise of organized crime in New England. The Boston Sunday Globe carried an extensive articled entitled, The Bug, The Baron and Raymond Patriarca, which noted that the listening devices planted in Patriarca's office had documented his commitment to the mob; "In this thing of ours," he told an associate, "your love for your mother and father is one thing; your love for The Family' is a different kind of love."

The devices also discovered that Patriarca had withstood all kinds of violent threats to his expanding kingdom but the "panther-like gangster" never anticipated the deadliness of such an incongruous combination of an FBI bug and a deal-seeking Barboza.

Omerta, the code of silence, had been intended to shield the mob from outsiders, each of its members swearing in front of their peers to "enter into this organization to protect my family and to protect my friends. I swear not to divulge this secret and to obey, with love and omerta." It wasn't working for the New England mob.

John T. Howland, Boston police superintendent, said Patriarca was "looked upon with awe as a smooth, sure and careful man." Suffolk District Attorney Garrett Byrne said the mob boss was "a man whose name you ordinarily hear whispered but nobody wants to hear out loud." Patriarca had been feared and was thought to be "too shrewd and too big" for the few law enforcement officials who challenged him.

While powerful committees in Congress had tried to get Patriarca in the 1950s and again in the 1960s, they never penetrated deep enough. The FBI's bugging of Patriarca's office and the solicited information from a willing Barboza did far more than the congressional investigators to disrupt Patriarca's criminal enterprise.

Patriarca had occasionally worried about a bug but dismissed it. He had talked freely in "The Office," while the FBI listened. The take from the microphone was rich in detail and intelligence about Patriarca and his New England crime family. Even though the government couldn't use the intelligence in court because the microphone had been placed as a result of an illegal trespass on Patriarca's property, the bureau certainly benefited from the intelligence it generated. Barboza and Kelley were needed to provide testimony in court.

The Sunday Herald Traveler reported that federal agents said no other Mafia family in the country had so many bosses in jail or facing trial as the New England mob. An unnamed federal agent was quoted in the article as saying, "We have so many informers that they have to stand in line." That may have been a bit of hyperbole but things were going well for the good guys and it was informants and cooperating subjects who were generating the success and Rico, whose cultivation of FBI informants had become legendary, was the person most responsible for it.

Court records and interviews show that Rico's success with informants had been absolutely critical to the government's success against members of the New England crime family. Many of the tools the FBI employs today in recruiting and maintaining critical informants and cooperating witnesses did not exist in the 1960s. Court authorized electronic surveillance that produced evidence that could be used in a prosecution, use immunity cases and the Racketeer Influenced and Corrupt Organizations Act (RICO) did not become available until the next decade. The witness security program was only in its formative stage.

As the New England mob was pressed further and harder, the person who was most responsible for its decline was clear. Rico's name kept appearing in local newspaper accounts of FBI successes and Mafia failures. Articles about Barboza's cooperation named Rico as the agent handling him.

When Boston lawyer John Fitzgerald was bombed in 1968 by Frank Salemme and Steve Flemmi while the lawyer was representing Joe Barboza, the local paper described him lying in the street calling out for Rico. When Kelley's cooperation became known, it was Rico who was interviewing him. At every step on the path to prison, Rico appeared to be handling the big cases and interviews. And it seemed that everybody who was anybody in crime knew him. After all, for many years, the veteran FBI agent had hung out where the leading figures in crime hung out and he knew them all. And they knew him.

Agents who worked with Rico at the time say the Italian Mafia came to "hate" Rico. They knew he was responsible for the charges and prosecutions that had been energized and they hated him for it.

As dangerous and deadly as many career criminals are, it is a rare thing that they decide to kill a cop, much less an FBI agent. In fact, of the 36 FBI agents killed in the line of duty since 1925, none died as a result of a criminal assassination that was planned in advance. Criminals know that the murder of an FBI agent sets off a critical response effort that includes a cadre of agents and support personnel who are experts in investigations, surveillance, the use of informants and tactical operations.

But in August 1969, perhaps the inevitable finally happened: the New England mob decided to take action against Rico, whose actions had sent many of the syndicate's leadership and top lieutenants to prison.

On Aug. 12, 1969, Rico was contacted by Richard "The Fat Man" Chicofsky, a veteran con man and longtime FBI informant he had interviewed in connection with those who worked for and with Kelley. Chicofsky told Rico and another agent that a couple of days earlier, gangland killer Maurice "Pro" Lerner had arranged to meet him in the parking lot of a Boston Restaurant, where Lerner questioned him about his meetings with Rico. Chicofsky said he told Lerner that another agent usually accompanied Rico when they met and they usually talked in a car. In that conversation, Chicofsky said Lerner wanted to know a lot of details: including whether they locked the doors, kept the windows closed and where they normally sat in the vehicle.

Lerner knew Kelley was talking and he expected to be arrested soon, so Lerner suggested a plan in which Chicofsky would call Rico and tell him it was urgent they meet at a pre-arranged location. When Chicofsky joined Rico and the other agent in their car, Lerner and three other hoodlums would approach the car, take control and kill the other agent. Chicofsky said Lerner thought that killing the other agent would demonstrate to Rico that they really meant business. Chicofsky said Lerner told him they would then force Rico to take them to the place where Kelley was being guarded by the U.S. Marshals Service, where they would kill Rico, the deputy marshals and Kelley.

Chicofsky said Lerner also talked about trying to find Rico's house in Belmont, Mass., and that he had been to the town trying to locate it.

Lerner was arrested the day before Chicofsky came forward, named in the murder of bookmakers Rudolph Marfeo and Anthony Melei, who were gunned down on the orders of Patriarca on April 20, 1968, while shopping at a market in Providence, R.I. The New England crime boss had been angered by the attempts of Marfeo and Melei to set up gaming operations without his permission. In addition to Lerner, seven others were charged in the killing including Kelley, although he agreed to cooperate and testify for the government. When he was arrested, Lerner told Rico, "You look just like your pictures."

If Lerner was hoping to intimidate Rico or the FBI he missed the mark. The FBI's reaction to such a threat was predictable to those who knew the bureau. The threat galvanized the FBI and officials at the bureau's headquarters in Washington, D.C., ordered the field offices to do what was necessary to ensure that vigorous action was immediately taken to bring Lerner's three associates who were still fugitives to justice. An FBI Headquarters teletype to the special agent in charge of the Boston field office ordered that Rico and his family be protected and the office to vigorously press their investigation to locate the three men. In addition, FBI Headquarters directed that obstruction of justice and assault on federal officer charges be pursued against Lerner and the three hoodlums.

When the Boston FBI field office advised that the Woonsocket, R.I., Police Department had a source who could produce the location of the three fugitives but needed $2,000 to pay the source, the amount was quickly authorized. By the end of August 1969, Lerner and his three hoodlum associates were all in custody. All four were held without bail.

With Lerner and his three colleagues in jail held without bail, the immediate threat to Rico and his family had been alleviated. In September 1969, another Boston informant reported that a new La Cosa Nostra plan was being developed. The informant said the Mafia was considering ways in which they could discredit, disgrace or embarrass Rico. At least you could say that they had identified their problem. But it was too late for the Mafia to take action against Rico. Their opportunity for revenge on Rico would come over thirty years later.

In the spring 1970, Rico was transferred to Miami. After he left Boston, the organized crime squad would change significantly and those changes would affect many people including Rico.

Chapter 13: Miami

ON APRIL 1, 1970, veteran FBI Agent H. Paul Rico came home from work and told his wife, Connie, they were going to be transferred from the bureau's Boston field office and they could go anywhere they wanted. The couple announced the pending transfer to the rest of the family at the dinner table that night and, at first, the children thought he was kidding—that it was an April Fool's Day joke. When he persuaded them it was not, Connie got together the maps they had and they talked about where they would like to live.

Rico was close to his family, which included not only his wife and children but various and assorted cousins, second cousins, uncles, aunts and even a few people whose precise relationship was unknown to Connie. Most of them lived in Massachusetts but they often visited Florida. The Ricos considered some of the more exotic places in the country but rejected them because they couldn't imagine that their relatives would make the trip to California, Hawaii or to many of the more distant places they considered. Miami was the place that met their requirements—it was tropical and their relatives would visit.

For agents accustomed to accommodating the "needs of the bureau," this type of transfer was a highly unusual occurrence. It was the highest form of recognition that an agent could earn. Under FBI Director J. Edgar Hoover, such a choice was acknowledgment that the FBI believed the agent's performance had been exceptional, and in Rico's case, was in danger. Although there was a real and continuing threat to harm the veteran agent, Rico never told Connie or his children about any pending danger.

The family never knew that Mafia hitman Maurice "Pro" Lerner had very real plans to kidnap and murder Rico because of his success in turning informants and enlisting cooperating witnesses in a number of high-profile cases involving the New England mob. Connie's mother once described her son-in-law as an umbrella to his family and friends, saying he always kept troubles off them.

The Ricos planned to stay in Miami for five years and then retire, returning to Belmont, Mass., just outside Boston, where they had been happy. Belmont was home to the couple. Rico had transferred from a private school to Belmont High School so he could play sports. It was there that he became one of the school's football stars and where he met Connie, the proverbial high school sweetheart he married after a stint in the U.S. Army during World War II.

Connie, upbeat as always, convinced the children, who then ranged in age from Joyce, 17, to John, 7, that they were embarking on a great adventure. They located a five-bedroom ranch style house in Miami Shores, just a dozen miles north of Miami, and moved in.

Rico told the children they would each have to commit to some outdoor activity. In response, Suzanne began to sail and the other Ricos took up golf. When their family and friends from Massachusetts would visit, they would host "The Rico Open" at a local golf club. In the family, Rico was in charge of "fun and funds" and Connie took care of all the other things. To keep things upbeat in their golfing outings, he made rules such as whining cost a stroke and tears cost five strokes.

The Ricos made friends quickly. Their house was constantly filled with kids. Connie thought it was like living in a club house. Rico had always wanted his children's friends to be around their house. He told them they could sleep over when they went to college, but until then he wanted them around their house.

Of all the lessons he taught, Rico was most insistent on honesty. His daughter, Christine, remembers that she once went to the local swimming pool by crossing railroad tracks where she had been forbidden to go. On the way, she fell and chipped her tooth but told no one since the fall had occurred where she wasn't supposed to be. In spite of the fact that her little brother, John, knew what had happened and he teased her with comments using the word chipped ("don't you want a chocolate chipped cookie, Christine"), she got away with it for several days. Finally, her mother noticed the chip and her secret was exposed. She was punished for not telling the truth rather than for going the forbidden way.

At the FBI's Miami field office, where during the 1970s white-collar crime, corruption and fraud were the primary focus, Rico was assigned the Criminal Intelligence Program. He had the responsibility of coordinating the Top Echelon Informant Program, which oversees those persons who are either furnishing high level information in the organized crime area or are under development to furnish such information. He also was detailed to the La Cosa Nostra Investigative Program, which targeted would-be informants inside the Mafia. He was loaned to the Metro-Dade Police Department's new organized crime squad, where he lectured on informant development. He also had liaison with the Florida Pari-Mutuel Wagering Division.

Over the next few years, in addition to his regular assignments, Rico handled several undercover operations. In April 1970, a truckload of 280 Winchester riot shotguns and 80 Marlin rifles was stolen from the Interstate Motor Lines (IML) truck terminal in North Branford, Conn. News accounts at the time speculated that "militants" and violent extremist groups were responsible for the theft. In January 1971, a source appeared in one of the Miami division resident agencies and told the FBI a former fellow inmate had approached him about disposing of some shotguns and rifles to subversive groups in the Miami area.

The source identified his contacts that were in New York City and worked with the FBI to place Rico in touch with them in an undercover role as a buyer. Rico's skills in dealing with gangsters and a variety of informants had prepared him well. He was at home and played his role effectively. After several meetings with the subjects, Rico arranged for them to take a rental truck and load the guns into it and then return, where and when he promised he would pay them. The subjects were followed to their drop site in West Babylon, N.Y., and there they loaded the guns into Rico's truck. Of course, FBI agents ultimately would take possession of the guns when the thieves were arrested, they certainly knew that somebody had to load the truck and deferred the arrests until the task had been accomplished.

In 1973, Rico was contacted by a former source who knew that a substantial amount of securities that had been stolen months before were available to be purchased. Rico saw at once the opportunity to make an undercover buy and directed the source to develop more information. In the process of negotiating the purchase, Rico had several telephone conversations with a known Miami fence. He learned that the U.S. Secret Service had an interest in the fence for counterfeiting and brought that agency into the investigation.

Rico's FBI personnel file says he met with two subjects in a local Miami restaurant while posing as a "flamboyant hoodlum buyer." With his penchant for dressing as a 1950s character out of Guys and Dolls, he would hardly have appeared as a "conservatively dressed hoodlum buyer."

The two subjects had spotted a police car as they entered the restaurant and were nervous. Rico overcame their fears, convincing them that they were not the objects of surveillance by the police. He learned that the securities were in their Cadillac parked outside. It was then revealed to the two sellers that while they were not under surveillance by the police, they were under surveillance by the FBI. They were arrested and $214,000 in securities was recovered.

In 1974, Rico was selected for one more undercover operation. He again posed as a corrupt buyer and was introduced to subjects who had counterfeited three million dollars worth of Sunbeam securities. After being introduced by a source as a possible buyer, he introduced a second undercover agent as a stock expert who would have to pass on the adequacy of the counterfeit securities. The two agents convinced the sellers that they were hoodlum buyers. They met several times and identified the printer and the press used to create the false documents. When the case was concluded, the subjects were arrested in possession of $2.2 million in counterfeit Sunbeam Corp. securities.

By 1975, financial obligations for the Ricos were becoming serious. Their children had started college and it was evident they were smart—all the Rico children attended universities and earned degrees. Rico insisted his daughters attend school and learn a trade in case they were widowed and had to go to work for themselves. It was an old fashioned view of the world and, while his first two daughters complied, they had greater ambitions.

The oldest Rico child, Joy, attended Florida State University where she majored in biochemistry. She later attended the University of Florida where she earned a pharmacy degree that would protect her if she was widowed. After working as a pharmacist, she attended the College of Medicine at the University of Florida, where she earned her medical degree as a doctor.

The next child, Melissa, earned a degree in nursing from the University of Florida that would protect her if she was widowed and then attended the University of Cincinnati, where she earned a law degree. The third child, Suzanne, was especially gifted in math and physics and attended Barry University in Miami while in high school. When she was 16, she entered the University of Florida without graduating from high school. The Ricos allowed her to go to the university at that age because her sisters were there and could look out for her. She earned a degree in engineering, which seemed to satisfy her father's concerns about her ability to take care of herself if she was widowed.

By the time Christine graduated from American University and earned a master's degree in New Hampshire, Rico had adjusted to the new world where women were on a more equal footing with men. The youngest child, John, graduated from Boston College and earned his law degree at the University of Miami School of Law.

Education at Florida's universities was very reasonable in 1975; undergraduates paid less than $500 a year tuition. With five children headed to college, costs would still mount up. As Rico approached retirement at age 50, he realized that he would receive 50 percent of his salary in retirement annuity payments. If he continued to work for the FBI in the job he loved, he would be working for 50 percent of his pay. If he worked in retirement, he would enjoy both the FBI retirement annuity and the salary for his new job. Retirement was the time when most agents were able to increase their income, pay their bills and enjoy a different paced life.

In the spring of 1975, Rico was contacted by an executive search firm seeking to hire a vice president for security for the World Jai Alai Company (WJA). He had been suggested by a retired agent who owned a company that handled security at several dog and horse racing tracks. Alan Trustman, chairman of the WJA Executive Committee, had insisted that retired FBI agents be hired since he knew they would have clean records and they would be able to advise him who he could talk to and who he should avoid in the pari-mutuel business. Rico was interviewed by the headhunter and then by John Callahan, the WJA president. He then flew to Boston with Callahan and met several members of the WJA executive board who lived there.

Rico was careful about taking this job; he did what agents of the time would have done. He called the FBI's Boston field office and had the office search its records for Callahan and several members of the executive board. At the time, field offices did not send all the information they developed to FBI Headquarters so it was important to check where the subject of your inquiry had lived and worked. Boston found no record concerning Callahan and nothing derogatory concerning its executive board members.

Callahan and Rico came to an agreement and on May 1, 1975, Rico ended his 24 years with the FBI and became the vice president for security of the WJA. It seemed like the perfect job for him.

Chapter 14: Retirement and Jai Alai

NO JOB EVER works out precisely as one expects but on the whole, now retired FBI Agent H. Paul Rico found that his new job at World Jai Alai Inc. (WJA) was a very good fit. There were many things about it he enjoyed. He loved the excitement of the business, he was making good money, he had a company car, his country club membership was paid, he had an expense account that included company-paid trips to Europe, and he could set his own hours and pace. Who wouldn't like a job like that?

Rico arranged his work schedule to be at the arena, or fronton, when the jai alai games were being played so he was there into the evenings. On Saturdays, his wife, Connie, would join him for dinner at the fronton and he often would invite some of the patrons to join them. The Ricos enjoyed these evenings.

When Rico started at WJA, one of the Boston owners complained that the company had experienced petty thievery by some of its employees; that, as an example, one of the managers was ordering more carpet and pictures than needed and putting the extra in his own home. The Boston owner told Rico it seemed impossible to find a manager who wouldn't exploit the system, but Rico assured him he had come to Miami to make sure the whole office building would be filled with honest people. He did so by hiring retired FBI agents to fill key management and security positions in the company. The petty thievery stopped.

In addition to his security responsibilities, Rico was named WJA general manager and while he may not have studied management theory, he managed as a person who practiced "Management by Walking Around." He walked around the place at a surprisingly quick pace stopping occasionally and talking to employees, including the police officers filling security positions. He greeted customers.

Robert Warshaw, then a young Miami police officer who would rise to become assistant chief of the Miami Police Department, worked in a second job as one of the 30 police officers handling security duties in the WJA fronton. He remembered that Rico was easy to spot, a "flashy dresser," tanned and always wearing a light colored suit. He said he was approachable, easy to talk to and thought competent by the police officers. At the time, the WJA fronton was "bone" clean and the crowd was composed of well-dressed affluent people who caused few real police problems.

As he walked about, Rico would find out what was going on and if something was wrong, he would bring people in to solve whatever problem he had discovered. Many of those who worked at the fronton said they could tell from his confident manner and the way that the employees reacted to him, that he was both well-liked by the employees and greatly respected by them. Rico appeared to some of the WJA employees as "everyone's grandfather."

His management philosophy was straightforward and simple. When his daughter, Suzanne, was assuming her first management position and asked him for advice, he told her it was simple. He said, "When you have a problem to deal with, call everyone together and tell them 'this is our problem. If we don't solve it, you will get some son-of-a-bitch in here that you don't like.'"

Rico was not a "small talker," but if you engaged him in a serious discussion, he revealed himself as an intelligent, thoughtful person. By nature, he was helpful and considerate. He was highly regarded—one former employee thought Rico was "brilliant"—but he wasn't focused on details. When dealing with areas such as the record and accounting systems, he relied on competent subordinates. His boss, Richard P. Donovan, was the WJA president; an accountant who focused on details. They were a good team.

Rico used his expense account and entertained frequently. The WJA owned jai alai schools in France and Spain and he traveled there periodically for the company. On occasion, he took Connie on his trips to Europe and, of course, she was careful to always pay her own way because she did not think it right for the company to bear her expenses. Connie would sometimes entertain her sister or a friend at the WJA but would always pay the bill from her own funds.

Many employees and others also described Rico as very gracious, who made the Jai Alai facilities available at a reasonable price to his former FBI colleagues for retirement functions and transfer parties and the like. When these events occurred, he would stop by and check to see if everything was going well and visit briefly with the group.

The job was not only fun but, as many of us find in groups that we like, the Ricos felt that the people made it great. Rico once told Connie he was extremely fortunate to have had two jobs where the people around him were so good.

In the 1970s, jai alai was at its peak and large crowds attended the complex and highly competitive games. The environment in which the sport operated was also complex and competitive.

The WJA was one of the oldest jai alai enterprises in the United States. In 1926, a group of Boston-based investors opened a jai alai fronton in Miami. Nine years later, they were joined by Richard Berenson when Florida legalized parimutuel wagering. By 1975, the WJA executive board, still composed chiefly of Boston based investors, contained some interesting people including two who were at odds over the control of the company.

One, Alan Trustman, a Harvard lawyer who taught at Boston University Law School and later wrote several screen plays for successful movies, became a friend to Rico. The other, Buddy Berenson, whose father had played a key role in developing the sport in the United States, was gradually forced out of the WJA management and for the next several years struggled to get back into the jai alai business. WJA management believed Berenson was attempting to publicly depict those competing with him as agents of organized crime, hoping to deprive them of the state approval required for involvement in pari-mutuel operations.

Just two years before Rico would retire from the FBI and join the WJA, the company was doing well and growing. It had frontons in Miami,

Tampa and Ocala, and by 1973 was considering expansion into Connecticut. The environment there looked good for jai alai. It was a small state geographically but it had a population of over 3 million. It was near New York and could expect to draw fans from New York City. Before the 1970s, The Hartford Courant, the largest daily newspaper in Connecticut, carried few articles about the sport of jai alai but those few were very favorable to the sport and depicted it as an exciting and glamorous activity.

A 1966 Hartford Courant news article headlined, "Legal Gambling Raises Millions for 'Good Works'" observed that gambling at jai alai "… is not sinister illegal gambling. This is open gambling which produces millions of dollars for state and city governments." The article went on to discuss gambling conducted by churches, fraternal orders, veterans groups and political clubs that raise millions of dollars for "good works" as if jai alai and its revenues were somehow related to such charitable endeavors.

A 1968 Courant article ran under the headline, "Jai Alai Big Action in Miami" and described it as a sport that combines "all the glitter of a Broadway opening, color of the bullring, drama of football and speed of hockey into one of the world's oldest ball games." And if that wasn't enough, the article gushed that the Miami fronton was one of the country's "most colorful sports auditorium(s)" that created a feeling of "ancient Spain and Mexico." It included a dramatic picture of two players in action with a caption that advised the reader that "Action at the Miami Jai Alai Fronton combines the grace of ballet with the speed of tennis in a spectacle as dramatic as the bullfight."

But these glowing reviews were destined to change.

In 1972, the Connecticut Legislature authorized the establishment of parimutuel betting facilities within the state that included jai alai frontons. A year later, the WJA began negotiations with Connecticut authorities and the Hartford City Council in anticipation of securing a license to open a fronton in Hartford. At the same time, WJA competitors also were exploring the possibility of establishing jai alai frontons in the state. As WJA proceeded to gain approval for an $11 million fronton in Hartford, The Hartford Courant suddenly editorialized extensively against the establishment of the WJA jai alai fronton there.

By 1973, The Courant's coverage began to contain references to organized crime and to cite a variety of problems jai alai would bring to the
community. The new negative trend in the reporting on jai alai is illustrated
by a March 25, 1973, Courant article that quoted a former police chief as
saying that "... organized crime has grown in Connecticut to a concentra-
tion that rivals any state in the union ... with jai alai here, we can well
expect the town will be a breeding ground for elements of this type." The
statement plays to a preconceived image in the public mind and would be
typical of Courant reporting about jai alai for the next 30 years. Although
little or no evidence for the allegation was set out in the article.

By the time Rico joined the WJA, news coverage of jai alai in
Connecticut had changed dramatically. As the date of the opening of the
Hartford fronton approached, The Courant predicted inconveniences such
as traffic jams, highlighted complaints of Hartford businesses and even discussed the worries of neighbors that gambling would change the "life style"
of the community. After the Hartford fronton was opened, The Courant
quoted restaurateurs as whining that their patrons had rushed off to place
bets at the fronton.

As the negative coverage in the press swirled around the business,
Rico was confronted with two predicaments at work. Both would receive
public attention. One appeared to be a relatively minor problem but the
other was clearly a major obstacle. Rico would resolve both.

The first situation occurred when Rico's new boss, John B. Callahan,
wanted to hire Bryan McNeely, a tough guy from South Boston who had
played football at one of the Big Ten universities. Rico wanted to hire
another person for the position and did not like McNeely. He searched
police records for McNeely in Boston and Florida but was unable to locate
any record of an arrest. Callahan was president of the company and, of
course, prevailed. McNeely was hired and assigned to the food service
operation. He quickly became a problem. He seemed to provoke problems
rather than calm things down. There is one story that after he was cautioned for fighting, he went to the Mutiny Club in Coconut Grove and got
in a fight with the bouncer there and threw him through a plate glass
window.

The second, and more serious problem, occurred in March 1976 when Rico's old FBI partner in Boston, Dennis Condon, called him and advised that the Connecticut State Police were trying to use some information about Callahan to generate negative publicity for the WJA. At the time, WJA was working to acquire the jai alai fronton in Hartford and any association of its managers with criminals would threaten the company's ability to secure the gambling license it needed.

Condon told Rico that Callahan had been observed by the police at the Playboy Club with a group of people that included James Martorano, the hoodlum brother of John Martorano—a mob hitman who would murder Oklahoma businessman Roger Wheeler five years later. The state police were working to deny the WJA its license. They advised Boston Police that while such a field observation was helpful it would not be enough to prevent Callahan from attaining a license. They suggested that a newspaper article about Callahan and his association with Martorano might help. They inquired if the Boston police had a friendly reporter who could write an article about Callahan being in touch with unsavory characters. If they could plant such a story, the additional publicity might help them bar Callahan and the WJA from securing a license in Connecticut.

Austin McGuigan, then an attorney in the Connecticut State Attorney's Office, was directing the police officers in their inquiry. Law enforcement sources inside the state police told a WJA investigator that McGuigan was a "barracuda mad for publicity." McGuigan was believed to be the source for a number of news articles alleging the corruption of jai alai.

McGuigan's role in obtaining a negative newspaper article about Callahan's associations appeared to be confirmed when, during the April 1976 Connecticut licensing hearings, Rico overheard the state gaming commissioner tell McGuigan, "you said to wait for a newspaper article."

While, of course, it was entirely proper for the Connecticut state police to have been checking with other police departments to determine if there was any negative information about the top management of a business seeking a license for gambling in their state, planting a story in the newspaper to build their case was going too far.

Rico immediately understood that this was a major threat to the WJA. If top managers were associating with known criminals it could have a devastating impact on the company's ability to operate. The company could be denied a license to do business after it had invested millions of dollars in its efforts to start a fronton in Connecticut.

Rico flew to Boston and met with the WJA attorney there, telling him of the information about Callahan's associations and making sure he understood its potential impact on the company. A meeting of the WJA executive committee was called and the directors considered the information. They had not been pleased with Callahan's performance anyway. Callahan had apparently lost interest in his job and had inexplicably ceased coming to work and remaining in contact with the WJA board. Previously, Trustman had tried to persuade him to resign. The information that Rico provided the company caused the executive committee to act. The committee agreed to terminate Callahan's contract as president and an officer of the corporation. After some negotiation, Callahan agreed to resign.

The Connecticut State Police officers involved in developing the information were reportedly angered over the fact that Rico had learned of their efforts and took the information about Callahan to the WJA board. They had hoped to deny the license and, when Callahan resigned, the issue disappeared. The state police realized their attempt to plant an article had been disrupted and they concluded that Rico was engaged in serving corrupt interests.

The Connecticut state police view of Rico's actions was most unreasonable. By planting a news article, the police were clearly abusing their authority. Rico was employed by WJA and, unless something improper or illegal was going on, he owed the company his allegiance. If he knew something about a top manager that threatened the company's viability, he certainly was obligated to provide the board that information.

The point of checking on such things was to keep people with corrupt associations out of the business. Rico's actions had served a legitimate law enforcement interest: Callahan had been removed from the business. Further, Rico had inadvertently prevented the Connecticut state police from committing an abuse of its power. It is hard to see how Connecticut authorities could conclude otherwise. Nevertheless they did and they held it against Rico for many years.

After Callahan left, Rico addressed the McNeely issue. He took it to Donovan and McNeely was fired. As it turned out, Rico did the right thing in both situations. He recognized from the outset that McNeely was not the kind of person who would be helpful to have around a business that catered to the public. Although he initially had found no police record for McNeely, after the fight in the Mutiny Bar, there would be a police record and he was clearly not the sort of person who was helpful to the business. As soon as he could, Rico terminated McNeely.

Rico had confronted the situation of the derogatory information about his boss with no hesitation. He moved swiftly to fulfill his duty and protect the company that employed him. A lesser man might have fretted over acting on the information. After all, the executive board might have backed Callahan. There is no evidence that Rico wavered. He simply did the right thing.

Following his termination, Callahan removed himself from the business and reinstituted his consulting company. Donovan, who had been serving as CEO of the WJA, began to exercise the powers of the presidency and after another executive search, Donovan was given the job.

Rico would get along well with Donovan, whose personality was quite different from Callahan's. Callahan, a quick wit as an accountant, was very gifted with financial matters. He enjoyed partying and drinking and possessed a warm, engaging, sometimes dominating personality. Donovan was a more typical CPA, displaying much the same laid back and subdued personality as Rico.

Chapter 15: The Hartford Courant

THE DAY OF gushing newspaper coverage of jai alai was over. The sport's very existence and that of the companies who brought it to the public was now shrouded in negativity. The naysaying that began in 1973 would continue unabated for the next 30 years, led by The Hartford Courant, Connecticut's largest newspaper, which published hundreds of articles about jai alai, many of which alleged corruption and infiltration of the sport by organized crime.

While it is not the responsibility of a newspaper to make any enterprise successful or to provide favorable coverage to any business, it is the duty of a free press to ensure that what it does report is both accurate and fair, to make sure that its stories are not overblown and misleading. The Courant's coverage of jai alai did not always measure up to those standards.

Much of it, certainly by design, tarnished the image of jai alai— reaching to describe some impropriety or corrupt act by someone in the business, real or imagined. A citizen in Connecticut who got their news from The Courant would have a negative view of jai alai.

Regrettably, the real world today does have problems and no business or large organizations are completely pristine. But the news coverage of jai alai, particularly in Connecticut, mixed legitimate news with a constant and often unnecessary repetition of allegations of corruption and infiltration by organized crime figures big and small. Austin McGuigan, the Connecticut chief state's attorney during much of the period, repeatedly commented about organized crime and jai alai—and those comments often ended up in print or were fodder for the evening rip-and-read news shows.

Connecticut licensed three different companies to operate three jai alai frontons; one each in Hartford, Milford and Bridgeport. A few real problems and many false accusations would arise in the jai alai business over the next few years and would be discussed at length in The Courant. The discussions often would include the allegation that organized crime had infiltrated the sport and the business.

In 1975, as jai alai was attempting to establish a foothold in Connecticut, one of the World Jai Alai Inc.'s competitors, David Friend, president of Connecticut Sports Enterprises Inc., told a representative of the Connecticut State Police he had paid $200,000 to a state official to assist in getting his company's gaming license. The official's name was ultimately cleared but there was intense media publicity on the charges. A judge ultimately dismissed a perjury charge against Friend on the grounds that pretrial publicity had precluded a fair trial. The judge also criticized state officials for using the press to create a "soap opera."

The state official the judge characterized as creating a "soap opera" was McGuigan. The situation justifiably drew attention of The Courant and other news organizations and produced a buzz of illegality and corruption in jai alai. It had, however, nothing to do with the WJA, but its executive board decided to make an effort to sell the business and since 1976 had been seeking a buyer. As the company pursued its sale, former FBI Agent H. Paul Rico, the newly-hired vice president of security at WJA, was protected with a severance package of one year's salary if he was terminated by the new owners. Discussions were held with a number of prospective buyers including Tulsa businessman and entrepreneur Roger Wheeler, but Ballys Manufacturing Co. offered the best deal. In 1977 WJA and Ballys reached an agreement in principal to merge and publicity became intense. If the deal was consummated, Ballys would pay the WJA stockholders $66 million in Ballys' stock.

When the deal was announced, a burst of news coverage in The Courant ensued. There were many references to allegations of Ballys' "connections" to organized crime. Courant headlines for a few of the articles that mentioned the sale included: "Fronton Seeker Has History of Shedding

Mob Ties," "Probers Confirm Loans Given to Crime Figures" and "Jai Alai License Probe Urged."

The concern about Ballys was serious and deserved coverage, as the company's origins definitely had organized crime connections. One of its founders had been a Mafia boss in New Jersey, but by the time it offered to buy the WJA, Ballys was a publicly held corporation and had purged itself of management figures that were associated with mobsters. But the issue of whether it should be licensed was one that should have been debated publicly. In order to buy the WJA, Ballys would have to obtain licenses in two states, Connecticut and Florida. Soon, however, it was apparent that the controversy over Ballys would not go away and the licensing process would take a long time. The Ballys deal was dropped.

During the coverage of the Ballys contract, The Courant learned that WJA owners had had dealings about the sale of the company with Jack Cooper, a part owner of the Flagler Dog Track in Miami. Rico and Alan Trustman, an attorney and WJA executive board member, had had several meetings with Cooper who was depicted in The Courant as a convicted felon and associate of mobster Meyer Lansky. Miami Metro-Dade police Sgt. David Green had photographed Lansky talking to Cooper in a restaurant in Miami.

In September 1977, when the Florida Department of Business Regulation considered Ballys application for a jai alai license, Rico was asked about the meetings with Cooper. He testified that he met Cooper as an agent investigating an extortion in which one of the owners at the Flagler Dog Track was the victim. He encountered Cooper when he visited Flagler to conduct interviews in the case. He knew Cooper had a conviction for tax evasion for which he served two and half months in jail.

Rico explained that Trustman had asked to meet Cooper. Since Rico knew him, he set up the meeting and accompanied Trustman. There were several meetings and Rico concluded that it was unlikely that any deal between the two would be consummated. His assessment proved to be correct.

Rico's responses revealed his attitude toward his responsibilities to the company. He had provided Trustman information about Cooper's conviction and association with Lansky. He let Trustman assess whether it would have a negative impact on the WJA if the word got out that he was meeting Cooper to discuss a deal to buy the WJA. Rico said he briefed Trustman fully on the subject but he thought the decision of whether to meet with Cooper should be made by the people who owned the company, not the vice president for security. He thought it was his responsibility to provide Trustman all the information available about Cooper and that Trustman should decide what to do.

Rico didn't think there should be adverse publicity for talking to an individual who was part of a parimutuel business licensed by State of Florida. He also said he didn't think people should be labeled "Organized Crime" by news media. Rico had higher standards for labeling a person as part of "organized crime" than The Courant.

The veteran agent was not naive. He had spent his working career around mobsters and certainly would not have been afraid to talk to a person like Cooper. Rico told Trustman that no matter what his reputation, Cooper had always been as good as his word around him. Trustman, who is mentally combative, taught law at Boston University and screenplay writing at Harvard. He was a partner in one of the largest law firms in Boston, and then successfully wrote screenplays for movies that had great appeal. He is not the sort of person who would be intimidated or afraid to meet with someone who spent two and a half months in jail for tax evasion.

In the end, nothing came of the Ballys deal but the image of jai alai as a corrupt business gained ground. WJA investigators suspected that Louis "Buddy" Berenson, who had been forced out of the WJA management and had soured on the Cooper deal, was telling law enforcement authorities in Connecticut and Florida that the WJA was dealing with organized crime figures. A WJA investigator learned from confidential Connecticut law enforcement sources that Berenson's allegations about the WJA were truly outrageous. Apparently, he told the police that Rico was tied into the "Irish" faction of Boston organized crime and it was to provide the "muscle" to keep other organized crime groups from encroaching on WJA's action. The tale didn't stop there. The story asserted that Arthur Anderson and Co. was engaged in training Irish Americans to operate parimutuel skimming on behalf of organized crime.

The allegations about Rico defy credibility: If he had been involved in criminal activity with organized crime in Massachusetts, how could Berenson know it when it seemed to escape the attention of all of Boston's law enforcement community for over 20 years? Is it possible that the Arthur Andersen, which was then one of the nation's "Big Five" accounting firms providing auditing, tax and consulting services to large corporations, would be involved in a blatant act of criminality such as training jai alai employees to skim. It defies credibility to the point of being laughable, but that and other rumors were taken as fact in Connecticut.

Perhaps as a result of the unsubstantiated whispers by Berenson, The Courant's coverage was a bit overblown; but Cooper was not exactly Charles "Lucky" Luciano, the Silician mobster credited with being the father of modern organized crime in America who, with Lansky, was "instrumental in the development of the national crime syndicate" in the United States. Cooper occasionally had breakfast with Lansky at Wolfie's Delicatessen in Miami but his only conviction had been for tax evasion for which he served 79 days in jail.

The Courant carried a number of articles that discussed Ballys' mob origins, along with Cooper's associations and opposition to the sale from various politicians. In spite of the fact that the deal was dropped, The Courant continued to write about jai alai, Cooper and Lansky for several years. As late as 1980, The Courant was still writing about Cooper and his associations. An article appeared in the Aug. 24, 1980, edition of The Courant under the headline, "Florida Jai Alai Figure Retains Links With Underworld Chief," reminding its readers that Cooper was still a convicted felon, friend of Lansky and other unsavory characters and he once had connections to jai alai. But Cooper had nothing to do with jai alai in 1980.

On Sept. 24, 1978, the "Systems Bettor" issue was reported by The Courant under a headline "Insiders Monopolized Super Jai Alai Payoffs." The article said that two-thirds of the winnings at the three Connecticut jai alai frontons went to out of state residents and that "much of it (went) to a privileged group of professional gamblers from Florida." According to the article, gamblers who were using a "systems betting" scheme won $1.12 for every dollar they bet. The tone of the article implied that something terribly wrong was going on. After all, money was going to out of state interests and the involvement of a "syndicate," particularly one from Miami, certainly sounded ominous.

But despite the headline and doomsday tone of the article, a careful reading of the facts shows that 65 percent of the payouts at the Bridgeport arena, the closest fronton to New York City, went—not surprisingly—to New Yorkers. Incredibly, people in the industry were quoted as saying that Connecticut bettors weren't "sophisticated" enough to get their fair share of the winnings. And while "systems betting" may sound evil, there was nothing illegal or wrong with a bettor developing his own method to beat the odds and then playing it. It is doubtful that these systems bettors made more than they lost but, even if they did, betting by whatever system a customer could dream up was entirely legal. And regardless of who made or lost money, the State of Connecticut always got its percentage of the bets placed. The systems bettor controversy was much to do about nothing but systems betting would reappear in news articles for years to come.

In November 1977, The Courant carried articles in which Harvey Ziskis, described as a former employee of the Hartford fronton, was quoted as alleging that a group of professional system bettors had received "special privileges." Another Courant article added impact to the allegations when it reported that Ziskis was being guarded by Connecticut State Police officers. Evidently, the state police believed Ziskis' life was in danger because he had come forward.

In February 1978, The Courant reported that WJA President Richard P. Donovan, Rico and another WJA vice president would be named in a complaint before the Gaming Commission because they failed to report Ziskis' allegations that he had several jai alai players on his payroll. In another story, Rico was quoted as saying that he never believed Ziskis' allegations of a player fixing scheme and did not think reporting them was necessary. From the time he emerged as a source about corruption in jai alai through 1984, Ziskis would be quoted in many newspapers making allegations ranging from systems bettors getting special privileges to fixing games.

Ziskis got a lot of ink, but just who was he? Harvey Ziskis had been fired by WJA after a two-month stint in the cash counting department. A couple of hundred dollars for which he had been responsible for counting had disappeared and he was unable to explain where the money went.

Thereafter, he became a self-described "professional gambler" and with unnamed partners, a systems bettor. In August 1977, Ziskis had approached a Hartford cashier and presented a winning ticket worth $478.20 for payment. He placed the ticket on the counter and, as the cashier was counting out the money, Ziskis asked if he gave the cashier $22, could he get an even $500. He then gave the cashier $22 and as the cashier was putting the money in the cash drawer, Ziskis picked up the winning ticket and put it in his pocket.

After Ziskis walked away, the cashier realized what had happened and notified the assistant chief of security who immediately searched for Ziskis. They found him at a betting window. When they approached him, Ziskis stated, "I know about the ticket. I am going to give it back." They retrieved the ticket and took Ziskis to the security office where he was interviewed by Jerry Coakley, a former FBI agent who Rico had hired as chief of security at Hartford. During that interview, Ziskis became irate and very loud. Coakley ordered that he be banished from the Hartford fronton. A month later, Ziskis appeared at the Connecticut State Gaming Commission and made a long series of accusations about the WJA operation. He was later hired as a consultant by McGuigan but before long had a falling out with him. An inquiry by the Gaming Commission largely refuted Ziskis' allegations.

Stories referring to Ziskis and his allegations about jai alai went on for twenty years. Even after he was discredited, The Courant and other newspapers continued to present him as a legitimate expert on the subject of jai alai. In 1999, The Courant reported that "professional gambler" Ziskis was locked deep inside a Florida prison where he was working on a book, "Licensed to Steal." Ziskis was serving eight years for a greyhound racing scam but faced another five years for escaping from a federal prison camp. McGuigan, who, apparently couldn't resist commenting about jai alai corruption one more time, was quoted in the story as saying, "I feel bad he can't stay out of trouble … He was on to something with jai alai game-fixing and skimming." Twenty years of no charges and no convictions in the WJA and McGuigan still argued that games were being fixed and skimming was going on.

The drumbeat of stories about the WJA and organized crime took its toll on the company and its reputation. In a Courant article in January 1979,

Connecticut State Rep. Christopher Shays (later to represent his district in Congress) was quoted as saying he was told by one of the state's gaming commissioners that "big league" organized crime was involved in legalized gambling. Shays later announced in a Congressional Committee hearing that McGuigan told him about "FBI agents who were working for jai alai operations in Connecticut and how they were retiring and then working for these organizations that were very much involved in organized crime, and that the FBI was working for organized crime." He was, of course, repeating a tale he had often been told by his friend McGuigan and reinforced in hundreds of stories in his local newspaper.

Connecticut convicted a few people at another jai alai business for game fixing in the 1970s but the WJA had an exceptionally clean record when Rico was its general manager. Despite the allegations by McGuigan, Shays and others for over twenty years, Connecticut's and Florida's law enforcement authorities were not up to the task of putting together sufficient facts to even identify the criminals, much less charge them. Either McGuigan and law enforcement were inept at addressing rampant organized crime in the business—an unlikely proposition—or rampant organized crime just wasn't there.

J. Patrick McCann is a retired FBI agent who served from 1973 until 1976 as a director of the Florida Division of Parimutuel Racing that oversaw jai alai betting and as the director of the Jai Alai Association from 1977 to 1982. He said he was aware of only two instances where serious criminal activities involving jai alai were alleged. Both instances involved game fixing by players; one instance in Connecticut and a second involving two players in a fronton in Northern Florida.

In spite of jai alai's public image, which suffered from repeated news stories alleging organized crime involvement in the business, McCann said former WJA Vice President John Callahan was the only person connected to Florida jai alai who was alleged to be an organized crime figure. And Callahan had been fired when the allegations about him surfaced. The allegations of organized crime involvement were always non-specific; there was never a specific organized crime figure named as involved in jai alai.

There is one constant and remaining fact: In spite of the plethora of stories and mountain of allegations, in the 22 years Rico was employed at

WJA, not a single employee was convicted of any illegal act relating to jai alai. In fact, during that time, no one employed by the WJA was ever even charged with a crime relating to jai alai.

That's because the WJA had detailed a number of specific procedures to be used to detect skimming, theft and game fixing. Annual audits were performed by a major accounting firm; bets were placed on a computerized system that tracked winners and ensured that winning tickets would be paid only once; and an undercover system operated by the accounting firm bought food and beverages, parking and other services and the receipts were checked to ensure the money had been received.

To prevent game fixing, players were paid bonuses to win, a "coach" watched every game to look for signs of game fixing, and a video was made of every game played. Off-duty police officers were hired to work both inside and outside the fronton and five retired FBI agents handled the company's security.

Chapter 16: Enter Roger Wheeler

WHEN A DEAL to sell World Jai Alai Inc. to the Bally Manufacturing Company in 1977 fell through, WJA Executive Board Member Alan Trustman told David McKown, vice president of First National Bank of Boston, to try to find another investor who would be licensable in Florida, acceptable to management and able to bring a new deal together. McKown was the logical person to assist in this since his bank had been financing the WJA since 1973.

McKown immediately revived discussions with Roger Wheeler, the Tulsa businessman, oilman and chairman of the Telex Corporation who previously had shown an interest in the business. The two men already knew each other, having met four years earlier during a private dinner at the Locke Ober Restaurant in Boston, called to acquaint Wheeler with the jai alai business. The dinner was attended by Trustman, McKown, Wheeler, WJA President Richard P. Donovan, WJA Vice President John Callahan, H. Paul Rico, WJA vice-president in charge of security, and five WJA board members. They all got to know each other.

McKown was close to Callahan and regarded him as a trusted business associate. He met Callahan when he became the chief executive officer of the WJA and, after his resignation, McKown hired him as a consultant to the bank.

Wheeler was a religious person who had never considered investing in a gambling business. He once told friends and colleagues he would vote against legalized gambling but as long as it was legal, he felt free to own and profit from such a business. Wheeler believed it was better for a responsible businessman to run the WJA than a gambling company. Bally at the time was the world's largest slot machine manufacturer and had been tied in the past to mob figures.

McKown also had tried to interest Wheeler in another gambling venture, the Shenandoah Corporation, which owned two West Virginia race tracks but the deal failed to materialize. McKown then directed Wheeler back to jai alai and was instrumental in sparking and maintaining Wheeler's interest in the WJA. He pitched the WJA as a "real money making machine." McKown facilitated the negotiations, which ultimately led to an acquisition of WJA for $55 million—financed by the bank.

Records show the bank loaned Wheeler between $45 and $50 million of the $55 million he needed to buy the company. To manage its risk, the bank negotiated several restrictions on Wheeler's supervision of the business. Although he acquired 100 percent ownership of the WJA, the bank required him to retain Donovan as president and if he was replaced, it retained the right to put the loan in default if the bank was dissatisfied with his replacement.

The bank also required Wheeler to agree to refrain from making any significant changes in the way the business was operated without the bank's permission. While these restrictions certainly limited the ability of Wheeler to change the management of the WJA, in light of the fact that he was inexperienced in operating a gambling business they were not onerous requirements. Donovan had demonstrated for two years that he could manage a gambling enterprise. Furthermore, with Wheeler's record for conflict and litigation over business deals, the bank was wise to place tight written controls on him.

Finally, the First National Bank of Boston took a $1 million fee to pay for "financial services rendered" in the deal. One Wheeler adviser described the fee as a "finder's fee," which was split, 55 percent to FNBB and 45 percent to Telex Corporation's lead bank, the Continental Illinois Bank of Chicago. Apparently, it was called a fee for financial services rendered because the charging of a finder's fee was a violation of the rules in effect at the time. The Comptroller of the Currency required banks to take no further part in negotiations if they were to charge a finder's fee for the deal.

One often-repeated but untrue myth about this transaction is that there was a requirement to keep Rico on the payroll as a condition of the sale. The only specifically named officer of the company that had to stay on was Donovan.

After the deal was completed, Wheeler showed little interest in jai alai or gambling and visited the Miami business infrequently. His sons, Roger Jr. and David, worked in Miami more regularly. Over time, Roger Jr. and Rico became friends and frequently golfed together. David, who had computer software training, was given a $50,000 contract to develop some computer software to be used in the business.

After three years of owning the WJA, Roger Wheeler Sr. was ready to sell it. His purchase of the company had been motivated by the substantial tax benefits it brought him. In 1978, when he purchased the WJA, the top tax rate on corporations was 48 percent and the top tax rate on individuals was 70 percent. Since Wheeler bought WJA as a partnership the tax deductions generated were passed through to his personal income, a big benefit since Wheeler's high income made most of his earnings taxable at the 70 percent rate. Wheeler's purchase price included players' contracts, which he valued at $15 million. Good players were an important draw for the frontons. Wheeler purchased the business primarily because the Internal Revenue Service (IRS) allowed him to depreciate the $15 million value of player contracts over a period of three years and realize a $5 million personal income tax deduction each year. In 1981, the benefit of the player contract deduction would end. So Wheeler began to look for a buyer.

According to several knowledgeable sources, Callahan was involved in constructing the deal that enabled Wheeler to purchase the WJA. In particular, Callahan developed the tax plan for deducting the value of the player contracts. One source said Callahan received, or was to receive, 1 percent of the deal, or $550,000.

In December 1979, Wheeler looked inward to the top WJA managers to find a buyer and suggested to Donovan that he put together a deal. Donovan and Wheeler negotiated and in June 1980, they came close. Donovan sent a letter to the Florida Gaming Commission advising that he and Rico would be purchasing the WJA from Wheeler. In July 1980, however, Wheeler declared the sale "null and void."

Rico was doing well financially but didn't have the resources to commit much money to the purchase of the WJA. He was included in Donovan's offer for a small percentage. A proposal to buy a company that includes key managers for some small percentage of ownership is not unusual.

As they continued to negotiate, Wheeler became concerned about cutting costs since his loans for the purchase of WJA were at a high interest rate, over 16 percent. He took a number of steps to assess the operation and cut its expenses. In March 1981, Wheeler sold the Hartford fronton to Louis "Buddy" Berenson, a former WJA president and chief executive officer who left the company in 1977. On May 20, 1981, Wheeler declined Donovan's offer to purchase the WJA and seven days later, Wheeler was murdered at the Southern Hills Country Club in Tulsa.

An Oct. 14, 2003, affidavit by Tulsa Police Sgt. Mike Huff, the lead investigator in the Wheeler case, said mobster Stephen "The Rifleman" Flemmi told him that Callahan, Donovan and mob associate John Martarano, who admitted pulling the trigger in the Wheeler killing, were attempting to purchase WJA from Wheeler. According to the affidavit, Flemmi and Callahan wanted Winter Hill Gang boss James "Whitey" Bulger and other gang members "to protect them from possible action by other organized crime groups." In return, the affidavit said, Callahan offered Bulger, Flemmi, Martarano and others $10,000 per week—which would have been skimmed from WJA parking concessions.

J. Patrick McCann, the retired FBI agent who headed the Florida Jai Alai Association, and Donovan traveled to Tulsa for the Wheeler funeral and to offer their sympathy to the family. McCann recalled that when Donovan got on the plane, he was terribly shaken. He appeared so shaken that McCann thought perhaps he had learned something disturbing about the murder from Callahan. He never learned the explanation for Donovan's reaction.

The Wheeler murder stimulated a new burst of news coverage. A few days after the killing, CBS News broadcast a report that Roger Jr. said his father suspected that funds had been illegally diverted, or "skimmed," at WJA's frontons. Roger Jr. publicly denied the news report the following day and Donovan wrote a memorandum saying that Wheeler Sr. had never

indicated that he had discovered or even suspected any skimming at WJA
jai alai frontons.

A few days later, Ted Driscoll, a reporter for The Hartford Courant,
called Roger Jr., telling him he had received information that his father had
expressed concern about the possibility of skimming at Hartford. Donovan
explained that the CBS report had been erroneous and that he had corrected it the next day.

Driscoll then called Marty Fleischman, the WJA director of public
relations, telling him he had received information that the Hartford Jai
Alai's concession receipts had substantially increased after it was taken over
by Berenson. Fleischman told Driscoll he understood the receipts actually
had increased, noting that Berenson received permission from the state to
charge for parking and, of course, that would have been a new source of
revenue. Finally, he pointed out virtually all the supervisory people who
worked for the WJA continued in their jobs under Berenson and Wheeler's
brother, Sidney, continued to work there as food and beverage manager.

That didn't deter Driscoll. On June 10, 1981, an article by the reporter
appeared under the headline, "Slaying Victim Suspected Scam at Fronton."
It said "reliable sources" had confirmed that Wheeler suspected skimming.
While Wheeler surely thought about the possibility of skimming at a business that handles so much cash and may have even asked about it, to say he
"suspected" skimming implies he had evidence or at least some indication
of theft. His son, quoted in the article, denied it and 25 years later no such
evidence has ever appeared.

Berenson's management concessions revenue rose dramatically after
he assumed control of the business from WJA. Driscoll made no mention
of the fact that during the entire time, virtually all the supervisory personnel
who worked for the WJA and Wheeler's brother continued in their positions under Berenson. The explanation provided by WJA spokesman was
not reported.

Driscoll, in his article, projected losses from skimming at Hartford at
$350,000 annually and said that if as much was skimmed from each of the
other WJA frontons, the business was losing $1.4 million a year. While
insisting that skimming was occurring despite denials from those in the
know, the reporter projected skimming losses that did not exist from the

Hartford fronton and used the supposed losses to compute overall losses for the entire business—despite the vigorous denial of the victim's son, who was the family member most involved in the business.

While Driscoll reported again that Callahan had hung out with mobsters, the former WJA executive's unsavory relationships were old news and he had been terminated long before Wheeler bought the business. In addition, Bryan McNeely, known at WJA for his fiery temper, who had been hired by Callahan and placed in charge of concessions, was fired—at Rico's urging—long before Wheeler purchased the business.

Many law enforcement officials have experienced questionable news coverage, seemingly less committed to the facts than to selling newspapers or increasing the overnight ratings. Rico had a negative view of the news coverage that jai alai was receiving but didn't think much could be done about it. He just did not worry about it.

Later that summer, Bob Lawson and Dick Garrity, both former FBI agents employed at the WJA, traveled to Tulsa in an effort to be helpful in the Wheeler murder investigation. When Lawson spoke to detectives investigating the killing, he said he concluded they had already convinced themselves that the murder had been caused by his association with the WJA. Lawson said he tried to persuade the Tulsa detectives to look elsewhere— he simply did not believe jai alai had anything to do with it.

While the FBI agents in the local Tulsa field office treated them courteously, when Lawson and Garrity visited they said they felt they were being greeted with suspicion by the police and most of the Wheeler family. Lawson recalls waiting for an hour or two to see members of Wheeler's family at their office and finally learning that they would not meet with them. Roger Jr. was friendly, seemed to appreciate their help and even invited them to play golf. The police took them to the scene of the crime but treated them more like subjects than former law enforcement officers who were trying to help. An FBI agent told Lawson their hotel rooms in Tulsa were bugged by the police.

The attitude of the police towards Lawson and Garrity was cold and suspicious and since it was very early in the case, it cannot be explained away as justified by anything their investigation had uncovered. Investigators in Tulsa and Connecticut had received a tip in July 1981, from Boston that Winter Hill Gang mob members were responsible for the murder. Since Callahan had associated with members of the Winter Hill Gang, it was not a stretch to suspect that Callahan and the gang had something to do with it.

Unfortunately, agents and detectives occasionally buy into a theory of a case before they have enough evidence to support it. But there is no justification for investigators at this early stage of the investigation to conclude that since Rico and other former FBI agents worked at the WJA, they must have had something to do with the murder.

Over the next few years, Huff—who pursued the Wheeler case for 22 years—came to believe that jai alai was thoroughly corrupt. He regarded the FBI field offices in Boston and Miami as criminal organizations that would protect their retired comrades at almost any cost. The fact that Lawson didn't see a jai alai connection and tried to persuade the Tulsa detectives to look elsewhere probably played into Huff's beliefs that all the agents working with Rico were dishonest. He thought they were trying to deflect his investigation away from their colleague.

The idea that an entire field office could be corrupted and would act in unison to protect a former agent is hard to believe. Any organization, particularly a law enforcement organization, composed of several hundred people simply could not successfully engage in stealing, skimming and murder or protecting people who do those things.

On the death of his father, Roger Jr. became more involved in the operations of the WJA. He and his sister, Pamela, ordered an audit by the accounting firm Cooper Lybrand—chosen because of Donovan's prior association with Arthur Andersen, which had conducted regular annual audits. The brother and sister tandem were concerned that in light of their father's murder, that the audit would be truly independent. No financial irregularities were uncovered. A good audit by an independent accounting firm was an important step in verifying that financial matters were being handled correctly.

In September 1981, Harvey Ziskis, a consultant who was analyzing parimutuel tickets used in jai alai betting and was a former employee of the Hartford fronton, called Pamela Wheeler and asked for a meeting, during which he planned to make several allegations: The WJA was involved in her father's death; there was skimming in the past as well as the present; that exposure of skimming would lead to her father's killers; and that the FBI and Roger Jr. were not to be trusted. Since no one working for the WJA was ever charged or convicted for skimming, the idea that disclosure of skimming would lead to Wheeler's murders was meaningless. Wisely, Pamela Wheeler did not meet Ziskis.

In October 1981, Connecticut State's Attorney Austin McGuigan hired Ziskis as a consultant at $500 a week to assist in his jai alai investigation—an incredible decision based on Ziskis' background and his many false accusations. A member of Ziskis' family told a WJA investigator that Ziskis had begun as a paid informant for Driscoll, the Courant reporter, and then moved to McGuigan's office. In a Courant article in January 1982, Ziskis was quoted as saying he was examining jai alai-related records and that his investigation had progressed to a point where "individuals could be arrested and convicted."

It remains unclear if Ziskis was speaking for McGuigan's office, but it is highly unusual for a consultant to a law enforcement agency to be given the leeway to make such public comments regarding the readiness of a case to be prosecuted.

In the midst of all this turmoil, the FBI called Rico and asked if he would come out of retirement for one more case.

Chapter 17: The Judge

ALCEE L. HASTINGS, a prominent Florida attorney, civil rights activist and state circuit court judge, was nominated by President Carter as U.S. District Judge for the Southern District of Florida in 1979, the first African-American to be named to the federal bench in that state. He was confirmed unanimously by the Senate. But within two years, Judge Hastings would be charged with accepting a $150,000 bride in exchange for his granting of lenient sentences in a racketeering case.

Brothers Frank and Thomas Romano were at the heart of the Hastings scandal; convicted in his courtroom on 21 counts of racketeering in their theft of $1 million from a union pension fund. A defendant in a separate case, William Dredge, was approached by William A. Borders Jr., a prominent Washington, D.C., lawyer and friend of Judge Hastings, who asked if he would find out if the Romanos were interested in paying the judge $150,000 to avoid a prison sentence and having the money they stole returned to them. Dredge reported the approach to the FBI.

You can be sure that an FBI investigation involving a federal district judge as its target is one that receives close attention and review in both the field office and at FBI Headquarters in Washington, D.C. After FBI agents interviewed Dredge several times, a decision was made to run an undercover operation. Since Borders had never seen him, an agent could pose as Frank Romano, an Italian American in his 60s. But FBI agents must retire at 57 and, as a result, none were available who were the right ages. The bureau made a decision to recruit a former agent who could play the role.

Selection of the right person to play the role in such a high-profile case would receive careful scrutiny at many levels of management. An experienced and mature person who could handle himself and the pressures of the endeavor was essential. Intelligence and good judgment were obvious qualities that would be critical to success. In these operations, the person in the undercover role is often on his own, away from support and guidance of the case agent and supervisor. He must think quickly and make good decisions.

Sean McWeeney, who at the time was chief of the Organized Crime Section at FBI Headquarters and later retired from the bureau at the rank of inspector in charge after 24 years, had worked with Agent H. Paul Rico in Boston. He knew Rico was in Miami and suggested the bureau recruit the now-retired veteran agent to play the undercover role. McWeeney was familiar with Rico from his assignment in Boston in the 1960s and had a high respect for him as both a capable agent and a person of integrity. The allegations in the newspapers about jai alai, Rico's new employer, had been only the most general accusations of "organized crime" involvement. In spite of all the stories, there were no facts or evidence that reflected poorly on Rico or World Jai Alai Inc. (WJA).

Anthony "Tony" Amoroso, the FBI's public corruption squad supervisor in Miami, also had worked with Rico when he was an active agent. Amoroso was a skilled investigator who played the key undercover role in the infamous ABSCAM case, which ultimately led to the conviction on bribery and conspiracy charges of a U.S. senator, five members of the House of Representatives, one member of the New Jersey State Senate, members of the Philadelphia City Council, and an inspector for the now-defunct U.S. Immigration and Naturalization Service (INS). Amoroso knew exactly what it took to be successful in a sensitive undercover role and he thought Rico had all the qualities necessary. He admired Rico's work and regarded him as an honest, dedicated and intelligent professional.

The FBI case agent, Bill Murphy, also thought Rico was the right choice for the role—describing him as a capable agent who looked the part. Rico was short, stocky and looked like he might be of Italian ancestry, although he actually was the son of a Spanish-American father and an Irish-

American mother. He spoke with a northeastern accent and clearly "knew his way around the streets."

Before undertaking the undercover work, Rico asked Roger Wheeler Jr., the son of Roger Wheeler Sr., the Tulsa businessman and WJA owner shot and killed in May 1981 at a private country club, whether he would have any objection to his involvement in assisting the government in what he only said was an "undercover case." Only after the case was disclosed publicly, did Wheeler learn that this was the investigation of Judge Hastings. Wheeler asked WJA President Richard Donovan why Rico would assist the government in this way and Donovan told him that if Rico saw something was wrong, he "wanted to make it right."

Connie Rico knew her husband was very discrete; he rarely discussed FBI business with her. When Rico undertook the Hastings case, he told her nothing about it. He simply set up an office in their home, installed a telephone and told her that under no circumstances should she answer it. One day she saw Rico taking the license plate off of their car. When she asked what he was doing, he explained only that he did not like it and was replacing it with something else. At the time, they had been married over 30 years and she trusted him; she knew her husband was very secretive about some things.

Rico volunteered for the undercover work but he needed a contract with the FBI to protect him from liability issues. Although he used the Justice Department attorney for most of the case, he had a personal services contract written by his attorney at his own expense. Under the contract, Rico agreed to do the work for $1. Murphy believed he was motivated by a desire to help the FBI.

Rico's personal attorney, William Cagney, a former federal prosecutor who also became the agent's close friend, drafted the personal services contract signed by Rico and the FBI for the undercover operation. Although Cagney was a close confidante who prepared the generic personal services contract for Rico to serve as an undercover operative, he knew only that it was an "unspecified operation." Even though Rico knew that Cagney had cases in Judge Hastings' court, Rico never told Cagney that Hastings was the target of the investigation until after arrests were made.

Throughout his life, Rico exercised remarkable control; he just didn't talk about things that were secret and didn't need to be discussed.

When they met, Rico easily convinced Borders that he was Frank Romano. In three meetings, he made two payments totaling $150,000 to Borders for Judge Hastings to fix the case. After he made the first payment of $25,000, Judge Hastings signaled that he was on board in the deal by releasing back to the defendants some property he had previously ordered forfeited. A short time later, a date for the final payoff in Washington, D.C. was set. On October 9, 1981, when Rico made this payment at a hotel near Washington's National Airport, he put the money in an expensive leather garment bag that was his personal property. After the bag and money were passed, Amoroso made the decision to arrest Borders and the money and the bag were taken into evidence. For years after, whenever Amoroso encountered him, Rico would always ask "where's my garment bag?"

Judge Hastings and Borders were indicted on charges of conspiring to solicit a bribe from the Romanos. Borders was tried first. He was convicted and sentenced to five years in federal prison.

Before Hastings' trial, the judge defended himself in the media by claiming Borders was lying; claiming he was targeted because of his rulings against the Reagan administration's Haitian policies; and arguing that he was singled out because of his race. At the trial, Hastings testified that he had never discussed with Borders the court order that was at the heart of the case. Apparently, when pressed to the wall, Hastings, like so many others, was willing to sacrifice his friend to save himself. The defense worked; Hastings was acquitted by a jury. An arrogant Hastings announced to the press after the trial, "I have no fear of impeachment." Borders went off to prison but the fight over Hastings' guilt continued.

Following the acquittal, then-Chief Judge John Godbold of the U.S. Court of Appeals for the Eleventh Circuit filed a complaint with the court's Judicial Council urging a separate investigation into the matter. After a four year inquiry, investigators concluded that not only had Hastings solicited a bribe but he had repeatedly lied at his trial.

The investigator's report was followed by the House Judiciary Committee's consideration of impeachment. The full committee voted 32-1 in favor of recommending impeachment to the House. In August 1988, the

House passed 17 articles of impeachment against Judge Hastings in voting 413-3 to impeach on the grounds of bribery and perjury. It was hard to argue that race was the motive for the charges; the Congressional Black Caucus voted 20–3 in favor of impeachment.

On Oct. 20, 1989, the full Senate met in a dramatic session to consider the case. The chamber was filled but the senators were quiet rising only to vote. In a series of roll call votes, senators rose and announced their vote as "guilty" or "not guilty." Hastings was found "guilty" by the Senate of eight articles of impeachment relating to engaging in a "corrupt conspiracy" to extort a $150,000 bribe in a case before him. The vote on the first article, which charged conspiracy, was 69–26. Hastings, who had bragged that he had no fear of impeachment, was the sixth judge impeached by the Senate in U.S. history. He lost his lifetime position as a federal district judge.

While the Senate had the option to forbid Hastings from ever seeking federal office again, it chose not to do so. Borders, the lawyer who served as the conduit between the Romano brothers and Hastings, was again sent to prison for refusing to testify despite a grant of immunity in the impeachment proceedings. He was among 140 persons to receive a pardon signed by President Bill Clinton on Jan. 20, 2001.

Agent Murphy thought Rico did an excellent job throughout the case, which lasted 8 years. Rico was called to testify throughout the entire process—first in U.S. district court, then in the House and, finally, in the Senate. Murphy recalled that at least one Rico vacation was disrupted by the demands of the case. The former FBI agent did it all without complaint and for no personal gain even though it occasionally disrupted his personal plans.

FBI Director William H. Webster wrote Rico on July 16, 1982, thanking him for his "invaluable assistance" in the case, saying he wanted to add "my personal thanks for your help." The director wrote that Rico's participation "was a critical factor in the success achieved," adding that the former FBI agent had "every right to be proud of the role" he played. Mr. Webster ended the letter by saying, "We are always pleased by the support and cooperation we receive from our former associates, and we are truly grateful for your efforts on our behalf."

A note on the letter indicated that the FBI's Criminal Investigative Division had agreed with a recommendation by the special agent in charge of the bureau's Miami field office "that a letter of appreciation be sent to Mr. Rico."

Following his impeachment, Hastings bounced back. In 1992, he was elected to represent the 23rd Congressional District in Florida in the U.S. Congress, which includes Palm Beach and Broward County. He has been re-elected nine times and currently serves as a senior member of the House Rules Committee, ranking Democrat on the Commission on Security and Cooperation in Europe and on the Congressional Black Caucus. Since his initial campaign victory, he has yet to face a serious re-election challenge.

Chapter 18: Another Murder

THE BADLY DECOMPOSED body of Boston business consultant John B. Callahan was discovered Aug. 4, 1982, in the trunk of his silver-grey Cadillac, parked at Miami International Airport. A parking lot attendant had noticed a foul odor and called police. The car had been there for several days. The initial news reports said Callahan, who served as president of World Jai Alai Inc. (WJA) from 1974 to 1976, had been shot twice in the head and three times in the body. He had been stripped of his jewelry and identification cards, and three shell casings were found lying on the body.

Several weeks after the murder, The Miami Herald reported in a major article that Callahan's wife and children did not know why he was in Miami or with whom he was meeting. He apparently kept his frequent weekend trips to South Florida a secret, usually taking flights on Friday night and returning in time to be in his Boston office on Monday morning. Metro-Dade Homicide Detective Shelton Merritt said Callahan's American Airlines charge account revealed frequent trips to South Florida although he had no apparent business interests in the area. "He never stated to anyone what he was coming down here for," Merritt said, adding that "everything points to World Jai-Alai." But a spokesman for the company characterized that comment as "ridiculous."

Sgt. David Green of the Florida Department of Law Enforcement, characterized by the FDLE as a gambling expert, was quoted as saying he heard about Callahan from sources on the street. "I kept picking up information about Callahan with the bookies, Callahan with the Boston family members," Green said. "If he wasn't a member of organized crime, he was certainly a close associate."

The Herald reported in its 1982 article that for the past two years, Callahan had been working as a consultant and serving as president of Heywood-Wakefield, a Michigan-based furniture company. WJA was among his clients. It bought seats for its frontons from Heywood-Wakefield.

When Callahan left the WJA, his former business partner, Richard Donovan, moved into his job as president. Callahan severed his ties with the company. The two ended their partnership when Donovan sold his share of the business to Callahan for $1. Callahan continued to talk to Donovan frequently but stayed away from the WJA fronton. The employees there do not remember him visiting.

Although Callahan once told his banker friend, David McKown, vice president of First National Bank of Boston, that his association with Rico was "close," this was probably an exaggeration—Callahan seemed to think he was "close" to many people. After he left the WJA, Rico may have talked to him from time to time but no one employed there remembers seeing Callahan in the fronton after he resigned. They were certainly not buddies who hung out together. Rico's secretary, Janet Dowd, remembers that Rico knew Callahan but that Donovan had a much closer association with Callahan. She could not remember ever seeing Callahan in the WJA.

On August 5, 1982, The Hartford Courant weighed in on the Callahan murder. An article reported that Brian Halloran, a hoodlum and associate of Callahan, told the FBI that Callahan at a meeting offered him a contract to kill Roger Wheeler, the Tulsa businessman who had purchased the WJA, but Halloran said he turned the job down. That meeting was attended by Callahan, Winter Hill mob boss James "Whitey" Bulger and a top associate, Stephen "The Rifleman" Flemmi. Halloran, who was killed gangland style in Boston after talking to the FBI, had been interested in obtaining a deal from the government but had lied about some things he said and lost his chance. He approached the FBI looking for protection and talked about several crimes. He said Callahan offered him a contract to kill Wheeler but he refused it. Halloran later learned that Bulger, Flemmi and mob hitman

John Martorano handled the Wheeler murder. The FBI agents and detectives dealing with Halloran knew he was lying about some of the other things he was telling them and when he refused a polygraph examination concerning his statements, they decided not to deal with him.

The FBI arranged for Halloran to stay at a safe house where he would be secure as long as he stayed away from his old haunts. When the word got out that he was informing and he couldn't resist his old Boston hangouts, he and a friend were shot and killed by Bulger as they walked from a restaurant to their car. Had he remained in the safe house, it is likely he would have survived.

The Courant reported as a fact that Wheeler suspected that skimming was going on and had expressed dissatisfaction with Donovan and Rico, then the company's vice president. The article pointed out ominously that both Donovan and Rico had been hired by Callahan. Apparently, in the view of The Courant, anyone hired by Callahan was tainted.

There is no evidence Wheeler was dissatisfied with either Donovan or Rico. He used Rico's investigative skills when he sent him to California to investigate a matter of interest to him. Wheeler once commented publicly that he was comforted by the fact that he employed several former FBI agents.

Significantly, in the Courant article, the reporter, Ted Driscoll, wrote that the "skimming" was coming out of the betting monies before the state and the winners were allotted their shares. Previously, the newspaper had reported that skimming revenue was from the food and concessions.

The facts prove there was no skimming of any significance going on at the WJA. There is no information that Wheeler ever suspected that the WJA operation was being skimmed, although the WJA had encountered an occasional theft by some employees. One of them was Harvey Ziskis, described in court documents as a disenfranchised systems bettor who participated extensively in investigations conducted by journalists and law enforcement agencies into the reports of corruption in the systems betting activities at jai alai frontons. He was suspected of stealing a couple of hundred dollars from the cash he was to count.

There was, however, no evidence that the skimming of thousands of dollars ever occurred.

Wheeler never had any reason to suspect that either Rico or Donovan were involved in any financial irregularities, although after the murder of his father, David Wheeler said he suspected that they were. On one occasion, David Wheeler alleged that the paper cup expenses were excessive at WJA and that Rico and Donovan were possibly obtaining kickbacks from the supplier. Roger Wheeler Jr. had an audit done and found that the cups at WJA were being obtained at a very low cost, probably lower than other locations where paper cups were used.

Donovan, who was running the company, said Wheeler never expressed concern to him about skimming. The Wheeler family was split over the issue. David Wheeler has said his father suspected skimming and appears to have been the source of the story that his father was dissatisfied with Donovan and Rico. Roger Wheeler Jr., who was more active in overseeing the business, said his father did not suspect skimming. The press preferred David's story.

Wheeler, as a responsible businessman, certainly would have thought about the possibility that corrupt employees could steal from the business and asked about it to ensure the company had the right controls in place. Such thoughts and concerns would be expected of anyone who owned a business that generated a large amount of cash. But such thoughts and deciding what measures to take against theft are standard in the gambling business. If, however, he didn't have any evidence that it was happening, then Roger Wheeler Jr.'s view was probably more accurate. In the almost three decades that have passed since Wheeler was murdered, no one has produced any evidence that skimming was taking place at the WJA.

The WJA was audited every year by Chicago-based Arthur Anderson and Co., considered at the time one of the country's "Big Five" accounting firms. Following Wheeler's murder, the company was audited by Coopers & Lybrand, which later merged with Price Waterhouse to form PricewaterhouseCoopers—one of the country's largest accounting firms. No serious financial irregularities were discovered. In addition, periodically Arthur Anderson would run an undercover operation designed to discover skimming. The firm would send people unannounced to the WJA. They would park, buy food and beverages and bet and then provide the receipts to Arthur Anderson. Auditors would then check to see if the money reflected by the undercover purchases had actually been recorded and received by the WJA. It always was.

Connecticut officials never notified the WJA that they suspected skimming. This may be because, in spite of frequent comments that he was investigating the suspected skimming, Austin McGuigan's, chief state's attorney in Connecticut, had no specific information about skimming. Apparently, the only thing he thought he knew was that "organized crime was skimming." Who the organized crime figures were or how their skimming was being conducted eluded him.

Records and interviews show that bets at the WJA were taken and recorded as they were being made on a program known as the Totalisator Computer System. The WJA system had excellent internal controls. Importantly, the company installed the Totalisator "sell/cash" system in 1978. In this system, all pari-mutuel transactions were processed and recorded in a single computer. When a bettor bet, the cashier punched the information into the system which issued a betting ticket that reflected the amount wagered, the match in question, the team or combination of teams chosen, and the cashier terminal. The impact on betting odds was instantly calculated and displayed publicly on a large board.

On completion of a match, the winning teams were keyed into the computer. With the sell/cash system, when a bettor presented a winning ticket, the cashier fed the ticket into the Totalisator computer which printed out the amount of cash to be paid. Theft through double stamping or double cashing of tickets is not possible with the sell/cash system.

Finally, since no Courant article on jai alai would be complete without a comment about McGuigan, it reported that the then-prosecutor had briefed the State's Commission on Special Revenue on Callahan's organized crime connections. Now that was an important piece of information to present to The Courant's readers.

On Aug. 16, 1982, Augustus Dibble, onetime chief financial examiner for Connecticut's gaming division, and Ziskis incorporated Pro-Tek Consultants, Inc., a gambling consultant. A couple of weeks later, Dibble signed an affidavit at the Connecticut Chief State's Attorney's office stating that a review of records from various Connecticut frontons, including the

WJA Hartford fronton, had indicated irregularities "consistent with illegal diversion of funds from their normal course or rightful owner."

Two days later, Dibble collaborated in writing a memorandum to an assistant state's attorney stating that "... our examination reveals that on numerous dates ... mutuel tickets have been cashed twice ..." and "... that more winning tickets are recorded as having been cashed than are recorded as having been sold ..."

A WJA investigator interviewed a Ziskis relative who advised that in September or early October 1982, Sgt. Green of the FDLE had traveled to Connecticut and spent three to four days as a house guest of reporter Driscoll. According to this report, Green worked daily with McGuigan and Driscoll in McGuigan's office.

On Oct. 1, 1982, Dibble ceased active employment at the Connecticut Department of Special Revenue and Ziskis resigned from his job as a consultant to McGuigan. On the same day, Connecticut state officials removed not quite a full truckload of state gambling records from Ziskis' home. News reports noted that McGuigan denied that any of these records were confidential grand jury records.

Something was up.

Paul Rico (#10) starred on the Belmont High School football team.

BOSTON COLLEGE CHESS CHAMPIONS, part of the team which recently won the national championship of Jesuit schools, practice at Boston College, for a match with Harvard on May 10, L. to R. Robert J. Foley, Somerville, Paul Rico, Belmont, John J. Hallahan, Dorchester, John J. White, Dorchester.

For Release Mon., May 8

Rico's Boston College chess team won the
national chess championship of Jesuit Colleges.

Rico's arrest of James J. "Whitey" Bulger in the 1950s
led to his conviction for three bank robberies.

Stephen Joseph "The Rifleman" Flemmi was Bulger's partner in crime.

Dennis Condon, Robert Sheehan and Paul Rico at his 1970 transfer party.

Paul Rico after retirement at the World Jai Alai fronton.

1987 Rico was happiest playing golf with friends

MOST
WANTED

JAMES JOSEPH BULGER Jr.

1994 Photos

WANTED FOR:

19 Counts of MURDER,
Numerous Weapons Offenses
& Violation of the RICO Statute

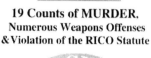

DOB:.................................9/03/29
Height:...............................5'-8"
Weight:.............................165lbs.
Hair:........................White / Silver
Eyes:.................................Blue
Complexion:..........................Fair
Race:................................White
Social Security:.....................
F.B.I.#:..........................169486A
Peculiarities:............Glasses / Balding
AKA's:...Thomas F. Baxter, Tom Harris,
Mark Shapeton, Thomas Marshall
Jimmy Bulger, Whitey

WANTED BY THE MASSACHESETTS STATE POLICE

After a lengthy investigation conducted by the Massachusetts State Police and Federal Drug Enforcement Administration (DEA), JAMES "WHITEY" BULGER, a once notorious "gangster" and a major organized crime figure in the Boston area was indicted in October of 2000 for his involvement in nineteen (19) Murders that occurred throughout the Boston area during his days as an Organized Crime Figure. BULGER is reported to be traveling with Catherine GREIG. BULGER is a very resourceful person and has cash at his disposal. BULGER should be considered Armed and Dangerous.

Massachusetts State Police: Violent Fugitive Apprehension Section
1-800-KAPTURE (1-800-527-8873) or Nights/Weekends (508) 820-2121
www.state.ma.us/msp/wanted/bulger.htm

"HE ESCAPES WHO IS NOT PURSUED" - SOPHOCLES

James J. "Whitey" Bulger was the last
Winter Hill Gang leader to be arrested.

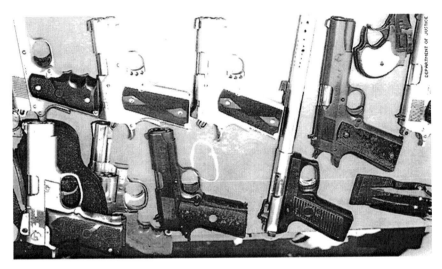

Guns found in Bulger's apartment after his 2011 arrest.

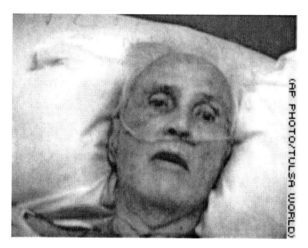

A feeble and dying Paul Rico was shackled to a bed by his jailers.

Chapter 19: The Search

WITH A GUN tucked in his belt, Sgt. David Green was an imposing character as he burst through the door of the second floor office of World Jai Alai Inc. President Richard P. Donovan. It was late afternoon on Oct. 4, 1982, and Donovan was meeting with his security chief, retired FBI Agent H. Paul Rico, and several other WJA employees at the Miami fronton. The switchboard operator had given Donovan a heads up, telling him several police officers were downstairs who wanted to speak to him when Green, Detective Shelton Merritt and a third officer entered the room.

"I'm Sgt. Dave Green of the F.D.L.E. (Florida Department of Law Enforcement) and I have a search warrant," the sergeant said, handing the warrant to Donovan.

Aware that Green and Merritt had recently visited the WJA's Orlando fronton with Augustus Dibble, the onetime chief financial examiner for Connecticut's gaming division, and Harvey Ziskis, a gambling consultant who participated extensively in investigations of the WJA by journalists and law enforcement agencies, Donovan looked over the warrant and then told Green, "You don't really understand what you are looking for. Let me get my attorney over here and we will approach this in an orderly way."

Green's response was short: "We don't need that. We've got our own expert CPA coming in from Connecticut to help us determine what is relevant and what to take." Donovan asked if Dibble was the CPA, saying, "If it is, I don't want him coming in here. He's a partner of Harvey Ziskis, who is a litigant against us in a Connecticut lawsuit." He said Dibble's participation in the search would lead to improper discovery in their lawsuit. Green confirmed that it was Dibble, but added, "That's the way it's going to be."

Donovan quickly called his key employees together and told them they had no alternative but to comply with the warrant. He directed them to give the police officers their full cooperation during the course of the search.

Within 20 minutes, the WJA attorney, William Cagney, arrived at the fronton, along with a caravan of reporters and news teams. The WJA spokesman did his best to answer their questions. A uniformed police officer announced, "We are seizing records in connection with an investigation of grand theft and the Wheeler/Callahan murders."

Roger Wheeler, who bought the Miami-based WJA for $50 million in 1978, was killed on May 27, 1981, after a round of golf at Tulsa's exclusive Southern Hills Country Club—shot in the head by a member of the New England mob. Boston businessman John B. Callahan was president of the WJA from 1974 to 1976. His bullet-ridden body was discovered on Aug. 2, 1982, in the trunk of his Cadillac in a parking lot at Miami International Airport.

Merritt had been the lead investigator in the Callahan killing and the FDLE was conducting an investigation of suspected corruption in the gaming industry.

Dibble arrived at the fronton dressed in short pants—after all, Florida can be hot in October. His movements were monitored by WJA employees who said he walked from one area to another, picking up a few documents and then—appearing to tire of his review and preferring to err of the side of inclusion—directing that all of the documents in any particular cabinet or receptacle be seized.

Daniel Lecciardi, operations manager for the WJA, expressed concern to Green that his officers were seizing winning tickets that had been received by the fronton in return for cash. He explained that Florida held the company responsible for all cash paid to winning patrons that cannot be verified by corresponding winning tickets. He tried to explain the fail safe features of the sell/cash computer system that prevented fraud and mistakes. Green rejected the point and said, "That's not what we found at some of the other places." It was apparent to the WJA employees that

Green, described as the FDLE's expert on organized crime and gambling, did not understand the sell/cash system.

At another point during the search, Lecciardi advised Green he was taking computer tapes that were the property of the Hialeah Race Track, not the WJA. Green responded by saying, "Fuck it, we're taking it." That seemed to be the prevalent attitude of the search team.

The search, which began at about 5:30 p.m., continued until the early morning hours of the next day. Green and Merritt seized thousands of documents and records and then carried them away in trucks. The Miami Herald reported that ten tons of computer tapes and records were taken. The WJA lost almost everything: pay records, time and attendance records, accounting records, tax returns, invoices, magnetic tapes, out-ticket ledgers, and creditor relationship information.

To experienced law enforcement authorities, such a wide ranging search indicates two things: First, the detectives had imprecise probable cause, meaning they did not have solid information that specific evidence could be found. If they had, they would have gone to the spot, located the evidence they sought, and left. Instead, they were dealing with a general allegation that something bad was going on and were left looking for information of theft or skimming or something else evil. They acted as if they were certain it was there but they had no idea what it was, how it was being done or where the evidence could be located. So they took everything they could.

Second, in conducting the search, Green and Merritt behaved like bullies. When a search is conducted and the people being searched are compliant, there is no reason to push them around. If the police do that, the people they are dealing with typically become angry and uncooperative. In working with people, even those they believe are criminals, agents and officers stand to gain more by being polite than roughly ordering them to get out of the way and comply. The demeanor and attitude of Green and Merritt was to demand compliance and to make no accommodation for them. As Green said, "Fuck it, we're taking it." As long as the people being searched are cooperating, there is no reason for the law enforcement officer to be anything but professional.

In bringing Dibble to the search site and allowing him to rummage through the WJA records was clearly inappropriate. As Ziskis' business partner in Pro-Tek Consultants, Inc., it was obviously unethical and when Donovan objected, Green simply rejected his argument and ordered him to comply. The records show that Green and Merritt took thousands of records and Dibble did very little to focus the search on those likely to produce the information the FDLE needed.

Veteran law enforcement officials agree that to take thousands of records and disable a company from doing business on the mere suspicion that something bad was taking place was the height of arrogance. More than anything else, it shows that Green and Merritt thought they knew what was going on and they never doubted themselves. In their view, the WJA was a corrupt criminal organization and they were sure of it. If they couldn't prove it, it was only because they hadn't yet found the evidence. They just knew it must be there. Good detectives and agents always keep an open mind about what the evidence shows.

In the end, 20 employees in the WJA accounting department were laid off because the records they worked with had been seized.

The raid was widely reported by the media to be connected to the Wheeler and Callahan murders. The FDLE spokesman said detectives were looking for clues in the probe of Callahan's death but the search warrant said the officers were looking for evidence of "grand theft." According to one theory advanced in The Miami Herald, Callahan was killed because he had knowledge of the secret diversion of untaxed gaming revenue.

Two days after the search, the federal government issued a grand jury subpoena for the records held by the police. The subpoena would allow the Internal Revenue Service and various fraud investigators to access the records and bring them before a grand jury that was to investigate the matter. This move also kept Cagney, the WJA attorney, from getting a state court to order the records returned so the company could operate.

The day after the search, the WJA decided it had had enough of Green, Merritt and the State of Connecticut and their unfounded allegations and suspicions, and headed to court—led by Roger Wheeler Jr.,—to seek justice. A federal lawsuit was filed by Wheeler, alleging that the business had been disrupted through seizure and retention of their records; and the seizure had been a violation of their civil rights, as it was an unreasonable search and seizure. The suit alleged that while Green and Merritt got a search warrant to search for evidence of grand theft they really were fishing for information on the murders of Wheeler Sr. and Callahan. It also alleged that the retention of the services of Ziskis and Dibble was of "doubtful credibility." The Miami Herald described Ziskis as a former WJA Hartford employee who resigned after some money disappeared in 1976.

Over the next four years, depositions of most of the prime players in the case were taken and many motions were made. The U.S. district court file for the case contains thousands of pages of documents, but concludes in a November 1986 note that it was settled with letters of apology from the State of Connecticut and from Green and Merritt. The two letters were accompanied by payments of $33,333 by Connecticut and $66,666 by Green and Merritt.

The letter of apology by Green and Merritt acknowledged that the search they conducted at the WJA on Oct. 4, 1982, resulted in a substantial part of the business records being removed and held by law enforcement agencies for approximately one year. It advised that "examination of the seized records failed to disclose any violations of any state or federal laws." It admitted that considerable portions of the search information and particularly significant parts of the information provided by Connecticut "have now been shown to be inaccurate or untrue." It went on to say that Green and Merritt had supplied it in the belief that it was true and in the belief that they were performing their law enforcement duties in good faith.

While the two detectives believed the information they provided was true, they were wrong. Their apology letter ended with the two detectives acknowledging their deep regret for the inconvenience and damage suffered by the WJA as a result of their search.

The letter of apology by the State of Connecticut was more artfully apologetic. It pointed out that the search was conducted by the FDLE and Metro-Dade police and that Green and Merritt had "acknowledged that examination of the seized records failed to disclose violations of any state or federal laws." But the one clear fact that remains is that the FDLE, Metro-Dade police and presumably the state police in Connecticut had access to the WJA records for over a year and had to admit they could not find a violation of any state or federal laws. While admitting that Connecticut authorities had passed information to Green and Merritt that was used by them in their search warrant application, the state denied that it knew at the time the information was relied on for the issuance of the Florida search warrant.

Significantly, the Connecticut apology included a statement that any inference of improprieties in the concession operations of the WJA's Hartford fronton from the information provided by the state would be inconsistent with investigations and audits since conducted. It continued, "... to the best of their information, no credible evidence has been uncovered by anyone of any wrongdoing, by WJA or by any of the agents, employees, or associates of the WJA, in connection with the operation of the WJA Fronton."

Apologies certainly have been offered on rare occasion by law enforcement agencies and officers for their actions to settle civil suits. But it would be difficult, perhaps impossible, to find any veteran law enforcement official who has ever worked for a police department, sheriff's office or federal agency to have found it necessary to offer a written apology.

Austin McGuigan, the chief state's attorney in Connecticut who had been relentless in his very public allegations that organized crime had penetrated the jai alai business, left office in 1985. His timely departure meant he was unavailable to sign the state's letter of apology. Two of his former subordinates, George Hyalls and Kevin Kane, signed for the office, along with representatives of the State Division of Special Revenue and the Connecticut State Police.

Timely, indeed, for a man whose peers often referred to as disorganized, extravagant, rude and too eager to trumpet his achievements to the media.

Chapter 20: Interlude

THE WINTER HILL Gang in Boston found new life in the 1980s and early 1990s following the mob murders of businessmen Roger Wheeler and John B. Callahan, both of whom were top officials at World Jai Alai Inc. Wheeler's ownership of WJA ended with his May 1981 assassination in Tulsa and Callahan, the Boston business consultant and former WJA president, was shot to death in Miami in August 1982.

Winter Hill boss James J. "Whitey" Bulger had welcomed home a close associate and one of the gang's key players, Stephen "The Rifleman" Flemmi, who had returned to Boston from his fugitive status in 1974 and was released on bail. Pending bombing charges against Flemmi later were dropped when mobster Robert "Bobby" Daddieco, on whose testimony the case rested, had a change of heart and declined to testify against him.

After Flemmi returned, FBI Agent Dennis Condon arranged for pending federal charges against the longtime mobster to be dropped. While Flemmi was grateful to the FBI and particularly to Condon, it was nothing at all. When Flemmi fled to avoid being arrested on the local bombing charges, he was charged with the federal crime of unlawful flight to avoid prosecution and a federal arrest warrant was issued. The charge is used by the FBI to enable it to pursue a state or local fugitive who has fled from one state to another. In such cases, when the fugitive is located the federal charges are always dropped.

Flemmi didn't understand the process and thought Condon had done him a favor, and the veteran agent wisely accepted the gratitude; he would never know when he might need to talk to Flemmi again and, if the mobster felt indebted to the FBI, then that was all the better.

Times also were good for Condon's former partner, H. Paul Rico, who left the Boston Office in 1969 for Miami and then retired from the FBI in 1975. Rico continued to work at the WJA for Wheeler—a relationship that lasted 15 years after the Callahan murder and for 11 years following the settlement of the WJA lawsuit against Florida Department of Law Enforcement (FDLE) Detectives David Green and Shelton Merritt. It was Green and Merritt who served a warrant to search the WJA offices in October 1982 that resulted in a substantial part of the business records being removed. The two detectives later signed an unusual letter of apology acknowledging that examination of the seized documents had "failed to disclose violations of any state or federal laws."

Rico retired from WJA in 1997 when he was 72 years old. These were the good years, with his children moving forward in their careers and trips to Europe, many cruises and Saturday night dinners at the WJA. Rico and his wife, Connie, had fun and enjoyed life. There would be the occasional news article claiming organized crime had infiltrated jai alai but Rico didn't worry much about things beyond his control. And the news seemed beyond everyone's control. His secretary, Janet Dowd, said he was never happier than when he was surrounded by current and former FBI agents, the people with whom he had the closest bonds.

Jai alai players went out on strike in 1988. When play resumed after a two-year strike, attendance was down and the sport never fully recovered the fans it lost to other gambling enterprises.

In Tulsa, the investigation by Police Sgt. Mike Huff into the Wheeler murder was going nowhere. Merritt's probe in Florida of the Callahan killing also was showing little progress. Both later claimed that the pressures of their investigations had harmed their lives. It is, however, well known that police officers and federal agents often are confronted with unsolved cases, some of which are very serious, and the fact that many of them get stalled is commonplace. The detective or agent who can't get used to or overcome that is in the wrong business.

In Boston, when the Winter Hill Gang's leader, Howie Winter, went to prison and several other potential leaders including John Martorano were charged with various crimes and fled, Flemmi and Bulger emerged as the gang leaders. Under their control, the gang engaged in loan sharking, illegal gambling, protection of narcotics distribution, extortion and, of course, murder. To protect itself, the gang corrupted law enforcement officials at every level: state, local and federal—an endeavor in which the gang was very successful. Bulger may have been the criminal mastermind between the two, but it was Flemmi who made the law enforcement contacts.

During the time when they were most active as criminals, both Bulger and Flemmi were operated as informants by FBI agent John Connolly who was compromised by them. Much has been said about Connolly, who was convicted in 2002 with Bulger and Flemmi on federal racketeering charges. Among the many allegations about him and his boss, John Morris, are accusations they provided Flemmi and Bulger with information about law enforcement investigations and compromised state and local organized crime cases. While their actions were serious and greatly damaged the FBI field office in Boston, corrupt police officers were surely a greater source of intelligence for the Winter Hill Gang.

Flemmi's brother, Michael, a Boston Police officer for 32 years, provided support to Flemmi's criminal activities. Once, when Flemmi was incarcerated, he called on his brother to move a stash of firearms including sawed off shotguns and machine guns from his mother's house to hide them from investigators who later searched the house. Michael Flemmi later was convicted of obstruction of justice for lying to a grand jury about his role in hiding the weapons and was sentenced to a prison term. Michael Flemmi provided support to his brother in more ways than hiding guns.

A more damaging penetration of law enforcement was conducted through a second police source, Massachusetts State Police Lieutenant Richard Schneiderhan, a 25-year MSP veteran who retired in 1984. He served in the state police's organized crime unit and, following retirement, continued in law enforcement by working at the New England State Police Intelligence Network, a federally-funded law enforcement information clearinghouse. Schneiderhan, who met Flemmi when both were children living in the same Boston neighborhood, was on the payroll of the Winter Hill Gang, which paid him a salary of $1,000 a month for many years. A federal investigation produced charges that in 1977 Schneiderhan helped

Martorano beat a test designed to match his voice to one recorded on a wiretap. The probe also showed he tipped Flemmi and Bulger to State Police bugging devices planted inside their headquarters and told Flemmi that his son had been profiled by investigators in Florida. Bulger was reported as saying that Schneiderhan "... saved our ass a hundred times."

Schneiderhan was almost infatuated with Flemmi. Investigators found letters he had written to his son to be opened after his death. In one, he referred to Flemmi by the code name "Paul" and provided his son Flemmi's pager number. He instructed his son to use the numerical code "131313" when contacting Flemmi. He asked that Flemmi attend his wake or mass and "sit up front with you as family." The letter advised his son that if he had problems and needed help he should contact Flemmi. "Trust him. He is one of the few people in the world that you can trust."

In February 1973, Connolly, who grew up in South Boston, was transferred to the Boston field office. Since it was an extraordinary transfer given much earlier than would be expected, it has generated accusations that "crooked agents" in Boston arranged it so that they could work with Connolly whom they viewed as a fellow crook. Howie Carr, the Boston columnist, wrote that although the transfer was purportedly as a result of Connolly's location and apprehension of Boston Top Ten Fugitive Frank Salemme, "his capture was a convenient way for crooked FBI agent H. Paul Rico to get (Connolly) back to Boston, where he could funnel information to the mob."

Carr might be surprised to learn that at the time of Connolly's transfer, Rico had been gone from the Boston Office for almost three years. The transfer actually came as a reward to Connolly for locating and arresting Salemme in 1972 in New York. At the time, Salemme was a FBI Top Ten Fugitive. Connolly had been assigned to the New York field office and desperately wanted to return to his hometown. Under normal conditions, he would have had to wait for years to move to the top of the "Office of Preference" list and become eligible for a routine rotation transfer home.

On Dec. 14, 1972, FBI Agent Tom Baker persuaded Connolly to accompany him on a brief mid-day shopping trip. The FBI's New York office was located at 69th Street and 3rd Avenue and Bloomingdale's had just opened a few of blocks away. Baker wanted to have a look in

Bloomingdale's to find a Christmas gift for his wife. Connolly was working diligently on paperwork, trying to get his cases in order so he could visit his family in Boston over the holidays. After much persuasion, Connolly gave in and agreed to go with Baker. He would be glad he did.

Connolly had followed cases in Boston closely enough to know that Salemme might be in New York. Salemme was the Mafia member identified by Rico as one of the two responsible for the car bombing of Joseph "The Animal" Barboza's attorney, John Fitzgerald, resulting in the lawyer losing his right leg below the knee. Salemme had made the big time; he was on the FBI's Top Ten Most Wanted List.

The Boston agents that Connolly knew sent him wanted posters with Salemme's picture, description and fingerprints. Connolly knew of Salemme's fondness for sports and hoped to bump into him at a Madison Square Garden sporting event. With all the people in New York, only a relatively naive new agent would expect to be able to find a fugitive, much less a Top Ten fugitive, on no more of lead than "he might be in New York."

As they left the New York field office, Baker took the lead and chose the route. When they had traveled a block or two, Connolly suddenly spotted Salemme on the sidewalk walking toward them. He hollered, "Hey, Frankie." When Salemme acknowledged his name, the two agents placed him under arrest. It was easy. The wanted poster was still folded in Connolly's pocket. Salemme was returned to Boston to face trial and the bureau was so impressed and pleased that Connolly was rewarded with a transfer back to his hometown.

There is no evidence, apart from Flemmi and Salemme's allegations, that there was any corruption in the FBI's Boston field office until Connolly arrived. Connolly, who was in the opinion of Rico, mismatched with Bulger in raw intelligence later was compromised by Bulger and Flemmi. There is no evidence he was spotted by other corrupt agents as a fellow traveler and brought in to continue the corrupt practices in supporting Bulger and Flemmi.

In the 1970s, the organized crime element of the Boston field office had changed fundamentally. Jack Kehoe, the vigorous, highly-effective organized crime squad supervisor, retired in 1970, the same year Rico was transferred to Miami. Morris, who was thought to be a "nice guy," arrived in Boston in 1972 and served as supervisor of the organized crime squad in late 1970s and early 1980s. Agents quickly learned that Morris was not the man Kehoe had been; he was a weak, ineffectual supervisor. Morris would not only fail in his responsibility to keep an agent under his supervision from engaging in criminal acts, but he himself would be corrupted.

In September 1975, three years after Connolly arrived in Boston, he arranged a meeting with Bulger and pitched him on cooperating. He used the same approach Rico had used on many other informants; he did not try to get information about Bulger's Winter Hill Gang but used Bulger to provide information about their rivals in the Mafia. In any case, cooperation with the FBI could be dangerous but, as Bulger apparently saw it, valuable to the Winter Hill Gang.

Over ten years after Rico left Boston, Connolly reopened Flemmi's informant file in 1980 as a Top Echelon informant, meaning he was someone who had the ability and access to provide the FBI with first-hand information about high-level organized crime figures. Connolly was then dealing with two very dangerous people. There certainly is nothing wrong with collecting information from any murderous thug as long as the agent handling the informant doesn't lose sight of the fact that the informant should always remain a target for prosecution for any of his criminal deeds. If the informant is giving up important information about high level Mafia activities, the FBI is not going to pursue trivial crimes, but the agent can't let the informant prey on other people or commit violence and murders.

Rico never lost sight of that, which can be seen in the fact that when his Top Echelon informant Flemmi bombed Fitzgerald's car he moved quickly to get Flemmi charged with the crime. Rico provided the information about Flemmi's culpability to another agent, identified the witness who could break the case and suggested a strategy that was successful in obtaining the information needed to charge the informant. When Flemmi was charged, Rico closed the informant file exactly as is supposed to happen. There was never a question in Rico's mind about what to do about Flemmi, and there is no information to show that Flemmi ever knew of Rico's role in his being charged.

Unfortunately, Connolly trusted and protected his two Winter Hill Gang informants and crossed the line when he did so. Having grown up in the same neighborhood with Bulger, Connolly liked the mob boss personally and had a strong interest in keeping him active as an informant. Flemmi and Bulger made Connolly a big deal within the FBI, giving him that unspoken status that comes from operating important informants. As his informants became more dominant in local criminal activity, Connolly didn't become aware of their more serious crimes or, if he knew about them, he ignored them and protected his informants from law enforcement. Where Rico knew what was going on with his informants and what to do when one committed a horrendous crime, apparently Connolly did not.

When Connolly's handling of the two informants began to receive negative public attention, Rico confided in a close associate that he thought Bulger was one of the smartest criminals he had known and he doubted that Connolly was his equal. Connolly operated Flemmi and Bulger as informants until he retired in 1990 and there is no doubt that they ruined him.

The key to what happened in Boston—and ultimately to Rico—was the corruption of Morris, Connolly's supervisor. An FBI supervisor is an integral component in the bureau's management structure, perhaps the most important one. A squad supervisor has the responsibility to ensure that the assigned agents are handling the right cases in the right way. When an agent develops an active and significant criminal as an informant, the supervisor must be alert to the informant's criminal activities and be sure the agents are not inappropriately ignoring serious criminal activity. A supervisor should particularly be attentive to an informant when he is being handled by an agent who knew him as a childhood friend.

Kehoe was an assertive organized crime squad supervisor who knew the cases and agents he supervised. He understood the strengths and weaknesses of the people who worked on his squad and made assignments accordingly. Unfortunately for Connolly and for the FBI, Morris suffered feelings of inferiority when he dealt with Connolly. Morris said, "He was my best friend ... he was like an older brother ... I trusted him. I respected him. I trusted him with my life."

Morris was impressed with Connolly who he thought to be more worldly and successful in developing the big cases and informants. Morris described Connolly as having "qualities I didn't have." He thought he was "mentally and physically tough" and being from Boston, "knew the streets." Morris didn't just fail to properly evaluate what was going on with Bulger and Flemmi; he became a part of their corrupt operation.

Agents operating informants may tend to minimize some of their informant's criminal activities, but the supervisor is a step removed from the "hands on" position that the agent is in and must ensure that the agent doesn't overlook much. Morris not only failed in that responsibility but he participated in crimes.

As the years passed, Connolly became closer and closer to Flemmi and Bulger and more protective of them while their criminal activities grew. When Rico left Boston, they were serious criminals. Twenty years later, in 1990 when Connolly retired, they were the dominant criminals in South Boston and had committed multiple murders. Connolly and Morris should have seen this and acted to stop it. If Connolly failed, it was Morris' responsibility to act.

In 1981, Morris was going through marital difficulties and had begun a romance with his secretary. He displayed astonishingly poor judgment by "borrowing" $1,000 from Bulger to pay for his girlfriend to travel to Georgia where he was attending a drug investigation training session. Bulger and Flemmi, who surely understood Morris' weakness and set out to exploit it, sent him a case of wine with $5,000 in it. In both instances, Connolly delivered the money. Morris later said these were "loans," but neither loan was paid back.

Borrowing money from an informant is strictly forbidden by FBI policies and rules for handling informants. Both Morris and Connolly were in too deep to get out. Morris had not only failed in his responsibility to oversee Connolly's relationship with his informants but he became an active force in continuing and protecting their corrupt activities. Without Morris' involvement, it is doubtful Connolly could have continued without being detected.

In 1983, Morris lied to the special agent in charge of the Boston field office about his relationship with his secretary and was moved to the drug squad, where he would no longer supervise Connolly or have responsibility for overseeing his work with Bulger and Flemmi. James A. Ring, who was appointed as the new Organized Crime Squad supervisor, was much more skeptical of Connolly and his two informants.

Connolly quickly tried to compromise Ring, as he had Morris, but found him an unwilling collaborator. After a couple of meetings with the informants, Ring became concerned about Connolly's relationship with them. Ring felt that Connolly talked too much and gossiped with everyone. He also thought that Bulger and Flemmi often exaggerated to make themselves seem to be at the center of everything.

Ring asked Morris if there was any reason Bulger shouldn't be continued as an informant. Morris lied and told him there was no problem. In fact, every time that something came up that threatened the two informants, Morris, the supervisor, worked behind the scenes to protect Connolly and the informants. Morris' dishonesty and abdication of his responsibility as a supervisor was the key component in continuing the corruption. His protection of Connolly and the informants became essential in ensuring that other supervisors and managers wouldn't identify the real problem.

After two meetings with Connolly and the two informants, Ring became disturbed about the relationship he had observed. He brought Connolly back to the office and asked him if he understood that the two informants were not "friends" or "consultants." Connolly gave all the right answers. That Connolly knew what to do was illustrated by the fact that when he made a video for the bureau discussing proper informant development, he was careful to point out that informants were criminals, not friends. Apparently, he thought that such rules applied to everyone else.

At the same time Connolly was giving Ring the right answers, he was conspiring with Morris and the informants to protect them and keep the relationship as it had been. Connolly had become much too close to his informants. And within the Boston field office he had the continuing clandestine support of Morris. Even after Morris had been removed as the organized crime squad supervisor, he actually hosted dinners at his house attended by Connolly and the two thugs.

On one occasion in 1985, he invited Condon, Rico's old partner, but failed to tell him the two informants would be there. Condon was surprised to find them at the house when he arrived and felt ambushed. He left immediately after dinner. For Morris to continue clandestinely his relationship with an agent he formerly supervised and his informants was an egregious violation of FBI practices.

After a few years of struggle with his new supervisor, Connolly retired in December 1990 and took a well-paying job with the local power company. Although Bulger and Flemmi were closed as informants, no one at the FBI told them since it wasn't the practice of agents handling informants to tell them that a file had been opened and that everything they were saying was being recorded in it. On the surface, things seemed to be rather peaceful and tranquil in 1990 when Connolly retired, but a storm was brewing.

Chapter 21: Batman

THE TWO PROSECUTORS painted such an imposing picture in the courtroom that Boston Magazine characterized them as "Batman and Robin," the caped crime-fighting crusaders who pitted their wits many times against a dastardly collection of villainous arch rivals. Assistant U.S. Attorneys Fred M. Wyshak Jr. and Brian T. Kelly were once again being asked to stave off a wave of organized criminals with fiendish designs and desires to control mob activities in the Boston area.

It was the early 1990s and federal prosecutors and the FBI had begun to focus their attention on James J. "Whitey" Bulger, boss of the infamous Winter Hill Gang in Boston, along with a couple of his top assassins, John Martorano and Stephen "The Rifleman" Flemmi. It would be the job of Wyshak and Kelly to assess the investigative reports to determine whether there was sufficient evidence to file criminal charges, to bring those charges to the court and to argue the case before a judge.

Wyshak had transferred to the U.S. attorney's office in Boston from Newark, N.J., and quickly was regarded by the FBI agents who dealt with him as very smart and aggressive but arrogant and obnoxious. He offended many people and seemed to have a strong dislike for the FBI. Kelly was a veteran prosecutor in the U.S. attorney's office in Boston who helped lead the federal investigation into and the crackdown of Bulger's criminal enterprises.

Described as "tall and big chested," the physically imposing Wyshak was said to be a prickly and brash Batman.

After a couple of unpleasant dealings, FBI Agent James A. Ring, then the supervisor of the Organized Crime Squad at the bureau's Boston field office, decided life was too short to deal with a prosecutor who was so abrasive and difficult. He approached the head of the Strike Force and asked that Wyshak not be assigned to FBI organized crime cases. Apparently, Ring's request was discussed with Wyshak and it further poisoned their relationship.

Wyshak relied on a team of investigators from the Massachusetts State Police and the Drug Enforcement Administration (DEA). His use of the state police investigators played into a longstanding "lack of a team effort" between the Special Services Unit (SSU) of the Massachusetts State Police and the FBI. The state investigators operated out of their own headquarters and focused on gambling and bookies, while the FBI's organized crime strategy de-emphasized gambling cases to focus on higher-level targets. The different investigative focuses could have been complimentary but, unfortunately, led to clashes between the agencies.

Since many FBI agents felt that most of the local officers and DEA agents who had gravitated to Wyshak's team harbored an animosity for the FBI, the relationship between the FBI and Wyshak and his investigators was troubled.

But 1995 would be an important one for the Winter Hill Gang, the FBI and, ultimately, for FBI Agent H. Paul Rico, one of the most recognized and decorated agents in the Boston field office. In January, arrest warrants were obtained for Flemmi, Bulger and Francis B. "Cadillac Frank" Salemme, a mob hitman. A joint effort was made by state and federal agencies to locate and arrest the men—an arrest that evolved into a strange affair that illustrated the dysfunctional relationship that then existed between the agencies. Normally when joint arrests were conducted, agents and their local counterparts would team up and work together sharing cars and communications. When Flemmi was arrested, the relationship between the agencies was so troubled that FBI agents discovered that while the state police could monitor FBI radio frequencies, the FBI agents were not provided access to state police communications. The relationship between the agencies had deteriorated to the point that not only were the investigators not teamed up but there was little communication between them.

In spite of the fact that Flemmi later claimed to have been told by FBI Agent John Connolly in Boston in December 1994 that he, Salemme and Bulger would soon be indicted and arrested, Flemmi didn't flee. He was spotted coming out of a restaurant and, although an FBI agent was about 200 feet away from him, the state police quickly swooped in for the arrest. Flemmi was placed in a state police vehicle and taken straight to their headquarters, where he was grilled about FBI corruption. The FBI was given no access to him.

Bulger was not found and his girlfriend, Theresa Stanley, who later was interviewed by the FBI, said she and Bulger were on their way back to Boston from New Orleans when they heard about Flemmi's arrest on the car radio. Stanley said they pulled into a motel in Connecticut, where they stayed for a few days and Bulger made numerous telephone calls. Shortly thereafter, in the middle of the night, Bulger snuck into Boston with Stanley, dropping her off and picking up another girlfriend, Catherine Elizabeth Greig. He and Greig then fled the city.

Bulger remained a fugitive for more than 16 years until his June 2011 capture in Santa Monica, Calif. He had been listed on the FBI's "Ten Most Wanted" list, which offered a $2 million reward for information leading directly to his arrest.

Wyshak rejected Stanley's story, believing the tale that Connolly had tipped Bulger to the arrest. The FBI agents who interviewed her thought she was telling the truth. Whatever the truth, Salemme and Bulger, who, according to news reports, had been seen in Boston the week before, both escaped. A few days after Flemmi was arrested, Martorano was arrested in Boca Raton, Fla., by the FBI and Massachusetts State Police. He had been a fugitive for 16 years. A week after Flemmi was arrested, he, Bulger and Salemme were indicted by a federal grand jury on 19 counts of murder, along with additional counts of conspiracy to commit murder, conspiracy to commit extortion, narcotics distribution, conspiracy to commit money laundering, extortion, money laundering and racketeering.

In August, the FBI and Massachusetts State Police located and arrested Salemme in West Palm Beach. At the time, Salemme was reported to be the head of the New England Mafia Family. He had been featured in an America's Most Wanted program and his location came as a result of a tip.

The agents in the FBI's Boston field office were at lost to explain why Wyshak seemed to be so uncooperative and confrontational. The story circulated within the FBI that Wyshak had had some unpleasant dealings with the FBI in New York or Newark when he was working in the U.S. attorney's office there and, as a result, he harbored an intense dislike for the bureau. Wyshak's motivation is unknown but it was apparent that during the investigation of corruption in the FBI in Boston, he offended a number of agents and was at the root of the resulting negative working relationship.

The Wyshak team focused on corruption in the FBI's Boston field office and saw the Winter Hill Gang subjects, primarily Flemmi and Martorano, as instruments to lead to the indictment of corrupt FBI agents.

In 1997, Barry Mawn was assigned as the new Special Agent in Charge (SAC) of the Boston office with orders to deal with the allegations of corruption there. By the time Mawn arrived, it was clear there was a serious FBI corruption problem that needed to be addressed. From the outset, Mawn tried to be helpful to the corruption probe. He had a good reputation for working successfully with other agencies and prosecutors. He was an experienced leader who could have been helpful to any inquiry. There was no hint that there was anything corrupt about Mawn or that he would do anything to protect a corrupt agent.

Wyshak was smart but often was unnecessarily provocative and confrontational. At one meeting in front of Massachusetts State Police officers and DEA agents, Wyshak directly accused Mawn of lying. After Mawn had spoken, Wyshak said, "Here's the FBI lying again." The remark led to a nasty confrontation and a "nose to nose" shouting match between the two. In spite of the difficult strained relationship, Mawn tried repeatedly to cooperate and participate in the investigation into corruption in his office. His efforts were rejected by Wyshak who seemed suspicious of everyone associated with the FBI.

Wyshak's group was initially focused on FBI Agent John Morris, due to the fact he was Connolly's supervisor and the higher ranking of the two agents suspected of corruption. Morris had retired from the FBI in December 1995 after reaching a senior executive service position and took a job with an insurance company.

Mawn believed Connolly was more of the driving force and, therefore, the more culpable of the two. He suggested that the focus of any investigation into corruption should be on making a deal with and turning Morris rather than Connolly. Ultimately, Wyshak followed the strategy Mawn recommended but excluded the Boston field office from the investigation. The state police and DEA agents handled the bulk of the inquiry.

When the FBI suggested approaching Martorano, Wyshak observed that he had killed 20 people and turned them down flat, saying "absolutely not." Four or five months later, Mawn heard that the Wyshak team had "flipped" Martorano. When Mawn confronted him with this, Wyshak told him Martorano wouldn't talk to the FBI because he didn't trust the bureau. Such an excuse is, of course, standard fare when a law enforcement official wishes to exclude another person, agency or department from its investigation. But such excuses are silly, almost childish—no one with any experience believes such an excuse. Moreover, Martorano was making a deal to save his life, deciding which agency he would talk with should not have been his choice.

As indictments drew closer, pre-charging meetings were held that included the FBI and Wyshak. Often these meetings ended up in shouting matches, with Wyshak frequently challenging the integrity of the FBI and the agents. Most often, Wyshak started his comments with "I find it hard to believe ..." which raised the tension immediately. Petty issues often surfaced and added to the poisoned atmosphere.

On one occasion, an FBI agent told Wyshak and the investigators he had closed a prison informant close to Howie Winter, one of the original leaders of the Winter Hill Gang, on the advice of a prison official who said the source's safety was threatened since he was telling too many inmates he was an FBI informant. The informant was providing no information of value and the prison authorities had decided to transfer him.

Wyshak became incensed that he had not been involved in this decision and accused the agent of being corrupt. Later the agent's decision to close the informant was cited by Wyshak to a Justice Department Task Force headed by John Durham as "evidence" of the agent's corruption. As a result, the agent was interviewed by the department's Office of Professional Responsibility (OPR) and all of his informants were interviewed to determine if he had had any improper dealings with any of them. He had not and the OPR case against him ultimately was closed.

Wyshak's small-mindedness harmed the FBI pointlessly. Corruption in a law enforcement agency is always damaging to morale of the people in the agency. The corruption of both an agent and his supervisor was highly unusual and would be extremely damaging when it was disclosed. Since the FBI has the primary responsibility for investigation of corruption in the federal government, the agency usually has played a lead role in cases dealing with corruption among its own employees. In fact, while the bureau has failed on occasion, overall it has an excellent record of dealing with corruption in its ranks. It has dealt successfully with agents who committed espionage, others who stole or embezzled and even with its own director—William Sessions—who was fired in 1993 by President Clinton as a result of an FBI investigation.

Wyshak hindered FBI participation in the investigation of Morris and Connolly. He used Massachusetts State Police and DEA agents extensively. Whatever his motivation or his methods, Wyshak was successful in bringing to light a serious corruption problem with Connolly and Morris. At the same time, his contentiousness contributed to a poisoned law enforcement atmosphere in Boston.

The news that Morris had accepted immunity and admitted he had taken money from Bulger and Flemmi was explosive. There seemed to be no end to the revelations. At one point, Morris admitted attempting to have Bulger killed. He said he leaked the fact that Bulger was an informant to a reporter hoping Bulger would be killed and he would be free of him. If you could believe that both an agent and a supervisor had been so corrupted then you could believe almost any other allegation that was made. You could, for example, easily believe that their corruption started with Rico.

In April 1998, Morris testified about Connolly and his corrupt relationship with their informants, Flemmi and Bulger. The news coverage was intense.

Abusing the FBI became routine. Mawn found it was very difficult in Boston during the inquiry into corruption. For example, after the FBI had turned over mountains of informant files and documents to U.S. District Judge Mark L. Wolf in a civil case related to the corruption, a Boston agent discovered a document covered by the judge's order that had not been disclosed. Mawn instructed the agent to alert the court and disclose the document. Later, he received a call from Judge Wolf's office saying the judge ordered him to come immediately to his chambers. When he arrived, he found Judge Wolf and several lawyers seated around a conference table. Judge Wolf berated him mercilessly and generally refused to allow him to speak.

Watching comfortably from the sofa and upholstered chairs in the judge's office were Flemmi, Martorano and Salemme. Mawn was extremely angry at being rebuked by a judge in front of a bunch of mobsters but there was little he could do about it. A judge who would berate the head of an important law enforcement agency in front of mobsters has lost his way.

One year after Morris testified in September 1999, Martorano pled guilty in federal court to killing ten people including Tulsa businessman Roger Wheeler on behalf of a racketeering enterprise. He said Bulger and Flemmi told him to kill Wheeler at an exclusive Tulsa golf club and that Rico had assisted by providing the information used to locate Wheeler. It was revealed that the longtime mobster had reached an agreement that called for him to plea to second degree murder charges in Tulsa and Florida, and provide information and testify against Flemmi, Bulger and any former FBI agents targeted in Wyshak's probe. Although Martorano confessed to another eight murders, the government agreed to recommend a sentence of 12 1/2 to 15 years imprisonment—a little more than 9 months for each murder.

The deal with Martorano was far too generous. He was a serial murderer who admitted to 18 murders. There are allegations he killed more than 20 people including randomly targeting and killing black people because of their race. The fact he faced trial for murder in two states that still execute murderers gave the government a huge hammer to hold over his head. There is no reason the government should have settled for a slap on the wrist with Martorano. They could have made him trade his life for his cooperation. Prosecutors, however, are often too nervous about the case they have compiled and too eager to make a deal to bring another witness on board.

Patrick A. Patterson, another FBI agent assigned to the Boston office, also was treated poorly by the Wyshak team. Patterson was an inspector during the 1997 review of the Boston office. Since the news was filled with stories about corruption in the FBI, Patterson interviewed Connolly to see what he had to say about it. During the interview, Connolly steadfastly denied having any relationship with Flemmi's defense team. Later, the FBI was able to show that this was a lie and one of the charges against Connolly was that he had lied during his interview with Patterson.

During the Connolly investigation, Patterson was called to testify before a federal grand jury. The prosecutors asked him to be at their office early in morning. Patterson arrived at 8 a.m. and waited there until about 10:30 a.m. when he realized they had no intention of using him that day. So he left and went over to the FBI office. The prosecutors did not use him at all that day and, in the evening, one told him they would use him "the first thing in the morning" so he could get out on an afternoon flight.

Patterson suspected that Wyshak's team had no real intention of putting him in early, so he made reservations to return home two days later. Sure enough, he waited all of the next day and finally testified at 4 p.m. The prosecutor with whom he was working said he hoped he hadn't made him miss his flight. Patterson told him he figured they wouldn't put him into the grand jury room until late in the afternoon so he made reservations for the following day. He told the prosecutor he would enjoy a nice dinner and would return in the morning. Patterson thinks Wyshak was poisoned by the Massachusetts State Police with whom he worked, all of whom hated the FBI and shared that hatred with Wyshak.

On another occasion, someone called in a tip on Bulger, advising that he had been seen in Paris. Wyshak told the tipster that if the FBI was advised of this he would prosecute the person for obstruction of justice. In spite of the fact that the FBI maintains an agent in the American Embassy in Paris, who has liaison with the French police, Wyshak made plans to send the Massachusetts state police to Paris to look for Bulger. What exactly would a state police officer, with no established relationship with French officials, do in France? Did they even have the authority to make an arrest in France?

Wyshak's actions and conduct are perplexing. He was leading a largely successful effort to address corruption in the FBI's Boston field office and deserves strong praise for that work, but his actions and those of his team were so petty on occasion with Patterson and abusive with other FBI executives that his reasons remain muddled. What was the point of making Patterson wait for two days? Patterson, Mawn and many of the agents in the Boston office were clearly on the side of ferreting out the truth. And Patterson had evidence to offer the prosecutors.

But Wyshak's harsh behavior was not limited to the FBI. He also was incredibly cruel to Wheeler's son, Roger Wheeler Jr. In June 2003, Wheeler Jr. willingly appeared for an interview by Wyshak, Tulsa Detective Mike Huff and two assistant Tulsa district attorneys. Wyshak began the interview by asking Wheeler to view gruesome autopsy photographs of his father to identify the body which Wyshak claimed had never been done. There could have been no need, 22 years after the murder, to have a son view autopsy photographs to "identify the body." It appears from the evidence and records that Wyshak was angry that Wheeler Jr.'s refusal to believe that Rico had anything to do with his father's murder and wanted to shock him into compliance with his theory of the case. Wheeler told Wyshak he would not view photographs of his father's body and terminated the interview.

In December 1999, Connolly, Flemmi and Bulger were indicted again for racketeering, racketeering conspiracy, obstruction of justice and conspiracy to obstruct justice. The charges were amended in 2000 when Connolly was indicted on a range of charges including providing tips to Bulger and Flemmi to enable them to eliminate threats to their operations and to misleading grand jury investigations.

In March 2001, Salemme agreed to be a witness against Rico, Connolly, Bulger and Flemmi. In May 2002, Connolly was convicted by a jury that deliberated for two days on charges he shielded the gangsters, accepted a bribe and tipped them to impending indictments. The jury found Connolly guilty of one count of racketeering, three counts of obstruction of justice and one count of making a false statement to the FBI. Interestingly, the jury must not have found the government's witnesses compelling; they found a number of charges "not proven beyond a reasonable doubt." The failed charges included accepting a diamond ring from Bulger; delivering a case of wine to Morris; giving Morris $1,000 from Bulger; giving $5,000 to Morris; and aiding and abetting the extortion of two citizens who were driven out of their liquor business by Bulger.

The jury also rejected allegations that Connolly alerted Bulger and Flemmi that two of his murder victims were informants; that former World Jai-Alai President John Callahan was being sought to testify before a grand jury; and that a federal grand jury would issue indictments against Bulger, Salemme and Flemmi.

Connolly was sentenced to ten years in federal prison.

In October 2003, a little more than a year after Connolly was convicted, Flemmi agreed to plead guilty to all counts in the federal indictment and guilty in both Oklahoma and Florida to the first degree murders of Wheeler and Callahan. He agreed that the appropriate sentencing guideline for his offenses was life imprisonment.

Dade County, Fla., agreed that Flemmi would be sentenced to life in prison without eligibility for parole for 25 years for murder in the first degree and that the sentence would be served in a federal prison. Tulsa County agreed to the same: guilty to first degree murder, life in prison and the sentence to be served in federal prison.

For a person facing the death penalty in two states, a sentence life in prison, particularly federal prison, looks pretty good. The deal with Flemmi was good on the surface but the real question was: Would he tell the truth or just what he thought the prosecutors wanted to hear? There is no record that Flemmi was ever subjected to a polygraph examination to judge the veracity of his allegations.

The record shows that Wyshak didn't polygraph Flemmi or any of the others who had signed up to join his team. Of course, there can be valid reasons why a prosecutor chooses not to use a polygraph. But in this case, Wyshak had gone on record with the First Circuit Court of Appeals with the claim that Flemmi had committed perjury in Judge Wolf's court. The Judge also found that Flemmi had made false statements under oath.

For a prosecutor to use someone with this background it would be expected that he had strong confirmation of the witness through a polygraph examination or development of strong evidence confirming his story. Apparently, Wyshak had neither.

Chapter 22: Mike Huff

THE CREDIBILITY AND judgment of the lead investigator in most criminal prosecutions is a side issue of varying importance, particularly when the government can offer compelling evidence of guilt. But in the Oklahoma prosecution of FBI Agent H. Paul Rico, a prosecutor and, ultimately, a court had to buy into the largely uncorroborated claims of two Mafia hitmen with serious credibility issues and much to gain by offering false testimony. This is when the skill, integrity and professionalism of the lead investigator assume much greater significance.

A naive interrogator with a fixed agenda, for example, might easily give away far too much information in posing leading questions to a calculating, street-wise hood. Then, once the jail-house witness feeds back a vague story that clearly pleases the investigator, the story "evolves"—conveniently disguised as improved recall to fit increasingly specific questions. The skillful liar incorporates as much truthful detail as possible, and any physical evidence or preconceived inferences presented to the witness are worked into the chronology. Eventually, the tale morphs into the witness's "incriminating" testimony and it becomes a matter of memorization and practice.

A review of hundreds of pages of court records, other documents and dozens of interviews with key officials in the Rico case shows that the lead investigator, Tulsa Police Department Sgt. Mike Huff, was the intrepid force who persisted over several decades to persuade a reluctant district attorney to charge the longtime FBI agent.

Experience has shown that there is much more to a case than what appears in the files—particularly in a prosecution that was never tested during a trial before a judge or a jury, or even a preliminary probable cause hearing. Only an interview with Huff and a thorough review of all of the case documents would show whether there was undisclosed evidence that might well confirm the sketchy claims of mob assassins Stephen "The Rifleman" Flemmi and John Martorano that Rico was involved in the May 27, 1981, murder of Tulsa millionaire businessman Roger Wheeler. Investigators sometimes use informants and cooperating witnesses with checkered pasts, like Flemmi and Martorano, but usually only after their information has been corroborated by tape recordings or some other incontrovertible evidence.

If Huff had such information or at least other, credible witnesses corroborating the key elements of the offenses charged against Rico—including evidence that implied his culpability by even a preponderance much less than "beyond a reasonable doubt"—those arguing that Rico's arrest and prosecution was a travesty would have to pack up their briefcases and leave this sordid tale alone.

But in interviews in June 2007 that lasted several hours, Huff was unable to do so, instead leaving the very strong suspicion that the case against Rico in Tulsa was far weaker than ever imagined. When pressed repeatedly for corroboration for Flemmi's and Martorano's dubious claims that they met with Rico at the World Jai Alai offices in Miami in August 1982, Huff offered only unspecified Miami Beach hotel records for an unknown female represented to be Flemmi's girlfriend. He could produce no other documents to corroborate the allegations. A warning issued by Huff himself during a telephone call to set up the interview had come true, there was no "smoking gun" pointing to Rico, even a significant lack of actual smoke relevant to the charge filed in Tulsa.

Instead, Huff sought to steer the conversation to tales of the many other Boston mob murders—as many as sixty—during the Irish Gang wars in the 1960's. According to Huff, Rico had "ordered" many of those hits when he was assigned to the FBI's Boston field office. He was as "certain" of that as much as he was convinced that Rico had commissioned the Wheeler murder.

As badly as the La Cosa Nostra mobsters in Boston and other assorted high profile crooks wanted to get rid of Rico because of the damage he had done personally to organized crime in New England—they even planned to kidnap and kill him—it is inconceivable that if he had been involved in any of the Irish Gang War killings that his ties to the deaths would not have come to light. Add to that the long-standing Boston law enforcement rivalries, rampant corruption in local and state agencies and the "cooperators" over the years anxious to trade prize information for leniency by the courts, a lack of at least other attempts to prosecute Rico is completely unexplainable. But Huff offered only his suppositions and beliefs and little or no hard evidence to back up his charges, certainly nothing that could or would have been presented in court.

During the interviews, Huff offered only second-hand uncorroborated rumors peddled by Francis P. "Cadillac Frank" Salemme, a Boston mobster and hitman who eventually served as boss of the Patriarca crime family of New England, which ultimately were discredited with Salemme's 2008 federal perjury conviction for false information given in the Rico investigation. Yet Huff had no trouble accepting Salemme's stories, which were just too good to pass up—including Salemme's allegations of three-way homosexual romps involving Rico, FBI Director J. Edgar Hoover and Hoover's deputy, Clyde Tolson. The rumors concerning Hoover's sexuality are longstanding, although never proven, but there is absolutely no evidence there were contacts or any relationship between Rico and Hoover. If Rico's criminal enemies had such proof, it would very likely have been put to good use.

As to Huff's claim that Rico ordered the Wheeler murder, not even Flemmi would back that up. Flemmi claimed to be the only available witness concerning the hatching of the Wheeler plot but would barely go so far as to say that John Callahan, former president of World Jai Alai who was later killed in Miami by Martorano, pitched Flemmi and Winter Hill Gang boss James "Whitey" Bulger to help with killing Wheeler for money and a promise of future cash payments. Flemmi alleged that he followed up with a call to Rico in Florida, in which Rico supposedly agreed with the murder. Martorano, the actual trigger man, claimed only that he got his instructions from Flemmi and Callahan and never met Rico until more than a year after the Wheeler murder. Martorano claims he never discussed the Wheeler killing with Rico.

Moreover, if Rico was, as Huff claimed, the true mastermind of the Wheeler murder, it made absolutely no sense that Rico would have no knowledge of the plans to kill Callahan in Florida in July 1982. Yet both Flemmi and Martorano have testified that Rico had nothing to do with the Callahan murder. So the claim of Rico as the "evil mastermind" was not sustainable even if one accepted Huff's own witnesses as credible. There was no internal logic to Huff's theories.

Questions also remain concerning the circumstances surrounding the arrest warrant presented to the only judge who would ever pass judgment on the probable cause to charge Rico. An examination of the probable cause statement in the affidavit shows that it is weak. There was no grand jury indictment, which would have been normal in a federal case of this nature but not unusual for Oklahoma. There was only a criminal information filed—a statement of the charge by the Tulsa District Attorney's Office.

Interestingly, Huff and Tulsa District Attorney Tim Harris chose to present a 22-year-old murder case of this significance to a Family Court "special judge," which would be similar to bringing it before a justice of the peace. It later was learned that the special judge had served as an intern in district attorney's office and was unlikely to refuse an arrest warrant sought by Harris. During the interview, Huff was very defensive on this point and said they chose this judge because he was someone who could be "trusted" due to his prior work at the district attorney's office.

A particularly troubling part of the stories told by Flemmi and Martorano was an account of their one and only alleged face-to-face meeting with Rico—14 months after the Wheeler murder.

There were a number of curious aspects to these two sketchy accounts:

First, Martorano claims this was his only meeting ever with Rico. If Rico was, in fact, the kingpin in the Wheeler killing as Huff believed, the former FBI agent had to know that Martorano was the shooter and a thoroughly dangerous killer. Further, if Huff's theory was correct and Rico was not going to pay off on the Wheeler hit, the last person Rico would want to meet anywhere was Martorano. Geometrically increasing the unlikelihood of this face-to-face get together was the fact that if Rico played the role Huff claimed, he had to know that Martorano, then a highly sought FBI fugitive, was teamed up with Boston mobster Joseph McDonald, then on the FBI's Top Ten list. Is it possible that if Rico were involved in a murder plot, he would invite these thugs into the WJA fronton which was teaming with 30 police officers and several retired FBI agents? One WJA official, Robert Warshaw, former assistant chief of the Miami, Fla., Police Department who later served as associate director of the Office of National Drug Control Policy, thought it would have been an unlikely place for such a meeting.

Second, Huff's arrest warrant affidavit dated this meeting as occurring in August 1982. Martorano later testified he killed Callahan a few days prior to the discovery of his body in the trunk of his Cadillac at the Miami International Airport on Aug. 3, 1982, a discovery that made the local news. The airport is virtually within sight of the Miami Jai Alai facility, making it an unlikely site for such a meeting. It would have been unlikely for Rico to meet any convicted felons—much less fugitives—at the Jai Alai premises under any circumstances because such meetings could jeopardize WJA's Florida gaming license. Add to this the risk of being seen in the company of co-conspirators being pursued by law enforcement, particularly with the "fresh heat" of the Callahan killing.

Third, Flemmi claimed to have called Rico long-distance from Boston to get Rico's authorization to murder Wheeler. Assuming the truth of that claim, it seemed unusual, to say the least, that Flemmi decided it was worth the effort to travel to Miami to meet with Rico for a few minutes just to find out if the sale of the WJA would go forward. Both Flemmi and Martorano claimed this meeting lasted only a few minutes and the Wheeler murder was never discussed. If anyone would have known whether the sale of the WJA was still an option, it would have been Callahan, who had just been killed by Martorano at Flemmi's behest. Also, Martorano testified elsewhere he fled South Florida immediately after killing Callahan and later testified that Callahan was intentionally killed far from Boston so that Flemmi and Bulger would have alibis. Again, why then would Flemmi place himself in the vicinity of the planned Callahan murder?

The lack of any corroboration for the only claimed meeting between Rico and the two witness/killers was troubling, to say the least. But far more troubling was Huff's account of one of his experiences in Boston during hearings before U.S. District Judge Mark L. Wolf. Huff said he dropped in unannounced to meet Barry Mawn, the new special agent in charge of the FBI's Boston field office, who had been brought in to deal with the Boston corruption allegations. Huff and Mawn exchanged pleasantries and Mawn gave general assurances of cooperation. Huff told Mawn of plans to interview the girlfriend of Kevin Weeks, a former mobster of Irish-American descent and a longtime friend and confidant to Bulger. Huff said the girlfriend had recently obtained a protective order against Weeks, which he thought might give Huff an opening to obtain her cooperation.

Subsequently, Huff went to see the girlfriend, buzzed her door, spoke to her through an intercom, responding to his announced arrival with something like "I was wondering when you'd get here." Then Huff described seeing a curtain move, leading him to conclude that Weeks was waiting in ambush. From these facts, Huff concluded that Mawn or someone very close to him had either tipped off the girlfriend or Weeks of Huff's plans. The Tulsa detective was outraged that his interviewers did not express anger at this obvious attempt by the Boston FBI to put his life in danger and Huff soon ended the interview.

Huff's leaps in logic were dumfounding, starting with the fact that the new special agent in charge of the FBI's Boston field office would even know at that point who Weeks was, where his girlfriend lived, and his role in the unfolding events, along with the inferences drawn from his observations. It remains unclear why Mawn would consider Huff to be such a personal threat that he would immediately try to endanger his life. Also surprising was the fact that the Tulsa detective would attempt to conduct an interview alone in a murder investigation in Boston where he had no jurisdiction or authority.

During the several hours of interviews, Huff advanced a number of theories, including his firm conclusion that Rico's exclusive hiring of former FBI agents and their wives in security positions at the Miami Jai Alai offices was just more evidence of a broad criminal conspiracy within the bureau. Huff also believed that Rico's former long-time partner, Dennis Condon, considered a straight arrow professional in Massachusetts law enforcement circles, had to be thoroughly "corrupt" because he spent so many years working with Rico. No matter that Condon had never been accused of any wrongdoing and was heralded in 2006 by former Massachusetts Gov. Michael Dukakis, who later appointed Condon as that state's Commissioner of Public Safety and Superintendent of the Massachusetts State Police, as the "finest public servant" Dukakis ever knew.

And Huff said he had interpreted alleged comments made by Rico during his arrest in 2003 in Miami as threats against the lives of Huff's children, although Huff acknowledged he never thought to report these "threats" to his Tulsa Police Department superiors or the prosecutors.

Huff also said he had been placed under surveillance by the FBI, saying that while he was surprised the bureau would conduct a surveillance of a fellow law enforcement officer, he attributed it to the competition between agencies. He could offer no evidence that any surveillance had ever taken place—a license tag or description—and said he did not report the surveillance to the FBI's Office of Professional Responsibility or to any other authorities.

Just who is Mike Huff, the lead investigator in the Wheeler murder who pushed the case against Rico for over 22 years and managed to sell the questionable stories of Flemmi and Martorano to the Tulsa District Attorney's Office and eager members of Congress?

Huff was a corporal in the Tulsa Police Department when he responded with other officers to an exclusive Tulsa country Club in May 1981 as part of a team of officers in the Wheeler murder. Twenty-one years later, in late 2002, when Huff testified before Congress about the killing, he had risen one notch to the rank of sergeant. One of his early supervisors estimated that Huff's career had peaked. His congressional testimony and later statements gave some indication as to why this was so.

Before the House Committee on Government Reform, chaired by Rep. Dan Burton, Indiana Republican, Huff began by giving a brief description of the Wheeler murder, which he said had been "empowered" by "corruption from within the FBI." He then hinted at what may have colored the decision to charge Rico on some pretty thin evidence: "Mob hits don't happen in Tulsa ... the Winter Hill Gang and associates chose

Tulsa, with an assumption that the Tulsa Police Department wouldn't solve the case," Huff told the committee. "They were wrong."

Describing his herculean efforts in dramatic fashion and drawing on a fertile imagination, Huff continued: "A task force of over a dozen dwindled down to me, the first detective on the scene. I became consumed and obsessed with this case. The stress of it all destroyed my family also … The investigation led us in the direction of the killers of Sheriff Buford Pusser, made famous in the Walking Tall movies, to international intrigue of CIA spies …"

Huff was later to claim "credit" for causing the murder of Callahan, the Winter Hill associate and friend of Martorano, who shot Wheeler and later killed Callahan.

Before Congress, Huff continued: "In July 1982, myself, my partner and detectives from the Connecticut State Police traveled to Boston to meet with the Massachusetts State Police to gain information on activities and whereabouts of John Callahan, the former president of World Jai Alai, who had been fingered by Brian Halloran and offering him the hit on Wheeler."

Huff later described for the committee what he characterized as a "sham" meeting with Justice Department officials in Tulsa, who were about to use the then-retired Rico as an undercover witness in a high-profile prosecution of U.S. District Judge Alcee Hastings. At the end of the meeting, federal prosecutors wanted to know if there was a case against Rico and, if so, said this information would have to be disclosed to defense counsel for Judge Hastings. Apparently, Huff had little to say in 1982, but in 2001 he recalled this as just another effort to obstruct his Wheeler murder investigation. Huff's lack of understanding of the need by the Justice Department for information at a time it was in the midst of an impeachment of a sitting U.S. district judge is appalling.

During his congressional testimony, Huff inexplicably responded to a direct question by Rep. William D. Delahunt, Massachusetts Democrat, by saying Rico had developed Bulger as an informant. This may have been just a mistake on Huff's part, but if so, it was a big one. In fact, Bulger was never cultivated as an informant by Rico, who was transferred to Miami because of Mafia threats to his life in 1970. In 1973, FBI Agent John J.

Connolly arrived in Boston and in 1975, he pitched Bulger. But falsely claiming that Bulger and Rico had such a close relationship had the effect of adding substance to the claims of their later long-distance collaboration in the murder of Wheeler. There is no other reasonable explanation for Huff's false testimony.

This testimony also raises another important issue. While Rico did develop Flemmi as an informant in the late 1960s, Rico closed Flemmi's file when he became a fugitive in the car bombing of defense lawyer John Fitzgerald, who was severely injured but survived the blast. Aside from Flemmi's claims of telephone contact with Rico, now assigned to the Miami Division, there was no evidence of any contact between Flemmi and Rico after Rico left Boston in 1970. Flemmi later claimed he called Rico in 1981 to get approval for the Wheeler murder. Rico, by all accounts was very smart and also readily familiar with the interception of telephone communications. It is questionable that he would have even obliquely discussed a murder long-distance on the telephone with a criminal he last saw twelve years earlier.

Add to this the fact that Rico was a widely acknowledged expert at turning hardened criminals into informants and cooperating witnesses, those Rico knew had no greater prize to offer than a corrupt law enforcement officer. Under the circumstances, if Rico received a telephone proposal such as described, he would immediately envision Flemmi on the other end of the line in manacles sitting in some prosecutor's office with a recorder running.

Huff also described for the committee a July 8, 1982, meeting with Jeremiah T. O'Sullivan, the lead federal prosecutor for the organized-crime strike force in Boston: "Retired FBI Agent Paul Rico, then vice-president of World Jai Alai, was described as a 'rogue agent' that caroused with the Winter Hill Gang members during his tenure in Boston ... I look back to the July meeting in this very building as an 'end of innocence' in my career in law enforcement. I had never been exposed to such a cesspool of dirt and corruption."

O'Sullivan was in the hearing room in December 2002, when Huff testified and the prosecutor's testimony immediately followed. O'Sullivan, who began his career as a federal prosecutor in 1973, three years after Rico left Boston, recalled no such statements. When asked by Burton if he was aware of the "cozy relationship" between Rico, Bulger and Flemmi, he said he was not. When pressed by the congressman on whether he had told Huff that during a meeting, the prosecutor said he "wouldn't have said that in a meeting with Mr. Huff."

O'Sullivan spoke of the "rumors I've heard around the street over a period of time primarily emanating from DEA," but said he had never worked with Rico, never saw him and rarely worked with Condon.

Since O'Sullivan did not start his career as a special attorney for the strike force until 1973, three years after Rico left Boston, and only a few years before Condon retired, this testimony is understandable. But what is not understandable is Huff's characterization of what he learned about Rico from his July 1982 meeting with O'Sullivan. Huff's testimony demonstrates that early on in his investigation—and throughout—Huff molded the facts to fit his preconceived notions rather than letting the facts unfold and shape theories as professional criminal investigators are taught. This flawed approach tainted Huff's investigation.

Another example of Huff's flawed logic can be found in his testimony about the handling of mobster Brian Halloran, a Bulger associate. Halloran was killed in May 1982 after the FBI tried to use him to obtain evidence incriminating Callahan, Bulger and Flemmi in the Wheeler murder. Halloran had offered to cooperate in the case because he was facing an unrelated state murder charge and, for several months, the FBI attempted to keep that cooperation a closely held secret—for good reason. But Huff made clear in his 2002 congressional testimony that he saw the FBI's handling of Halloran and the strike force's refusal to admit Halloran to the Witness Security Program (WSP) as more FBI-orchestrated obstruction.

"Yes, sir. It was what has become known as the Halloran story ... where Flemmi, Bulger, Martorano were involved," Huff testified. "They cut him loose and they never told us about him while they had him and he was still alive. Shortly after they cut him loose he wound up dead here in Boston ..."

But Huff did confirm that O'Sullivan had mentioned that Halloran refused to cooperate against Winter, one of the original leaders of the Winter Hill Gang. A refusal to cooperate fully in the investigation of all subjects, including the person considered the most significant at the time, along with the provision of incomplete or untruthful information, are well-established grounds for exclusion of a person from WITSEC.

However, when O'Sullivan testified, he also provided a more specific reason, having nothing to do with the FBI or the Wheeler case: "... At the time Mr. Halloran was cooperating with the FBI, he was under charges of murder in the Suffolk County, Massachusetts. It would have been contrary to Department of Justice policy to sponsor somebody against whom there was a murder case pending ... in the witness protection program. However, I did approach Suffolk County District Attorney Newman Flannigan and asked him whether, in fact, he would consider removing the murder charges or in some way dismissing the murder charges if Mr. Halloran would cooperate with him."

O'Sullivan said Flannigan turned him over to Assistant District Attorney Thomas Mundy, who was in charge of his homicide unit, who told him Halloran had claimed to have information regarding murders committed by the Winter Hill Gang, but it proved to be inconsistent with the physical evidence. O'Sullivan said Mundy recommended that, "I get away from Mr. Halloran because they thought Mr. Halloran was lying to them."

O'Sullivan testified that he told Huff he didn't believe Halloran because of the statements of the Suffolk County officials, adding that that "was the only basis on which I made the statement to Mr. Huff."

And so Halloran met the fate of others before and since who have tried to play both sides in a sometimes very dangerous game. Once again, Huff's assumptions, the inferences he drew from what he observed, and his conclusions were all shaped to fit his preconceived notion of a huge FBI conspiracy—one that included Rico at the center.

Huff announced his retirement from the Tulsa Police Department in May 2011 after 37 years with the agency. A local radio station paid tribute to the veteran detective, saying he had "dedicated his life to putting killers behind bars." The headline on the station's web page was even more direct, "Tulsa killer catcher calls it quits."

The Tulsa World reported the retirement under the headline, "Tulsa police legend says farewell," noting in a lengthy story the Wheeler case had defined Huff's career and his life. The newspaper also noted that a senior officer in the Tulsa department had warned Huff that taking the lead in the Wheeler inquiry could get him killed, but instead "his perseverance led to charges" against Rico and others.

"If you talk about putting a decorated FBI agent in jail who was a personal friend of J. Edgar Hoover, there's a price with that ... a lot of hassle, a lot of stress. Sure, it changed my life," Huff told the newspaper.

Ironically, Huff's retirement came 30 years to the day of the Wheeler murder.

Chapter 23: The Wolf Hearing

IN ASSISTANT U.S. Attorney Fred Wyshak's own words, longtime Boston mobster Stephen "The Rifleman" Flemmi's testimony in a 1999 case was "belated, inconsistent and inherently implausible." The veteran prosecutor called Flemmi a "lifelong organized criminal," adding that he had "repeatedly lied" during testimony at a pre-trial hearing. The prosecutor's harsh comments came on March 13, 2000, in the government's successful challenge of a 1999 pre-trial victory handed to Flemmi by U.S. District Judge Mark L. Wolf in Boston.

As criminal informants often do, Flemmi found himself on the wrong side of a serious criminal indictment. His pre-trial victory in Judge Wolf's courtroom had come after a lengthy, largely unsuccessful effort to convince the judge that FBI agents in Boston had effectively granted Flemmi immunity from prosecution when he first began his work as a bureau informant.

Since that work began with Flemmi's recruitment in 1965 by Agent H. Paul Rico, the now-retired FBI veteran testified early in the lengthy 1998 suppression hearing—but did so voluntarily, under oath and without a grant of immunity. He flatly denied that Flemmi had been given any assurances of "protection" of any kind. But Rico also testified that, in accepting the informant's tips, the FBI tacitly agreed not to use Flemmi's information against him, a standard arrangement without which no informant relationship could function.

Long a fixture in Boston's organized crime hierarchy, Flemmi's work as Rico's informant ended in 1969, when the mobster—a close associate of

Winter Hill Gang boss James J. "Whitey" Bulger in Boston and later a top echelon informant for the FBI—later became a fugitive from state charges in the car bombing of John Fitzgerald, a lawyer representing Patriarca mob informant Joseph "The Animal" Barboza. Fitzgerald survived the attack, but lost his left leg. Flemmi surrendered in Boston in 1974—four years after the bureau had assigned Rico to Florida.

A short time after his arrival, FBI Agent John Connolly, who had transferred into the bureau's Boston field office, initiated a new arrangement with Flemmi. At the 1998 Wolf hearing, the bulk of Flemmi's immunity claim focused on his work for Connolly in the late 1970's and '80's. By 1998, Connolly was eight years into retirement and under the gun, resulting in his invoking his Fifth Amendment right against self-incrimination and refused to testify.

Judge Wolf's ten-month pretrial proceeding was virtually unprecedented. What was supposed to be a hearing on four defense motions in a racketeering prosecution of Flemmi and several co-defendants became a one-man inquisition aimed at exposing alleged FBI misconduct. Judge Wolf's real target was the use of informants in the "relentless effort by the [FBI] to infiltrate, and eventually to smash, the New England branch of La Cosa Nostra (LCN)," as the Court of Appeals put it in its reversal of Judge Wolf.

The judge's mammoth 661-page opinion makes clear that he was painting on a much larger canvass than the United States v. Flemmi. It is best left to others to decide whether the lengthy hearing was an egomaniacal enterprise borne in part of Judge Wolf's personal pique over what he saw as the flouting of "his" informant guidelines—ghost-written for Attorney General Edward Levi in the 1970s when Wolf worked as a whiz-kid special assistant—or legitimate judicial fact-finding. Whatever the judge's motivation, the fallout was huge, leading to unprecedented congressional hearings over 2001–2002 that took the first line of Judge Wolf's opinion—"Everything Secret Degenerates: The FBI'S Use of Murderers as Informants"—as the title of its final three-part report.

The consequences for Rico, of course, were immeasurable. Then 73 and almost 20 years retired, he voluntarily testified before the committee without immunity, telling Committee Chairman Dan Burton, Indiana

Republican, that his lawyer had advised him to take the Fifth Amendment "until you people agree to give me immunity," but he said he had decided that "I have been in law enforcement for all those years and I'm interested in answering any and all questions." Rico told the committee he operated Flemmi as an informant for nearly four years beginning in late 1965 and that he promised Flemmi only, as he did all his informants, that the relationship would be kept confidential.

Flemmi, in pursuing dismissal of his pending criminal indictment, claimed that Rico guaranteed him "protection" along with confidentiality, a claim that Rico steadfastly denied. Rico was without peer in playing off the self-interested motivations of informants and cooperating witnesses to accomplish the FBI's mission. Flemmi saw personal advantage in providing intelligence that could be used to thwart La Cosa Nostra, a competitor in the New England underworld.

Rico was only too happy to take Flemmi's information and see that it was put to good use. That was the agent's job, and he was good at it. Attorney General Robert Kennedy and the FBI had given Rico, as his top priority, the destruction of La Cosa Nostra and the veteran agent very clearly recognized Flemmi for what he was—an opportunistic criminal. But Rico also knew that Flemmi was in a position to provide a "continuous flow of quality criminal intelligence information regarding the leaders of organized crime." This was the FBI's very definition of a Top Echelon Criminal Informant. It aptly described Flemmi, exactly the type of person Rico was charged with cultivating.

Thirty years later, Flemmi found himself in the jackpot and was grasping for anything he could find to escape a federal indictment that ultimately would lead to life in prison. So, in front of Judge Wolf, Flemmi claimed that the government—beginning with Rico—had promised him blanket immunity from criminal prosecution in exchange for information on La Cosa Nostra. Even Judge Wolf refused to buy this. Although largely irrelevant to his ultimate findings, Judge Wolf went out of his way to credit one of Flemmi's claims that personally hurt Rico. Based solely on Flemmi's desperate and dubious assertion, Judge Wolf branded Rico a criminal, guilty of "aiding and abetting the unlawful flight of a fugitive." Aside from that highly unusual "finding," Judge Wolf's published commentary about Rico had the effect of forever enveloping the veteran agent in the generalized ether of supposed widespread "Boston FBI corruption."

Flemmi testified that in September 1969, Rico tipped him and his co-defendant, Francis "Cadillac Frank" Salemme, that they would soon be indicted for the attempted murder of Fitzgerald, allowing both to flee. As the government pointed out, there was simply no evidence for this beyond Flemmi's claim. Rico denied it under oath and, in fact, as we later learned, Rico was largely responsible for ensuring that Flemmi was charged with the attempted murder at all. Beyond that, there was a Boston detective on the Winter Hill payroll with a direct interest in the case (and ultimately indicted but acquitted) who secretly met with Flemmi and Salemme in New York while they were on the lam. The detective was in all probability the source of the leak pinned on Rico.

In a real sense, it was difficult to justify crediting Flemmi's abjectly self-serving account against Rico's denial, particularly in view of the fact that Judge Wolf explicitly rejected other, similar Flemmi claims as perjury. Judge Wolf specifically found that Flemmi had lied about allegations the mobster made about illegal leaks of investigations by then-U.S. Attorney Jeremiah O'Sullivan in Boston, who also served as chief attorney for the Justice Department's New England Organized Crime Field Office, and FBI Agent James Ring, who supervised the bureau's organized crime squad in Boston, among others. In a breathtaking decision, Judge Wolf converted Flemmi the perjurer in the same proceeding into a credible accuser for the purpose of smearing Rico. The judge tipped the credibility scale in Flemmi's favor by citing a 1988 ruling from the Rhode Island Supreme Court.

According to Judge Wolf, the Rhode Island court "found ... that Rico had urged one of his informants to lie under oath, in part to mask another of Rico's informant's role in a murder." The judge might justify relying on this 1988 ruling for deciding Rico's credibility in terms of deciding Flemmi's claim of FBI "protection." For the Boston judge to take the next leap in proclaiming that Rico had committed a federal crime in 1969 by aiding and abetting the flight of a fugitive, is another matter altogether. Judge Wolf may not have foreseen the consequences of his reckless abuse of judicial power, but he likely did not much care what might lie ahead for this retired FBI agent.

But this gratuitous, unjustified "finding" of Rico's criminality had real consequences. It had little relevance to Judge Wolf's ultimate and over-turned rulings and it irreparably damaged something a career law enforcement professional such as Rico takes a lifetime to build—his reputation. What makes Judge Wolf's malfeasance all the more sinister is that he well knew that Rico, as a witness, had absolutely no recourse. A witness has no appeal rights and judges enjoy absolute civil immunity in these circumstances. That may have been in the mind of Appellate Judge Bruce M. Selya at the U.S. Court of Appeals for the First Circuit who wrote the majority opinion reversing Judge Wolf:

"Many of the particulars of this uneasy alliance are disputed, and Flemmi often attributes promises and assurances to FBI agents who deny having made them. For present purposes, we accept the district court's resolution of these conflicts-but we do so arguendo without critical examination of the supportability of the court's findings."

In an unusual notation, Judge Selya noted that the appellate court intended to "recount the background facts, focusing on the circumstances relevant to this appeal," and referred those who "hunger for greater insight into the seamier side of law enforcement to the district court's more exegetic treatment." The judge also noted that the information Flemmi and Bulger provided "enabled the FBI to make significant progress in its investigation and prosecution of major LCN figures."

"Many of the particulars of this uneasy alliance are disputed, and Flemmi often attributes promises and assurances to FBI agents who deny having made them. For present purposes, we accept the district court's resolution of these conflicts—but we do so arguendo, without critical examination of the supportability of the court's findings. Flemmi claims that his initial FBI handler, Agent Paul Rico, promised him protection against prosecution. When a state grand jury indicted Flemmi in 1969 for a car bombing and a murder, Rico supposedly suggested that he flee," the judge wrote.

In overturning Wolf's decision, the appeals court prompted Flemmi's deal with Wyshak, thereby transforming Flemmi into Wyshak's leading—now credible—government witness. As part of Flemmi's eventual plea agreement, that among other benefits saved him from death sentences in

Oklahoma and Florida, Wyshak sponsored Flemmi as Rico's chief accuser in the Tulsa murder of businessman Roger Wheeler. But while Flemmi's boarding of the G-train as a newly minted "Good Guy" was a significant step in the Rico story, Judge Wolf's labeling Rico an unindicted criminal and part of a wide web of corruption was probably more consequential. It was the real genesis of the perfect storm that ultimately consumed and killed the aging lawman.

For anyone trying to find the truth about Rico and what kind of man he was, the Rhode Island claims of perjury and cover-up could not be ignored. Did Rico tell one of his informants to lie under oath in a murder case? Did the former FBI agent cover up the involvement of yet another informant in the crime? When in 1969 Flemmi was charged with the attempted murder of Fitzgerald, did Rico help Flemmi evade capture? If this was all true, it would be so much easier to believe that Rico could be guilty of other crimes—including conspiracy to murder Wheeler.

So, what was the truth about Rhode Island?

Chapter 24: Perjury in Rhode Island

THE SIGNIFICANCE OF FBI Agent H. Paul Rico's role in crippling the leadership of La Cosa Nostra and the Raymond L.S. Patriarca crime syndicate in New England is difficult to exaggerate. While accomplishments such as Rico's may seem somewhat routine to the uninitiated, most career law enforcement professionals know what it means to put together a solid murder case on someone like Patriarca and his top lieutenants. Rico did it—twice, at a time Patriarca's control had extended throughout New England for over three decades and he was considered one of the most powerful crime bosses in the United States.

Ultimately, decades after Rico successfully put the New England mob leadership behind bars, understanding Patriarca's complete power over the notoriously corrupt Rhode Island government could be the key to explaining Rico's untimely 2004 death in a Tulsa jail. To reach that conclusion, however, some facts that may have been entombed with Patriarca's 1984 death from a massive heart attack at the age of 76, and the death five years later of Joseph Bevilacqua, chief justice of the Rhode Island State Supreme Court, might have to be unearthed. What can be known about this strange chapter in Rico's amazing career is told here.

Critically important in the search for truth about Patriarca's obvious domination of Rhode Island's government officials can be found in a brief exchange between Rep. Christopher Shays, Connecticut Republican, and Rico during the veteran agent's appearance before the House Government Reform Committee in May 2001. Cutting through some minor, mutual confusion about decades-past events and witnesses, the gist of it was summarized in a startling question posed by the congressman: "In 1988, the Supreme Court of Rhode Island found that FBI Special Agent H. Paul Rico, you, suborned the perjury of John Kelley, the state's principal witness in the 1970 murder trial of Maurice 'Pro' Lerner. Apparently at your instigation, Mr. Rico, Kelley altered two facts directly dealing with the murder and the extent of the promises that you made in exchange for Kelley's testimony. When asked why he perjured himself, Kelley said my life was in the FBI's hands, and this is in brackets, Special Agent Rico, end of brackets, said I had no alternative. Mr. Rico, why did you suborn the perjury of the state's main witness John Kelley in the gangland killing of Anthony Melei?"

Under oath before the committee, Rico flatly denied suborning Kelley's perjury, responding to the congressman with a simple declarative statement: "I did not suborn perjury." Asked for an explanation, Rico suggested that Kelley greatly feared Lerner, described as "a very competent killer," and suspected that Kelley's change of heart 13 years after the original murder trial in Rhode Island was a successful attempt to help Lerner years after Kelley was cleared of prosecution for his own criminal activity.

"I have always been able to say to everybody that was a witness or a potential witness the same thing, that we will bring whatever cooperation you bring to the attention of the proper authorities," Rico told the committee. "There's nothing else that I have ever said concerning eliciting testimony."

In concluding his questioning, Shays displayed an amazing burst of unsubstantiated allegations, claiming that the hearing had been "a fascinating day" for him.

"I think the thing I'm most surprised about is that it's clear to me that the FBI became as corrupt as the people they went after and it's clear to me that you have the same insensitivity that I would imagine in someone who is a hard and fast criminal," Shays said. "No remorse whatsoever. Cold as can be … No tears. No regret … You have gotten just like the people you went after. What a legacy."

Supreme Court opinions referring to FBI agents by name are extremely rare; but such a decision accusing an individual agent of subornation of perjury is undoubtedly a very big deal. It could not be overlooked, and indeed it had not been. Along with the congressional inquisitors, one court after another has understandably accepted the strongly worded 1988 Rhode Island decision as definitively tipping the credibility scale against Rico.

To find against Rico in various proceedings, use of this decision was a judicial necessity. Courts were faced with a confident, unapologetic former FBI agent testifying under oath without seeking immunity or hiding behind the Fifth Amendment. In writing opinions, the Rhode Island decision was very useful in justifying findings in favor of claims by admitted perjurers, murderers and thieves and, in at least one Boston federal court, hearsay from one such deceased outlaw offered from the mouth of disgraced, disbarred attorney F. Lee Bailey.

As we have seen, U.S. District Judge Mark L. Wolf in Boston, in his important but reversed 1999 decision highly critical of FBI informant procedures, gave conclusive weight to the Rhode Island opinion. Rico voluntarily testified in Judge Wolf's hearing, denying a claim by mobster Stephen "The Rifleman" Flemmi that Rico had tipped him off, along with an associate, Francis P. "Cadillac Frank" Salemme, concerning their 1969 state indictments, allowing them to flee. In an extraordinary part of Judge Wolf's ruling that found that Flemmi had made false sworn accusations against other law enforcement officials directly to the judge to bolster his claims, Judge Wolf nevertheless credited Flemmi's testimony against Rico. Why? Judge Wolf gave a detailed citation of the 1988 Rhode Island decision.

Similarly, in 2006, U.S. District Judge Nancy Gertner, also in Boston, gave substantial weight to the language of Judge Wolf's 1999 decision crediting the "finding" of the Rhode Island high court. Their ruling was, in fact, a foundation of her decision to credit the second-hand recantation of the deceased Joseph "The Animal" Barboza offered by Bailey in the 2006 civil case. Looking back, it is safe to say that some 10 years after it was handed down, the proclamation of the Rhode Island Supreme Court greatly accelerated the whorl of the perfect storm that ultimately engulfed Rico.

So what exactly happened in Rhode Island and how did its Supreme Court come to write in 1988 that Rico had suborned Kelley's perjury?

First, it is important to understand the lengths to which the Rhode Island court went to criticize Rico personally and the FBI in general. This is striking in its own right. In the 1988 eight-page opinion, Rico personally is singled out no less than 14 times in phrases such as "[Kelley] testified that his perjury was elicited by Paul Rico, a special agent of the Federal Bureau of Investigation" and "[h]aving determined that a serious due-process violation was brought about by Special Agent Rico ..."

But aside from the repeated, directly personal criticism of Rico, there is one other very remarkable aspect of this decision: There is a complete lack of any evidence for any wrongdoing by Rico noted in the opinion, beyond the claims made by Kelley in 1983. It would be difficult, if not impossible, to find an example of something like this in a decision of a state's highest court anywhere in the United States. Certainly what sets this June 1988 Rhode Island opinion apart is not its reference to questionable testimony, but its strident repetition of an accusation of criminal misconduct by a law enforcement professional based solely on a single witness thoroughly discredited by the court's own words.

It is not only that the sole source of the allegations against Rico was an admitted perjurer, murderer and thief, but also the court's own prior decisions strongly suggested that the same source, Kelley, also was suffering from Alzheimer's. In two separate rulings, in 1985 and 1987, the court overturned a murder conviction of mob boss Luigi "Baby Shacks" Manocchio because defense counsel had been given insufficient opportunity to probe Kelley's mental infirmity. Commenting in its 1987 decision in Rhode Island vs. Manocchio, the court wrote that "[a] very strong suggestion could have been made ... that Kelley had experienced on occasion difficulty of distinguishing between fact and fiction."

The court's wording of its 1985 decision also is illuminating: At the time of Manocchio's trial, Kelley was 68 years old, testifying about events that occurred fifteen years earlier. Defense counsel was understandably concerned about his present ability to remember and relate accurately the circumstances surrounding Manocchio's alleged involvement in the two murders. Counsel's apprehension grew when Kelley was asked by Manocchio's defense counsel if he was suffering from any disease that affected his mind and memory. Kelley responded by saying, "Yes. Yes," and then started to cry. Asked to tell the court disease he had, Kelley said,

"I have—I'm, I'm being treated for many different things, and premature Alzheimer's, I think it is."

Manocchio's defense team continued, getting Kelley to admit on the stand that his ailments affected his memory, his thought process and his ability to recall certain events. "When I tell you I can't remember a thing, it's an honest answer," Kelley told the court.

Later in the 1985 opinion, the court quoted from defense counsel's cross-examination of Kelley at trial:

> Question: Yesterday you told us you were taken to the House of Corrections in New Bedford. Do you remember saying that yesterday?
>
> Kelley: I don't recollect that.
>
> Question: You don't recollect saying New Bedford yesterday?
>
> Kelley: I don't recollect now.
>
> Question: Do you have a problem with your memory?
>
> Kelley: Yes, I do have problem with my memory.

Later in the opinion, the court noted that Kelley had acknowledged having difficulty remembering what had been asked of him two questions earlier, including where he was when he met with Rico. Defense counsel had asked, "So that if I were to ask you to repeat your answer as to where you went with Mr. Rico, you would have forgotten your answer?" Kelley responded by saying, "That's a possibility."

In ruling as it did, the court went far beyond the factual findings by the trial court, declining to remand the case for further fact-finding, perhaps fearing the outcome of such a proceeding. That explanation is certainly plausible, even likely, in light of the facts on the record.

Kelley died several years after testifying for Manocchio in the Lerner case, suffering from Alzheimers. It is disturbing to think that this was the witness whose uncorroborated accusations against Rico the court was willing to credit. What was even more disturbing was to find that there was substantial evidence on the record contradicting Kelley. All of this was available long before Rico had the opportunity to squarely deny Kelley's accusations, without immunity and under oath before Congress in 2001.

The first order of business was to track down the facts underlying the 1988 Rhode Island decision since the omission of any information corroborating Kelley's claims about Rico's criminal conduct could have been no more than sloppy drafting. Any law student can tell you that more than a few Supreme Court opinions lack clarity or even factual accuracy. The lawyers who handled both sides of the Lerner case shed a great deal of light on what actually happened.

The former Rhode Island prosecutor who tried the Manocchio case and first heard Kelley's proffered "change of heart" in 1983, the former assistant attorney general who lost Manocchio's and Lerner's appeals in the Supreme Court, and the public defender who won Lerner's freedom all agreed on one point—Kelley was a "reluctant witness" who, for all they knew, may have testified truthfully in the original 1970 trial. The primary issue that confronted them all in 1983 was what to do with the fact that Kelley was then saying that he had lied in the 1970 trial.

By far the most helpful was Barbara Hurst, who, as a young public defender, won Lerner's freedom, an achievement she considers one of the capstones of her career. She now serves as the second-in-command deputy public defender in Rhode Island. Hurst immediately retrieved and forwarded a wealth of material, including the pleadings and trial transcripts, that were key in answering the important questions about Rico. She recalled, and the pleadings confirmed, that the state attorney general's office did almost no fact-finding concerning Kelley's claims about Rico. The state attorney general "hung his hat" primarily on the concept that any federal misconduct could not be pinned on the original state prosecutors. Their strategy was to challenge Kelley's claims on the existing record and alternatively shift any residual blame to the FBI, arguing that state prosecution should be held harmless.

One significant discovery early was that the trial court that first heard Lerner's claim for post-trial relief—and denied it—also declined to find that Rico had committed or suborned perjury. The State Supreme Court later "found" that fact all on its own. What soon also became apparent was that Kelley's accusations of misconduct by Rico were almost entirely without foundation. To understand how this can be proven, it is necessary to deconstruct the substance of Kelley's primary claims in his 1983 "recantation" individually, both of which have been repeatedly uttered by the courts and Congress.

The first oft-repeated tale told by Kelley and accepted by the Rhode Island Court and others concerns a sawed-off shotgun used in the original murders. As Judge Gertner summarized this story July, 2007:

"Rico's Methods Are Exposed—By 1988, the FBI should have had even greater concerns about its LCN initiative and the methods employed. That year, the Supreme Court of Rhode Island ... found, among other things, that Rico urged one of his informants to lie under oath, in part to mask another informant's role in the murder ... The court found that in the trial of Patriarca Family member Luigi Manocchio, Rico's informant John Kelley admitted that in a related case (a case against Maurice Lerner) he had testified falsely—at Rico's direction ... Kelley testified that he had personally 'cut down' the shotgun used in the murders. However, during the Manocchio trial, Kelley stated his armorer had actually 'cut down' the shotgun. Kelley said Rico had directed him not to mention the armorer's role in the murders because the armorer was a valuable FBI informant that Rico wanted to keep on the streets."

Judge Gertner went on to say that the Rhode Island Supreme Court had "credited Kelley's testimony," and found that "Rico had caused Kelley to lie about the promises that Rico had made to obtain his cooperation." She wrote that the Supreme Court also had noted that Kelley's explanation of why he had lied under oath was because "Agent Rico told me ... that I should just do as he said, and everything would come out all right."

From the perspective of any FBI agent reading this, the most obvious flaw in Kelley's claim on its face is contained in the portion that alleges Rico's reason for this perjury—namely that Rico told Kelley the armorer was Rico's informant. Assuming this "armorer" existed at all—Kelley conveniently identified the man as recently deceased when he told this story in 1983—and assuming the "armorer" was an FBI informant, the last person on earth to whom Rico would have imparted such information was Kelley.

FBI agents in general are a discrete lot and among agents, Rico was one of the most discrete. A longtime Rico friend and Harvard-educated lawyer, Alan Trustman, said, "Rico wouldn't tell you if your hat was on fire." Agents learn early that they only share informants' identities on a strict need-to-know basis within the FBI and almost never outside the bureau—not even with federal prosecutors. In testimony before the same Congressional Committee that heard Rico, former Boston strike force chief and U.S. attorney Jeremiah O' Sullivan testified it "would have precipitated World War III if I tried to get inside the FBI to deal with informants. That was the holy of holies, inner sanctum ..."

Judge Wolf, who heard Rico's unimmunized testimony, cited the same portion of the 1988 Rhode Island opinion used by Judge Gertner. Judge Wolf used the case to justify crediting the testimony of Flemmi over Rico, after finding that Flemmi had repeatedly lied in Wolf's courtroom. But Judge Wolf missed at least one glaring inconsistency in his own lengthy decision; He credited Flemmi's allegation against Rico based solely on the Rhode Island court's statements in 1988, quoting Kelley's excuse that Rico forced Kelley to lie about cutting down the shotgun to keep another LCN informant "on the street." But in the summary at the very beginning of his ruling, the judge comments that "Rico and the many other past and present members of the FBI who testified regarded [promises of confidentiality to informants] as 'sacred.' ... Strictly adhering to this principle ... the FBI has regularly refused to identify its sources even to prosecutors and other Department of Justice officials ..."

Further confirmation of this came from congressional testimony given by U.S. District Judge Edward F. "Ted" Harrington in Boston, who testified that during his entire career, he never knew the identity of any FBI informant. The judge explained that absolute confidentiality was "... fundamental ... especially in the deadly world of organized crime ... and any breech thereof would have I think dire consequences."

If Rico had the inclination to and capability of shaping Kelley's 1970 testimony to the degree later claimed, he could have given Kelley any reason—or no reason—to keep someone out of the case. Rico knew that the life expectancy of a mob informant whose identity had been disclosed to the likes of Kelley could be measured in weeks or months at most. It remains unclear why so many supposedly sophisticated officials bought this claim without at least some proof.

Vincent "Vin" Vespia Jr., now chief of police of Kingston, R.I., was a state trooper for 25 years and, as a young detective, was assigned to assist with security at the 1970 Patriarca trial. He spent a substantial amount of time with both Rico and Kelley. Vespia described Rico as a "classy" guy who epitomized what an FBI agent should be. Kelley impressed Vespia as the "most impressive criminal" he has encountered in 50 years in law enforcement, and someone who could have easily become legitimately wealthy if he had chosen a different path.

Describing Kelley as the "consummate criminal planner," Vespia said Kelley once told him of a planned Brinks robbery that was never executed, but was carefully planned. Criminal associates grabbed a Brinks guard, brought him to an apartment where they put him in a chair facing a wall. Kelley questioned the guard from behind to preclude his identification for several hours about company procedures before releasing him. Kelley described in great detail for Vespia how he modified the shotgun used in the Marfeo/Melei murders, cutting the gun down in his basement so it could be slung concealed under a coat, specifically identifying that gun as the one used in the murders. Vespia has no doubt that Kelley personally modified this shotgun.

With regard to Kelley's bare claim 13 years after the trial that he lied about personally modifying the shotgun and that Rico told him to lie to protect Rico's informant, there is nothing in the record to show that any effort was made to identify the dead man named by Kelley as his "armorer" or to determine whether that person—if he existed—was an informant for any law enforcement agency. The record is clear that at the time, the most anyone had was an allegation by Kelley, whom the Rhode Island courts concluded was suffering from Alzheimer's and who also was unhappy about his relocation. He also, undoubtedly, was fearful of Mannocchio, whom he rightly suspected was in line to replace Patriarca as head of the New England Mob. Aside from that, there was no corroboration for Kelley's later claim about Rico telling him to lie.

Kelley's second primary claim, and actually the only supposed perjury found by the Rhode Island Court to be material to Lerner's case, was the testimony concerning benefits he got in the form of witness protection. Both Boston judge's ruling on cases dealing with Rico's conduct relied on the 1988 Rhode Island finding summarized in both decisions using identical language: "The [Rhode Island Supreme Court] found that Rico caused

Kelley to lie about the promises that Rico had made to obtain his cooperation ... In addition, it stated that, 'Kelley's [perjurious] testimony [at the Lerner trial] was then corroborated in all material aspects by Special Agent Rico.'"

First, the actual wording of the Rhode Island Court on this particular issue is important: "At Lerner's trial, Kelley was asked several questions about the benefits he was receiving in exchange for his testimony. He stated that Special Agent Rico promised him only immunity and 'protection for his family.' He stated he was not promised income from the federal government, a new identity or relocation. Kelley's testimony was then corroborated in all material aspects by Special Agent Rico. However, at the Manocchio trial, Kelley admitted that before the Lerner trial, Special Agent Rico had in fact promised him income from the federal government for the remainder of his natural life, a new identity, and relocation."

Now, one problem for the court is that the sworn testimony in both Lerner's 1970 trial and Manocchio's 1983 trial directly contradict these "findings." According to the transcript of the Lerner trial, Rico testified he told Kelley the Justice Department had informed him that the U.S. Marshals Service would protect him and that the FBI did not have the authority to offer any protection or security. The transcript also shows that Kelley testified he did not have any source of income and was not being paid any money by the government. He also said that while he was testifying, the government was moving him through a number of hotels and that he was being fed.

In a separate exchange, the transcript shows that Lerner learned that Kelley's every need was being met by the government and that this would continue as long as necessary. The records show that approximately two months after the trial, in May 1970, the Marshals Service formally enrolled Kelley in a witness security program, although it was not until October 1970 that Congress passed legislation authorizing what is now known formally as the Witness Security Program (WITSEC).

Kelley's 1983 recollection of his security arrangements in testimony at Manocchio's murder trial clearly demonstrates just how weak the foundation for a claim of 1970 "perjury" concerning protective benefits was:

Question: Were you always [as of 1970] under the control of some particular police agency?

Kelley: I was in protective custody.

Question: Now, at some point, did you come under the control of the United States Marshals Service?

Kelley: Yes.

Question: And at some point in time, without telling us where, did you become settled in some other part of the country?

Kelley: Yes.

Question: When did you first become aware that that would happen, that you would be settled somewhere under a new identity?

Kelley: That had been said through these proceedings. I have no idea just when. I can't place a time. That was part of the talk and considerations.

Question: Now, is there something—or was there something— that you were made aware of with respect to your future that you did not make known to the Courts and jury in 1970 and '72?

Kelley: Yes.

Question: And would you tell us what that was, sir?

Kelley: I can't remember all of the things, but the subsistence and agreements for protection for the rest of my life, and different things like that. I'm not sure, but the general thrust was in that way, but I'm not sure of the exact content of the conversations.

Question: And who made you aware of this?

Kelley: Paul Rico of the FBI.

Question: And what did you at that time understand would happen?

Kelley: At the time, I understood from what he said to me was because of my age, my wife's age, our ill health on both of us, that I would not be—ever be able to go on the street again, and that government would subsidize me.

Question: Now, you mentioned your wife's age. What's her age in comparison to your own, sir?

Kelley: She's older than I am.

Question: Now, did you, in fact, receive something in the form of a subsistence allowance?

Kelley: Yes.

Question: And can you tell us, sir, about how much that was?

Kelley: Yes, I can.

Question: What was that?

Kelley: Approximately $800 and a few dollars. Might have been $810, or $812 a month to pay all my rent, and all my bills out of that; food. Everything had to be paid out of the $800 a month.

Question: And was that for both yourself and your wife?

Kelley: Yes.

Question: And for how long a period, sir, did this continue?

Kelley: I'm not sure of the exact time, but up until, I think in the vicinity of 1980. I think it continued until that time.

Question: Now, is there some particular reason, sir, why you did not make known back in 1970 and '72 your understanding with respect to what you were told by Agent Rico?

Kelley: Yes.

Question: And what was that?

Kelley: Agent Rico told me I shouldn't tell all of these things because it looked like I was being paid; that I should just do as he said, and everything would come out all right.

It is little wonder that the trial judge, who first considered this record on Lerner's 1983 post-trial challenge, refused to find that Rico committed or suborned perjury. The records show that the judge reasonably chose to accept the witness's own claim that he committed perjury, but, as this judge also well understood, that is a far different matter from crediting the admitted perjurer's thirteen-year-old claim of criminal conduct by someone else.

Beyond that, there is no evidence on the record that Rico misstated anything of any significance. In 1970, he testified that "the United States Government had agreed to give [Kelley] personal security." Rico gave no time limits or particulars and likely did not even know the particulars, as he clarified that this arrangement was specifically with the Marshals Service and Rico's discussions were with a senior prosecutor. In fact, the exact details of Kelley's living arrangements, according to the U.S. Marshals, were not finalized until at least two months after the March 1970 Lerner trial. The formal WITSEC Program, administered by the Marshals, was not even authorized by law until October 1970. As many protected witnesses do, Kelley ultimately became unhappy with the transition from a life of crime involving murder and multimillion dollar robberies to the equivalent of the life of a clerk living on $800 a month. He left the program in 1979 or 1980. Records of the Marshals Service show that Fiscal Year 1980 (beginning October 1, 1979) was the last year funds were expended in support of Kelley. A total of $2,984 in subsistence expense and $1,036 for housing was spent in FY 80. Records show that for the prior ten years, beginning in October 1970, an average of about $10,000 per year was spent on Kelley by the government. The highest dollar amount in a single year was in FY 1976 when $11,250 was spent for subsistence and $3,496 for housing.

The record flatly contradicts Kelley's allegations and supports Rico's denial, under oath and without immunity. But Rico's denial was too late to undo the damage.

The question remains as to why Kelley would become, in 1983, just another reluctant witness? Why would the Rhode Island Supreme Court go to what appear to be extraordinary lengths to set Manocchio free from two consecutive life sentences plus ten years. He was until recently the reputed boss of the New England mob, replaced, interestingly enough, by Peter Limone, flying high on his multimillion dollar award by Judge Gertner. Why would the court do the same for Lerner, Patriarca's primary hit man, to whom Patriarca is said to have selected for a CIA contract on Fidel Castro? Why would they go to such effort to personally smear Rico?

Placing these events in the context of Rhode Island politics and corruption over several decades shows that the breadth and depth of Patriarca's control and influence over the levers of government in Rhode

Island may have been unparalleled. In the early 60s, Patriarca was comfortable enough to pick up the telephone and call Gov. John Notte to change his son's university class schedule. When Attorney General Robert Kennedy declared war on organized crime, Patriarca had already been "king of the rackets in New England" for over a decade, as State Police Colonel Walter Stone told a 1963 Senate subcommittee. Four years later, largely due to the efforts of a young FBI agent named Rico, Patriarca was wearing handcuffs for the first time in thirty years—and charged with murder.

Patriarca's sphere of influence necessarily included the courts. As a result, in part, the five-member Rhode Island Supreme Court saw two chief justices resign under threat of impeachment in years between 1986 and 1993. Certainly some parts of that story will never be publicly known. But what is known is rich with potential to explain the court's treatment of Manocchio, Lerner and Rico.

At the core is Patriarca's good friend, the late Joseph Bevilacqua, who served as chief justice of the Rhode Island State Supreme Court. While Patriarca had many "good friends" in state government, Bevilacqua was among the most well-placed. First elected to the House of Delegates in 1954, he rose to become Speaker of the House in 1969. From that lofty post, he felt secure enough to send a letter on Patriarca's behalf to parole officials in 1973, vouching for the mob boss's "integrity" and "good moral character." Six months after election by the State's General Assembly as chief justice in 1976, he presided over the wedding of Patriarca's chauffeur. A judicial ethics inquiry over that went exactly nowhere. Bevilacqua lasted as Chief Justice until 1986, when he resigned under threat of impeachment.

While the motivation behind Manocchio's surprising surrender in Rhode Island in 1979 is unknown, many believe the 1976 ascendancy of a Patriarca crony to a position of dominance over the Rhode Island court system as chief justice could have played a role. Manocchio's release on bond after 10 years in the wind on a case such as this was unusual, curiously timed with Kelley's decision to leave the Marshal Service's protection. Records show that Manocchio did not go to trial until 1983. Kelley was testifying at the time against Patriarca's future replacement as head of the New England Mafia Family. Kelley was either on his own without protection or with an unknown arrangement with the New England Mob. Either way, Kelley suddenly changed his story and went out of his way during cross-examination for Manocchio to claim complete memory lapses.

Apparently overlooking or discounting Kelley's claims of perjury and his memory problems, the jury convicted Manocchio on all charges. The trial judge upheld the convictions and sentenced Manocchio to two consecutive life terms plus ten years. Manocchio appealed. The 1985 Supreme Court ruling, with excerpts of cross-examination of Kelley concerning his "mental disease," has as the last line the following statement: "The chief justice participated in the oral argument and in the decision of the court but he did not participate in the publication of the formal opinion."

This is a reference to the fact that Chief Justice Bevilacqua was then under investigation and threat of impeachment for his ties to Patriarca and his associates. In 1984, Patriarca died of a heart attack and about the same time, the Providence Journal published an expose' of Bevilacqua's underworld ties. By the time the 1985 ruling was published, Bevilacqua was on a "leave of absence" while a commission headed by former U.S. Justice Arthur Goldberg investigated.

The 1985 Manocchio decision temporarily overturned his murder conviction and life sentences. The attorney general of Rhode Island, however, appealed to the U.S. Supreme Court, which took the case and remanded it to Rhode Island for reconsideration of the supposed defects in Manocchio's trial as "harmless error," probably a suggestion that the High Court thought the conviction should stand. This resulted in Rhode Island's review of the 1985 decision and a 1987 ruling by the Rhode Island Supreme Court that the error was not "harmless" and the murder conviction was again reversed.

At this point, prosecutors negotiated a plea to conspiracy that had the net result of releasing Manocchio almost immediately. "Beating" this murder case greatly enhanced Manocchio's stature in his world and probably contributed to his ascension to boss of the Patriarca family in 1996, a position he held until he was reportedly replaced in 2009 by Peter Limone, fresh from winning the $100 million jackpot awarded by Judge Nancy Gertner. He recently was described as "a legend" in the underworld who lives quietly as a 79-year old Federal Hill bachelor, reaping the financial rewards of being boss but rarely getting involved in details.

Then there is the strange presence throughout the chronology of the larger-than-life F. Lee Bailey, whose true role in the attempts to undo the work of law enforcement and the courts in fighting the mob may never be fully uncovered. Records show that Bailey somehow ended up in the middle of both the Kelley "recantation" and re-recantation of Barboza, who was key to Patriarca's conviction in the first, federal prosecution in connection with the other Marfeo brother. Bailey showed up again with Kelley and later, only months before his disbarment in Florida and Massachusetts for the theft of millions of dollars and offering false sworn testimony, Bailey was peddling tales of misdeeds by the FBI and Rico to eager members of a congressional committee.

In May 2001, Bailey testified that he sought out Barboza after Patriarca and others had been sent to prison. He said a contractor named "Frank Davis" had hired him to find Barboza, but Barboza later told Judge Edward F. Harrington, then a prosecutor, a different story. Harrington testified that Bailey came to Barboza on Patriarca's behalf, offering a cash bribe for a change in testimony. In the hearing, Bailey alleged that Rico and his FBI partner, Dennis Condon, had encouraged Barboza to give false testimony against Patriarca and other mob members.

During the congressional hearings and following an introduction by Rep. William Delahunt, Massachusetts Democrat, who described the soon-to-be-disbarred Bailey as having "unimpeachable" integrity, Bailey's testimony began:

> Mr. Bailey: And before more FBI bashing, let me say I am a big fan of the FBI. Judge Webster and Judge Sessions are friends. But the FBI is like the little girl with the curl; when they're bad they are horrid. In this case [Barboza' testimony] I believe the testimony was furnished. When the FBI decided who they wanted to target, it just happened to be the right-hand man of Raymond Patriarca … And one particular agent [Rico] not only did it in this case but did it in another …
>
> Mr. Delahunt: You know, that's a very serious statement.
>
> Mr. Bailey: It is.

Mr. Burton: Could the gentleman yield real quickly? You said they did it in another case?

Mr. Bailey: Yes.

Mr. Burton: Would you care to be a little bit more specific? I'll grant the gentleman the time.

Mr. Bailey: Certainly ... [defense attorney Joe Balliro] and I were engaged in defending what Congressman Delahunt will remember as the Great Plymouth Mail Robbery, then the largest in the history of the country. All these men were acquitted. The purported leader, John J. Kelley, whom I defended, was caught a year later in a Brinks truck robbery, nailed cold. And he was told—and I talked with Mr. Kelley about this extensively. He was told, you are such a big fish, that to get a deal you're going to have to give us somebody bigger. And there are only two people we can think of, F. Lee Bailey and Raymond Patriarca. He chose Mr. Patriarca, was helped to make up a story about Mr. Patriarca orchestrating a homicide, testified falsely in federal court, and obtained a conviction. The manager of that witness as well was Paul Rico, who came to my office attempting to intimidate me after Kelley turned, and I threw him out.

Mr. Delahunt: Well, again, [the alleged FBI coaching of Joe Barboza] is suggestive of subornation of perjury, Mr. Bailey.

Mr. Bailey: It is, the penalty of which is life.

Mr. Delahunt: And that particular statute does not have any statute of limitations, does it, Mr. Bailey?

Mr. Bailey: It does not ...

A few minutes later, Shays asked Bailey to further characterize Rico, and he had a quick response: "My only personal contact with Paul Rico was when he came to my office shortly after John Kelley had become a government witness ... Prior to testifying in the federal case, which he appeared as a witness who had organized an escape route for a murder requested by or ordered by Raymond Patriarca, and he later told me that story was one that he was told he would have to tell. Since he was unwilling to implicate me in my felonies, Patriarca was the only acceptable trade for his freedom, which he got. But I saw him many times after the trial was over. The only other knowledge I have of Mr. Rico's activity was one of which I am highly suspicious, and that was in his attempt to convict your colleague, Alcee Hastings. [Rico] was up to his ears in that."

Among the comments made by Bailey was the statement that he had talked to Kelley "many times after the trial was over." It is difficult to imagine any legitimate reason for such conversations. Who initiated the contacts? When and how many meetings? What was the proximity in time to Kelley's departure from the Witness Security Program, Manocchio's return from Europe and Kelley's changed testimony offered in 1983? The reference to the Hastings case also is of interest. The Rhode Island Supreme Court's June 1988 opinion, gratuitously critical of Rico, was issued just prior to the Senate trial of then-judge Hastings, where Rico was an important witness.

The overwhelming weight of the evidence is that Kelley testified truthfully in the 1970 trial of those involved in the 1968 mob Marfeo/Melei murders ordered by Patriarca. It also is clear that in 1983, no longer under the protection of the U.S. government, Kelley was either a very "reluctant" witness or doing his best to help the future leader of the New England mob. Other than Kelley's naked assertion, there is no credible evidence that Rico suborned perjury by Kelley or anyone else.

Rico was a remarkable, skilled and dedicated special agent, who enthusiastically accepted the mission given to him by the FBI. The record shows that he took on the most powerful combined power of the New England mob and the governments and lawyers it corrupted. He did enormous damage to the La Cosa Nostra and its allies and, in the end, he paid a terrible price.

Chapter 25: Congressional Hearing

THE HOUSE COMMITTEE on Government Reform set its sights on the FBI beginning in 2001, targeting what its then-chairman described as "injustices" by agents in the bureau's Boston field office. During a series of high-profile hearings, both Democratic and Republican committee members prattled endlessly about the suspected misdeeds of agents—looking, of course, to surf a wave of popular sentiment and perpetuate the media line that the "evil" FBI had somehow gone far out of its way to frame a minor league hood more than 30 years earlier.

In an attempt to cast light on what Committee Chairman Dan Burton, Indiana Republican, said was a "terrible wrong that was done to one man and his family," the committee focused on the 1965 murder of Boston mobster Edward "Teddy" Deegan, a low-level burglar for the violent Winter Hill Gang in Boston. He was shot to death in an alley in Chelsea, Mass., on March 12, 1965, after showing up for what he thought was going to be the gang-sanctioned burglary of a finance company.

The committee had become interested in the Deegan murder case because of the involvement of Joseph "The Animal" Barboza, an FBI informant who testified for the government and helped win death sentences against four men in the Deegan killing, which later were converted to life. At the center of the committee's concern was Joseph Salvati, convicted as an accessory to Deegan's murder and on two counts of conspiracy. He was released after 33 years in prison when a federal judge ruled the FBI had withheld evidence in the case.

"The reason Joe Salvati went to prison was because an FBI informant lied about him, which is unthinkable. But the reason he stayed in jail was because the FBI agents knew their informant lied and they covered it up, and that's much worse," said Burton, a former real estate salesman best known for using his own pistol to blast a pumpkin to bits in his backyard in 1998 in an unsuccessful effort to debunk forensic evidence in the suicide of Clinton White House Deputy Counsel Vincent W. Foster.

"The informant who put Joe Salvati in prison was Joseph 'The Animal' Barboza ... a prized FBI informant. He was considered so valuable that they created the Witness Protection Program to protect him," the congressman said, playing to a full house on Capital Hill. "Joseph Barboza was a criminal. You would expect him to lie, but the FBI is another story. They are supposed to stand for the truth."

Burton, with much fanfare, accused the FBI in general and then-FBI Director J. Edgar Hoover in particular of hiding documents and suppressing evidence that would have proven Salvati and others innocent of allowing Barboza to testify even though the bureau knew he was lying, of preventing Barboza from recanting his testimony when he tried to in 1970, and of ordering the longtime mob assassin to fire his infamous attorney, F. Lee Bailey, or "spend the rest of his life in jail."

"So the FBI once again was trying to protect their tails and cover this thing up. I think that is just criminal. Not only did the FBI conceal the evidence that they had on Joe Salvati that Joe Salvati was innocent, they went out and actively suppressed other evidence. To say what they did was unseemly was an understatement. It was rotten to the core," the chairman said.

And, according to Burton, the ringleader of all this corruption, deception and deceit was now retired FBI Agent H. Paul Rico, who choreographed Barboza's testimony and railroaded the four men into an unjustified murder conviction.

While Burton set the tone for the May 3, 2001, hearing, it got much better.

Rep. Christopher Shays, Connecticut Republican, demanded that the FBI apologize to Salvati, calling him a "citizen whose liberty was stolen from him for 30 years by his own government.

"So profound an injustice is almost unimaginable. But it takes very little imagination to reconstruct the sordid saga of official malfeasance, obstruction, brutality and corruption that brings us here this morning," Shays said. "In this tragic tale, ends justified means, cascading down a legal and ethical spiral until both the ends and means became utterly unjust. Protecting criminals in the name of catching criminals, agents of the Federal Bureau of Investigation became criminals, willing accomplices in the problem they have set out to solve, organized crime."

Burton quoted Thomas Jefferson and the Reverend Martin Luther King Jr. in describing the ordeal faced by Salvati, his wife, Marie, and their four children when the lowly mob associate was sentenced to prison for life in the Deegan murder. The congressman lamented over the fact that Salvati had missed birthdays, first communions, proms, graduations, weddings, the birth of grandchildren and other "priceless events in the life of a family, forever denied him because the FBI considered his freedom an acceptable cost of doing business with mobsters."

Shays spoke directly to Salvati as he sat in the congressional hearing room: "Thank you for being here. As a fellow citizen of a land that holds liberty sacred, let me say that I am profoundly sorry for what has happened to you. We can never replace what has been taken from you, but we are grateful for your openness and your willingness to share what you have."

Then turning to Salvati's wife, Shays said: "Your story of faith, incredible faith, Marie, incredible faith, family, your story of faith, your story of family, your story of courage and perseverance is a gift to your nation, and we cherish it. Your testimony will help ensure no one else has to endure the outrageous indignities and injustices you, Mr. Salvati and your family, Marie, and your family have suffered."

The congressman also spoke to Rico, who likewise was in the audience at the hearing. He had come to testify under oath and without a grant of immunity. Shays asked out loud during his opening statement how the former agent was able to sleep at night, describing his participation in the affair "disgraceful ... one of the greatest, if not the greatest failure in the history of federal law enforcement."

Also getting a free shot at the FBI was defense attorney F. Lee Bailey, who—according to Burton—had told the Massachusetts Attorney

General's Office that his client, Barboza, had lied and the wrong man was in prison. Bailey regaled the spellbound committee members and the audience with dramatic tales of murder, machine guns and FBI skullduggery, featuring Rico center stage. The famed legal personality told his eager listeners that Rico should spend the rest of his life in prison for suborning the perjury of Barboza, a ruthless killer Bailey had represented as "a favor" to two mobsters. It is easy to envision the distinguished lawmakers leaning forward in their high-backed chairs as Bailey told them how he dissolved the mad killer into tears by demanding Barboza remove his hat while the brawny lawyer grasped a .38 in his desk drawer.

Confirming the teaser preview of the chairman at the opening, Bailey colorfully explained how Barboza told him of succumbing to the FBI pressure to frame La Cosa Nostra Mob Boss Raymond L.S. Patriarca and others, and how Barboza wanted to recant and take a polygraph test. The bureau and Rico put a stop to that, of course, according to Bailey, who claimed that "... the FBI [told Barboza] to fire Bailey and don't take the polygraph test or you're here forever. And I'm quite satisfied that happened, since I was terminated."

None of the committee members or their lawyers questioned this account or Bailey's credibility, although they should have. The record shows that Rico had been transferred from the FBI's Boston field office months before any of the events described by Bailey had occurred and that neither Rico nor his partner, Dennis Condon, had any discussions with Barboza about his recantation or polygraph. When Barboza's brother called the FBI office asking that agents visit Barboza to discuss his contacts with Bailey, the FBI sent no agents. Instead, two federal prosecutors, including Strike Force Chief Theodore F. "Ted" Harrington, visited Barboza, who told them that Bailey was negotiating on behalf of Patriarca to purchase Barboza's recantation.

When the now-aged Rico quietly emerged from the gallery to take his place at the witness table, Bailey's booming baritone must have still been echoing through the congressional hearing room. Rico was 76 years old, in failing health and knew that at least one Oklahoma detective had a bull's-eye on his back. Burton asked him if he wished to proceed and Rico responded, "My counsel advised me to take the Fifth Amendment until you people agree to give me immunity. I have decided that I have been in law enforcement for all those years and I'm interested in answering any and all questions." Rico had been on the right side of things all his life.

His willingness to testify under these circumstances before an obviously biased committee was not the behavior of a person with something to hide. The record revealed a self-confident former agent proud of his FBI career doing his best to recall events thirty years or more in the past. He was generally respectful, but steadfastly refused to provide the melodramatic mea culpa that apparently was the goal of some on the committee. Shays made his suggestion: "... if I were you I would get down on bended knee in front of this family and ask for eternal pardon."

The retired agent may not have been what his interrogators expected, but his answers were truthful. He had a realistic, humble view of his role in the system. It was his job to find the facts and witnesses to the extent he and the FBI were able to do so, to provide them to the prosecutors and other authorities, and then let the justice system work. As Rico simply put it, he had "faith in the jury system" and it was the jury's job to decide guilt or innocence. "[W]e have a justice system and however it plays out it plays out. I don't think we convict everybody that is guilty and I don't think we let everyone go that is innocent."

Burton began the questioning by asking if Rico knew Salvati was innocent of the murder for which he had been charged and convicted. Rico responded by saying he was aware that Salvati had been tried and convicted. He said he had heard for the first time "today" facts that led him to believe that Salvati was innocent. Burton then asked about "Mr. Flemmi" and Rico responded:

> Rico: At one time, I had Steven Flemmi as an informant. He has admitted that before Judge Wolf and all of the contacts were exposed between my contacts with him and those contacts that were written—were introduced before Judge Wolf.
> Burton: Did you know he was a killer?
> Rico: No.

Burton: Did you not know he was a killer?

Rico: I knew that he was involved in probably loan sharking and other activities but, no.

Burton. Well, it's testified here by several witnesses, including the last two, that it was fairly well known on the north side of Boston that he was to be feared and that he was killing people, but you in the FBI didn't know about that?

Burton, certain that Rico was a scoundrel, revealed his lack of understanding of the facts in the next exchange.

Rico: Are we talking about Stephen Flemmi or Vincent Flemmi?

Burton. Vincent Flemmi, Jimmy Flemmi.

Rico: Oh, Vincent Flemmi. I think when I was in Boston I would have known that Vincent Flemmi had committed homicide.

Burton: Did you have any dealings with him?

Rico: Not really, no.

A little later in the questioning, Burton referred to an exhibit he thought was an informant report that Rico had sent to FBI Headquarters in Washington. Rico glanced at it and recognized that it wasn't an informant report but a report of something overheard on a microphone. Further, he hadn't sent it to Washington or anywhere else.

Rico: I don't see where, I don't see where I sent this. I can see what it says, but I don't see where I sent it.

Burton: It's exhibit No. 7. It was from the head of the FBI office there in Boston.

Rico: Yeah, right.

Burton: So that would not have been you at that time?

Rico: No, I have never been the head of the FBI office.

A short time later, Burton asked about Barboza. He wanted to know if Rico had used him as an informant after he knew he was involved in murder. When Rico responded that he never had him as an informant, Burton asked, "Who did?" Rico said that he didn't think anyone had him as an informant.

A thoroughly confused Burton, whose public statements showed he was sure Rico had framed Salvati, had begun talking about Stephen Flemmi when he meant Jimmy Flemmi. He didn't understand the difference between an informant and a cooperating subject, like Barboza, who is going to plead guilty to a crime and testify in court. He did not recognize what a microphone report was and thought it to be an informant report. He did not know that Rico was an agent assigned to conduct investigations and not the squad supervisor and certainly not the special agent in charge. Still Burton was confident he knew what was going on.

After more questioning by other members of the committee, Burton reentered the fray, asking about informant information that Rico had received more than two years before the Deegan murder. Burton said breathlessly that "Barboza was a known killer" and that he was "the only person who testified at the trial that put these people in jail for life and they were going to get the death penalty." He wanted to know why the informant information did not come out at trial. Rico explained that it was disseminated to the Chelsea Police Department, which had investigative responsibility for the case.

While key information from informants, such as the fact that Deegan was the target of a murder plot, was verbally disseminated when necessary, raw informant information was almost never released to outside agencies. It was not the bureau's practice to routinely hand over such reports to prosecutors (many of whom join the defense bar) in part, because most such information was hearsay of varying reliability. Furthermore, routine dissemination always carries risk of compromise, important to both the safety of the informant and his continued usefulness.

One key to Burton's and the committee's misunderstanding of these events was their view of Barboza as the "only person who testified at the trial that put these people in jail for life ..." In fact, although Barboza was no doubt important to the state's case, a great many witnesses testified at the trial, which lasted more than two months.

According to a hearing transcript, members of the committee appeared to have difficulty with Rico's responses. They either did not, or did not want to understand the FBI's role in the Deegan murder case. Rico did exactly what he should have done. He developed a witness and when it appeared the witness had information needed by the Chelsea Police Department, he passed that witness to the police. Rico made the witness available to local detectives, who—with the district attorney's office—questioned the witness and put together the trial plan.

Rico testified that his point of contact was John Doyle, a Boston detective who investigated the case for the lead prosecutor, John Zalkind. Rico also testified that he warned Doyle that Barboza could be expected to withhold information about his close friend, Jimmy Flemmi, and that Doyle was fully aware of the Barboza/Flemmi relationship. Zalkind, the district attorney, and another attorney who assisted him, James McDonough, both testified later that they—not Rico or the FBI—prepared and tried the case against Salvati and the others. The attorneys counted on Doyle and ten police officers detailed to the District Attorney's Office. In fact, during the Deegan case, Barboza was "kept in a safe house which was run by the Suffolk County District Attorney's Office," according to McDonough, who never had a single conversation with Rico. The detectives prepared a "booklet of events," or prosecutive summary, for the prosecutors, who had almost no contact with Rico or Condon:

"Mr. Zalkind. When I put this case in to the grand jury—and it was really, really voluminous—then I spent, Mr. Chairman, the next six months speaking with [Barboza] at least four or five times a week, with a detective with me at all times, going through every phase of the case. And I told [Barboza] over and over again, if I ever find out that you put someone in here that doesn't belong here, or you left someone out, that's perjury in a murder case; and I'll put you in. I mean, I made it so clear. I thought I had done everything that was humanly possible to keep the story straight."

Further confirmation of the fact that the FBI agents saw their responsibility in trial preparation as working with prosecutors preparing Barboza to testify in the federal prosecution of Patriarca came from Judge Harrington:

"When [Barboza] was interviewed on the Patriarca case, those statements were taken by FBI agents. When [Barboza] was interviewed with respect to the state Deegan murder case, those statements were taken by the District Attorney's office."

Zalkind told the committee he knew Barboza, having prosecuted him on two prior charges, and knew him well. He said he neither liked nor trusted him. Additionally, Zalkind had recently filed a habitual offender charge against Barboza that subjected the killer to a potential 84-year prison sentence, thus providing a large incentive for cooperation.

When a congressman advanced the committee's view that the prosecution "was based solely on [Barboza's] testimony," the district attorney protested that this was untrue, and that their investigation produced a great deal of corroboration for Barboza's testimony, much of which the prosecutor detailed.

The committee took the position that since Rico and the FBI were in possession of informant reports that Jimmy Flemmi was involved in the murder and no information about Salvati, the bureau had an obligation to disclose this as exculpatory. First, at the time there was no Justice Department or legal rule obligating or even allowing Rico to disclose those reports. As Zalkind explained, "What is considered exculpatory under Brady today was not the law in 1968. It had just come into effect; and what's exculpatory and what isn't has changed ..."

Moreover, McDonough greatly discounted the importance of the informant reports both from the police and the FBI as inadmissible hearsay of little value at trial. But regardless of the reports' actual usefulness to the defense, McDonough testified that "Barboza, in this trial, was cross-examined extensively about [James] Flemmi and the information in [one of the police reports]." It was apparent to McDonough that, during Barboza's six and one-half days of cross-examination by defense counsel, they were aware of Flemmi's involvement in the Deegan murder.

Rico was questioned closely by Burton and others about Barboza and the conflicts between reports from informants both before and after the Deegan murder. Several times Burton incorrectly referred to Barboza as an "informant" and was eventually corrected by Rico, who explained that Barboza was always a witness and never an FBI informant. During the questioning about the conflict between Barboza's testimony and the informant information, Burton said, "He's also a killer who didn't have much credibility." Rico responded, "I'm not one of his biggest boosters." A little later, Rico added, "I've never been a big supporter of Joe Barboza, but he was the instrument that we had. He was a stone killer, and he was put in a position he decided he wanted to testify. So we let him testify." Several months later, Harrington backed Rico up, testifying that, as the federal prosecutor who handled Barboza, Harrington—now a federal judge—knew that everyone up to and including the attorney general knew who they were dealing with. "They all knew it. That is why he was important. He was a cold-blooded killer for the Mafia. That is why we used him."

Rico frequently demonstrated his professional, ethical objective to secure untainted, truthful information from witnesses. Barboza was no exception. Rico declined Fitzgerald's offer to write Barboza urging him to cooperate against the Mafia because he thought that such pressure might not be helpful in getting the truth. He understood that cooperating subjects' information had to be corroborated. His relationship with informants and cooperating subjects was friendly and cordial but underneath he understood clearly that they can be dishonest. His handling of Stephen Flemmi when he learned that his important informant had bombed a lawyer's car clearly shows his detachment from informants and cooperating subjects. Rico generated the investigation and strategy that resulted in Flemmi's indictment.

If Burton gets the award for misunderstanding the issues and facts at hand, Shays gets the prize for most doggedly obnoxious pursuit of a preconceived theory. When his turn came, Shays jumped right in:

> Shays: Mr. Rico, I have been watching you for the whole day. I have known about you for 20 years. You are a person who basically worked for the FBI and then worked, in my judgment, for organized crime when you worked for World Jai Alai. That is my view of you. My view of you is that you sent an innocent man to jail.
>
> Rico: Your what?
>
> Shays: My view is that you sent an innocent man to jail and you knew it.

A review of the committee hearing transcript shows that Shays was not saying that as a result of performing his job, a bad thing happened or that Rico made a mistake or that he was negligent, but that Rico intended to convict an innocent man. It is not clear how Shays could have arrived at such a conclusion.

It might make sense to someone who believed Rico worked for an organized crime dominated company where all sorts of thievery was going on. And if you were a resident of Connecticut, like Shays, and read The Hartford Courant, you could certainly conclude that World Jai Alai Inc. (WJA) was a company dominated by criminals. You could think that any FBI agent who retired and went to work there was corrupt. And Austin McGuigan, the Connecticut state government official who couldn't resist being quoted on the subject, shares in the responsibility for Shays' misunderstanding of the facts.

Could or should Shays have known that the State of Connecticut apologized in writing for its search of the WJA fronton and the seizure of its records? Did Shays understand that Connecticut officials said they found no evidence of wrongdoing or criminal activity by the WJA? The simple fact was that there was never any prosecution brought anywhere that demonstrated any connection between WJA and organized crime.

Shays also demanded that Rico show remorse.

Shays: Let me ask you this. What does it feel like to be 76 years old, to have served in the FBI and know that you were instrumental in sending an innocent man to jail and you knew it? What is it like? What do you feel? Tell me how do you feel? I asked what it was like for Mr. Salvati to be in jail. I asked what it was like for his wife to know her husband was in jail. I want to know what it's like for you.

Rico: I have faith in the jury system and I feel that the jury should be able to decide the innocence.

Shays: This is what's fascinating.

Rico: Why? You think you can make a decision as to who's innocent?

At that point, Shays erupted: "You don't seem to give a shit. Excuse me. You don't seem to care."

Rico appeared to be surprised at the language and asked if that was on the record. Shays replied that it was and he was happy to have it on the record. Shays then began a series of questions in which he was trying to get Rico to say he was remorseful or sorry. He launched into a series of allegations, saying, "You don't seem to care. Where is your remorse? ... Tell me how you feel about Mr. Salvati and his wife. I would like to know ... You hold on a second. You can just wait. I wanted to know how a retired FBI agent feels about the facts that you learned today ... Why wouldn't you feel incredible remorse that you had a role to play, and you're saying it's ignorance but you had a role to play in the fact that an innocent man spent 30 years of his life in jail. Why no remorse? ... You have no remorse. Do you have any remorse that his wife spent 30 years visiting him in prison even though he was innocent of the crime? I want a word. I want something ..."

Finally, after this barrage of questions, Shays got an answer he wanted in the following exchange:

Shays: Do you have any remorse?
Rico: Remorse for what?
Shays: For the fact that you played a role in this.
Rico: I believe the role I played was the role I should have played.
    I believe that we supplied a witness and we gave them to the
    local police and they're supposed to be able to handle the case
    from there on. That's it. I cannot—
Shays: So you don't really care much and you don't really have
    any remorse. Is that true?
Rico: Would you like tears or something?
Shays: Pardon me?
Rico: What do you want, tears?

Shays did not want a conversation. He wasn't trying to find the truth. He never stopped for a moment to consider anything that Rico said. Shays wanted to make a headline and he could do that by portraying Rico as a corrupt agent and provoking a sound bite for the news. His constituents would see he was the defender of the little guy. So he tried to verbally beat up a man who had consistently done the right thing.

While the hearing was about the Deegan murder trial, Barboza pled guilty. He certainly was guilty. Defendants Henry Tameleo and Louis Greco were Mafia members who showed where they stood when they tried to persuade Barboza to decline to testify by bribing him and even offering to "whack" the victim of his stabbing. Why would anyone think they were not guilty?

Patriarca and Underboss Gennaro Angiulo had clearly authorized the murder. Limone, who was second in command to Angiulo in Boston, testified but had no alibi. The fact that Limone would be the one to direct Barboza to commit the murder was consistent with the way the Mafia operated. Boston mobster Ronald Cassesso tried to negotiate the perjury of Robert Glavin, who had been serving a sentence for first degree murder, in order to confuse the case. Mobster Wilford Roy French admitted he was there with Deegan.

Salvati, who was not a known member of the La Cosa Nostra, testified on his own behalf but couldn't remember where he was on the night Deegan was murdered. Significantly, none of the defendants availed themselves of any of the information contained in the notes derived from the FBI electronic surveillance of the office or cross examined any of the other defendants. No one brought up the fact that Patriarca had authorized Barboza and Jimmy Flemmi to commit the murder. One of the risks you assume if you become affiliated with the Mafia is that you may not be able to use information that would incriminate the boss in your own defense in a criminal trial.

Tameleo, Limone and Greco were Mafia members. To join that club, you had to demonstrate what you were made of by committing a murder yourself. If they were murderers and their boss approved the killing, why would it be hard to believe that they were involved?

Vincent Teresa, the Mafia soldier, wrote in his book, My Life in the Mafia, that Barboza hit Deegan on orders from Limone. He said French convinced Deegan he could make a big score if he went on the burglary with Barboza, Cassesso, and Greco. Teresa differs with Barboza on Tameleo and Salvati saying that Tameleo didn't authorize the hit and Salvati was just a flunky.

The case was weakest against Salvati, who may not have been guilty. There is a theory held by some familiar with the details of the investigation that Salvati was Cassesso's "gun guy" and delivered his gun to him before the murder and hid it after. But the case was tried in front a jury and the jury believed Barboza, who they observed for eight days on the stand. Apparently, the jury didn't believe Salvati.

Harrington, at the time of the trial the chief of the Organized Crime Strike Force, testified before the committee a few months later. He had no responsibility for the Deegan murder prosecution but did successfully use Barboza as a witness in the federal prosecution of Patriarca and others in a murder conspiracy. After reviewing the voluminous appellate record on the case, Harrington testified he believed that all of the defendants were probably guilty, although he had some doubt about Salvati.

And finally, many years after the trial, it was suggested that Rico must have covered up for Jimmy Flemmi because he had targeted him for development as an informant. Flemmi probably was involved in the murder—the FBI's electronic surveillance showed that he and Barboza were seeking approval to kill Deegan and all the informants seemed to agree Jimmy Flemmi was involved. But Barboza made it clear at the outset that he wouldn't testify against Flemmi who was his friend and Rico documented that as well as his informant reports that Flemmi was involved. The prosecutors certainly knew that Barboza had said he wouldn't provide information about Jimmy Flemmi.

Jimmy Flemmi had been "under development" as an informant and had been met only five times during a five-month period ending in September 1965. No one had a great stake in Jimmy Flemmi; he hadn't turned out to be an informant. Rico certainly didn't protect him then from charges of armed robbery with intent to commit murder. Why would he suddenly reverse himself and protect Flemmi from charges in the Deegan murder case? Although Rico would not know this because he did not participate in the Deegan trial, Barboza did testify about Jimmy Flemmi's participation in the murder. Harrington pointed that out for the committee in his February 2002 appearance:

Harrington: [Barboza] testified in the Deegan case that Flemmi
was involved in the scheme. The fact that Flemmi was not
named as a defendant, there could have been a lot of reasons,
but I think that question should be propounded of the district
attorney who made the judgment and not an assistant U.S.
attorney who had nothing to do with the case.

Harrington also testified that FBI agents told him at the outset that
Barboza was not willing then to give up his good friend, Jimmy Flemmi.
This probably was of little concern to Harrington because Flemmi was not
a target of the federal investigation aimed at Patriarca. And once Rico had
informed Doyle, the lead investigator in the state's Deegan case, that
Barboza had expressed this reluctance concerning Flemmi, Rico correctly
believed that his obligation was met. Rico certainly had no cause to go
around the local investigator to the district attorney.

The bottom line was, however, that Harrington, after studying the
voluminous record of the Deegan murder trial in preparation for the congressional hearings, was not then prepared to testify that Barboza lied during his trial testimony:

Harrington: I have learned more about the Deegan murder case
in the last 5 or 6 weeks than I have known in the last 35 years,
but he was on the stand for 8 1/2 days and was corroborated
to some degree by three other witnesses. So at this time, I am
not prepared to say that [Barboza] lied.

Rico did not even know who Salvati was until he was charged in the
case. Why would he single him out to be convicted of a crime he did not
commit? Apparently, Salvati was a guy who hung around the Mafia guys. In
the order of things, he was nothing. The convictions that counted were the
ones secured against the made members of the Mafia. The striking thing
about the committee is that for all the energy they expended these things
never occurred to them.

Rep. William Delahunt, Massachusetts Democrat, next probed about Rico's knowing Winter Hill Gang boss James J. "Whitey" Bulger, and Stephen Flemmi when Flemmi ordered the murder of the retired agent's employer, Roger Wheeler. Rico responded as follows:

Rico: You want to tie me into Bulger. I can tie myself into Bulger for you.

Delahunt: Go ahead.

Rico: Bulger …

Delahunt: Mr. Rico, I think I need full disclosure here because somebody will, I'm sure, discover that years and years ago I went to Saint Agatha's Parochial School with John Martorano.

Rico: I knew that.

Delahunt: I figured you did know that. So I really wanted to be forthcoming. And you should also know that John Martorano and I served mass together for Cardinal Cushing back in the eighth grade. So there are coincidences in life.

Rico: OK.

Delahunt: If you want to proceed, Mr. Rico.

Rico: The last time that Jimmy Bulger was arrested, I arrested him. I arrested him for two bank robberies and he pled guilty to three bank robberies. And that's my Bulger experience.

How disappointing the facts must have been to Delahunt. He and his committee colleagues may have imagined there was some relationship between Rico and Bulger. After all, Bulger was an informant for the Boston FBI. The truth is that the only relationship between the two was the one he referred to. Rico arrested Bulger the last time Bulger went to prison.

Delahunt was eager to get something so he asked if Rico had introduced FBI Agent John Connolly to Stephen Flemmi. Rico told him that was not correct. Rico, in fact, had departed the Boston field office for the bureau's Miami office three years before Connolly was assigned to Boston. The two men may have met once or twice but they never worked together.

But in the end, Shays was undaunted. He summed up the day:

"This has been a fascinating day for me, Mr. Rico. I think the thing I'm most surprised about is that it's clear to me that the FBI became as corrupt as the people they went after and it's clear to me that you have the same insensitivity that I would imagine in someone who is a hard and fast criminal. No remorse whatsoever. Cold as can be. The fact that a man spent 30 years in jail, no big deal. No tears. No regret, and yet you were responsible for that man being in jail for 30 years. You have gotten just like the people you went after. What a legacy."

Shays completely disregarded everything Rico had said. His summation set the tone for the committee, which seemed convinced that Rico and his partner, Condon, had knowingly conspired to send an innocent man to prison.

Condon was not called to testify. He had serious health problems and he gave a deposition. He was questioned about an "innocent" man, Salvati, being convicted as a result of his and Rico's work. He responded:

"Now, if you want to analyze things that I didn't do, or should have done, we are talking about 35 years ago; that's your judgment. As I sit here, I know that I did nothing to bring about such a thing. If innocent people were convicted and went away to jail, it's horrendous; and I never, never would have any part of that, or do anything along those lines. Not only because of the people involved, but for self motivation, too. How could I stand myself, or live my life, knowing that I had done anything to bring about an unfair, an unjust conviction? It wouldn't have been worth it to me; never mind the serious thing of innocent people going to jail."

It remains unclear what the committee said or did when they read the Condon response, but their appetite for bringing him before the committee was greatly diminished—despite a promise by Burton that the committee would be calling Condon despite his poor health.

"I understand he is in very poor health, but that does not excuse the things he is accused of doing and we have still have a lot of questions to ask him," Burton said. "I can assure everyone that one way or another, we will be interviewing Mr. Condon."

A review of the available evidence offers no support for allegations by the committee that the FBI framed anyone in the Deegan murder, including an unknown mob associate like Salvati. The bureau and Rico had taken the war on the Mafia very seriously, racking up convictions of important La Cosa Nostra bosses like Patriarca. Salvati was no prize for anyone, much less a legend like Rico. And at that, one would have to assume that Rico was willing to risk life imprisonment for suborning perjury in a capital case to nail a guy he had never heard of.

If the FBI wanted to frame Salvati, it would be ludicrous to suggest that Rico and the bureau would have made Barboza available to prosecutor Zalkind and a detective for grilling four or five times a week for six months of trial preparation? How could anyone in on the supposed "perjury plot" be sure Barboza could hold up in a lengthy trial, over what turned out to be days of cross-examination by some of the best mob lawyers in the area? There were no FBI agents monitoring the trial. The witnesses were sequestered. Rico never set foot in the courtroom. Condon testified briefly on one discrete issue, apparently as a state rebuttal witness. How could the agents know that someone like Barboza would not just fall apart under fire or rejoin the defendants, and expose them all?

Nothing contradicts the fact that Rico testified truthfully, under oath, to the best of his ability about the events surrounding the use of Barboza and the Deegan murder trial. Rico was willing to face the committee without immunity, without counsel, because he feared no question.

Chapter 26: The Princess and the $100 Million "Pea"

A FORMER HIGH school cheerleader and runner-up as homecoming queen, Nancy Gertner ultimately finished as valedictorian of her class. Later, at Yale University where she received a law degree in 1971, she became friends with fellow students, Hillary Rodham and Bill Clinton. Twenty-three years later, then-President Clinton named her to the federal bench. A self-proclaimed liberal known for her support of progressive causes, she published her personal stories in 2011, entitled "In Defense of Women: Memoirs of an Unrepentant Advocate."

In a May 2008 article, the Federal Lawyer, a publication of the Federal Bar Association, which represents more than 15,000 federal attorneys and judges, said Judge Gertner "analogizes her commitment [to justice] to the folk tale 'The Princess and the Pea,' the story about a princess who is able to feel a pea through 20 mattresses ... 'The just result ... may or may not be consistent with formal rules, provisions and standards.'"

A few months later, she said in a separate interview that judges need to understand where their personal values end and their judicial role begins. She used the story of the princess and the pea as an example.

"The real princess, so the story goes, had no trouble feeling the 'pea' under twenty mattresses and featherbed. I have no problem looking for the 'pea'—the just result—notwithstanding the layers and layers of legal rules that constrain me. Sometimes I can accomplish that result consistent with my oath, and sometimes I cannot," she said. "And the struggle has become more acute in recent years."

But the pitfalls of treating the rule of law as an obstacle, an impediment to the discerning judge who seeks a "just result," are on display for all to see in Judge Gertner's decision in Peter J. Limone et al. vs. the United States of America, in which she awarded $102 million to Limone, the right-hand man of La Cosa Nostra Underboss Gennaro Angiulo, and several others. Ironically, Judge Gertner's "findings of fact" may stand as a smear of an entire generation of FBI agents because of other judges' fealty to the law she so readily cast aside.

The swirling controversy, fueled by U.S. District Judge Mark L. Wolf, the media and Congress, spawned the inevitable rush of civil lawsuits. There was an endless parade of FBI "victims" anxious to reach into the federal government's deep pockets. The mobsters "falsely convicted" in the murder of Theodore F. "Teddy" Deegan championed by House Government Reform Committee Chairman Dan Burton, hit the jackpot when Judge Gertner drew their case. Much as Judge Wolf went out of his way to brand FBI Agent H. Paul Rico a criminal, guilty of "aiding and abetting the unlawful flight of a fugitive" in a 1999 case, knowing the elderly agent had no recourse, Judge Gertner knew that, unlike her legal rulings, her factual findings carried only slight risk of revision by a higher court. Lower courts' findings of fact are only rarely overturned as the trial courts are presumed to be in a much better position to evaluate the evidence before them.

In condemning the misconduct of the FBI she said ran "all the way up to the FBI director," Judge Gertner ordered the federal government in August 2007 to pay $102 million for the bureau's role in the wrongful murder convictions of four men nearly 30 years earlier, saying in a 228-page ruling that the charges against the FBI were "shocking" and the government's defense against them "absurd."

"Now is the time to say and say without equivocation: this 'cost'—to the liberty of four men, to our system of justice—is not remotely acceptable," Judge Gertner wrote. "This case is about intentional misconduct, subornation of perjury, conspiracy, the framing of innocent men."

Two of the men, Louis Greco and Henry Tameleo, had died in prison. The others, Limone and Joseph Salvati, spent three decades behind bars. Salvati was awarded $29 million and Limone was awarded $26 million, the rest going to the estates of the deceased plaintiffs, their wives and family members.

Judge Gertner, in her ruling, said Rico and his longtime partner, Agent Dennis Condon, knew that mob informant Joseph "The Animal" Barboza was lying when he said Limone, Salvati, Greco and Tameleo were involved in the Deegan murder in a Chelsea, Mass., alley in 1965. The judge said Barboza's story "contradicted every shred of evidence in the FBI's possession" but that Rico and Condon encouraged him to testify anyway.

No story about Rico would be complete without an accounting of this unprecedented lawsuit. But to clearly understand this part of the story, it is necessary to understand the known facts. This is the only way to understand what Judge Gertner did with the facts.

Rico's success in convincing Barboza to become a government witness was a very big deal at the time, the rough equivalent of the decades-later turning of Sammy "The Bull" Gravano against Mafia boss John Gotti. Barboza, motivated in part by the Suffolk County District Attorney's Office filing of habitual criminal charges subjecting him to a possible 80-plus year prison sentence and, in part, by personal revenge over the theft of his bail money by fellow criminals, decided to testify for the government. Barboza was seen by federal prosecutors and investigators as a gold mine of information about mob murders and other assorted crimes. Federal prosecutors and investigators, with the primary assignment given by Attorney General Robert Kennedy to force New England La Cosa Nostra Boss Raymond L.S. Patriarca out of business, focused their efforts on using Barboza to put a federal racketeering case together against Patriarca for the April 20, 1968, murder of bookmaker Rudolph Marfeo, who along with his bodyguard, Anthony Melei, were shotgunned to death in a Providence grocery. Ultimately, Barboza was used successfully as a key witness in that case and Patriarca was convicted, the first mob leader of that significance convicted since the 1940s. Barboza's truthfulness in the federal prosecution of Patriarca was never challenged.

Federal prosecutors and FBI agents agreed to make Barboza available to the Suffolk County District Attorney's Office and the local investigators responsible for the investigation of the Deegan murder, in which Barboza was a direct participant. While participating in the local prosecution, Barboza was kept in a safe house run by the Suffolk County District Attorney's Office. Assistant District Attorney John Zalkind ran the prosecution, assisted by a member of the State Attorney General's Office and a team of detectives and police officers. Zalkind testified that using a lengthy report assembled by local detectives—led by Boston Detective John Doyle—he questioned Barboza under oath before a state grand jury, which returned murder indictments against Limone and the others. Then Zalkind and the detectives spent "six months speaking with [Barboza] at least four or five times a week ... going through every phase of the case." Neither Zalkind nor his legal assistant, James M. McDonough, recalled having one substantive conversation about the case with either Rico or Condon.

Neither prosecutor considered Rico or Condon—or any FBI agent— to be part of the district attorney's investigative "team." Any questions Zalkind had were directed to Doyle, his lead detective, not the FBI. "We did nothing with the FBI that I can remember," Zalkind told Rep. William Delahunt, Massachusetts Democrat, during testimony before the House Government Reform Committee.

In her ruling, Judge Gertner would have none of this. The clear and compelling testimony of the two prosecutors that the FBI was not involved persuaded the judge that while the bureau was not orchestrating the entire investigative effort in the Deegan case, "Given Barboza's significance in the LCN 'war,' it is inconceivable that the FBI would have taken a back seat ... Rico agreed that he and Condon were 'on top of the [Deegan] case right from the start,' ... that he worked closely with the state authorities, providing them with information, helping them develop their prosecutions."

The implication of her ruling was clear: Rico, Condon and the FBI must have been behind the inquiry, remotely controlling every response by Barboza to the hours and days of interrogation by Zalkind and the Boston detectives behind closed doors over six months.

Zalkind testified that he was certain Barboza was telling the truth because "all the things that Barboza told me checked out piece by piece, and they were all right." Zalkind also stated unequivocally that no FBI agent ever pressured him to prosecute the Deegan case or to use Barboza as a witness. Although Barboza refused to implicate his close friend, Vincent "Jimmy" Flemmi, in the murder, Zalkind investigated Flemmi's involvement and was satisfied with Barboza's testimony, as was the trial jury.

Flemmi, also known as "Jimmy The Bear," was a mobster who worked for both the infamous Winter Hill Gang in Boston and the Patriarca crime family. In the 1960s, he and Barboza were so feared in Boston that newspaper photographers would attach notes on the back of their arrest photos saying "No Credit," for fear of being killed. He died in 1979 in prison of a heroin overdose while serving an eleven-to-18-year sentence for assault with intent to commit murder.

During the two-month trial, Barboza spent eight days on the witness stand, beginning with his entering a plea of guilty to the Deegan murder. Six and one-half days of testimony by Barboza was cross examination by defense counsel, including well-known Boston defense lawyer Joseph J. Balliro. According to a number of Massachusetts courts, including the Supreme Court, defense counsel's questioning of Barboza indicated that they were very familiar with the allegations that others beyond the accused were involved in the Deegan killing.

Barboza was very thoroughly questioned but Balliro and the others carefully steered clear of potentially troublesome topics such as what they knew about Patriarca's authorization of the murder. Balliro and one other attorney knew this because the logs of FBI intercepts at Patriarca's office had been turned over to them by the U.S. attorney's office in a previous case. Additionally, Balliro knew from his representation of Flemmi that, in fact, Flemmi had participated in the murder as law enforcement suspected. And Barboza, in fact, was questioned about Flemmi during the cross examination, with the defense also referring to the missing defendant in closing argument.

According to the testimony of the state prosecutors, Rico never stepped foot into the courtroom during the two-month trial and Condon testified only briefly on one collateral issue. Aside from that, Condon was also absent from the trial. Their presence frequently in the district attorney's office was attributed by Zalkind to the agents' responsibility for attorney

John Fitzgerald, a witness in the case and target of a La Cosa Nostra attempted murder. Other than that, they said, the agents had no role.

It is Fitzgerald's testimony during trial that may have been important to the jury's decision that Barboza was telling the truth about the involvement of two of the defendants, Tameleo and Greco. Fitzgerald, whom the LCN tried to murder while he represented Barboza, testified that Tameleo and Greco tried to pass a bribe through him to keep Barboza from implicating them. Fitzgerald told the jury that the bribe attempt occurred prior to Barboza revealing Tameleo's and Greco's involvement in the Deegan murder, something the jury likely saw as "consciousness of guilt" and corroborative of Barboza. Incredibly, Judge Gertner discounted Fitzgerald's account of the bribe attempt as relating only to the two defendants' desire that Barboza not implicate them in the federal case, where the two might face five-year sentences, and not out of concern that Barboza might send them to prison for life or the death chamber in the Deegan case.

In her ruling she noted that Zalkind had agreed that "Fitzgerald, a critical witness for the prosecution, was the FBI's 'boy.' ... It was up to Rico and Condon to 'tak[e] care' of Fitzgerald, 'right up until the point where Fitzgerald testified in Deegan and afterwards." She also wrote that Zalkind had called Condon to testify to "impress upon the jury that Barboza had not been coached or had been given any of the facts of this case by the FBI." Regardless of Zalkind's sworn testimony, Judge Gertner's view was that Zalkind "had absolutely no idea whether this was true" and given the way Barboza's story "changed in critical ways having to do with the plaintiffs, given what the FBI knew ... I believe that it was not."

This was a very thick mattress for sure, but not too thick to defeat one judge's extraordinary quest to feel the "just result."

On Aug. 25, 1970, Boston attorney F. Lee Bailey filed a petition for a court order allowing Barboza to take a polygraph examination. Bailey claimed that Barboza wanted to recant his testimony and produced what a Massachusetts court later characterized as a vague statement signed by his new client. Bailey also later claimed that he had been contacted by an interested party, a construction contractor named "Frank Davis."

Early the next morning, Barboza's brother called the FBI Boston field office and got a message to Condon, telling the agent that Barboza wanted to see agents and the federal prosecutors without Bailey's knowledge. The FBI refused to send agents, but passed the information to Assistant U.S. Attorney Edward F. "Ted" Harrington and Strike Force Chief Walter Barnes. They reported in writing to the Organized Crime Section at the Justice Department that Barboza told them that Bailey had "made [Barboza] sign an affidavit" but that he had no interest in recanting his testimony at the Deegan trial, which had been truthful.

Barboza also told the federal prosecutors he had been given money by Davis, who was a "front" for Patriarca. Bailey actually represented Patriarca in negotiations for Barboza's recantation. After learning of Barboza's "secret meeting," Bailey dissociated himself from his former client.

While openly skeptical of any information produced by the government, Judge Gertner displayed little difficulty accepting Bailey's word—although he was disbarred in 2001 in both Massachusetts and Florida for theft and perjury. Beyond that, what Bailey offered was 33-year-old hearsay from Barboza, whom Bailey himself characterized as a lifetime "chronic liar." All inferences from the available facts were drawn by Judge Gertner to show some form of FBI culpability in preventing Barboza from recanting his testimony.

"The FBI needed to keep its skein of lies from unraveling. That is, exposure of one piece threatened to expose the entire enterprise," Judge Gertner said in her ruling. "If Barboza came forward about his Deegan testimony, he would undermine the LCN prosecutions and expose the Top Echelon program and the wire. And so the FBI protected him, supported him, intervened when he seemed poised to recant ..."

While the record is full of detailed reports to FBI headquarters about the chronology of events involving Barboza, Bailey and the prosecutors, there is literally no evidence suggesting the FBI's involvement in any of the decision-making. Judge Gertner herself noted that the FBI sent no agent to meet with Barboza once Bailey announced he was representing Barboza, and the bureau refused to intercede with the district attorney's office to get new charges dropped.

"Barboza told [the federal prosecutors] how 'disturbed' he was about the probation revocation warrant, and how much he wanted the DA to withdraw it," Judge Gertner said in her ruling. "The [FBI] memorandum noted that the FBI had decided not to do anything to help. In fact, a subsequent [FBI communication] reported that even though Barboza's 'parole violation time' was about to run out, the 'DA's office' planned to continue his probation hearings, ostensibly to ensure his presence in the area."

The FBI was paying attention since Barboza was an important, high-profile mob witness, but the evidence shows the bureau did not call any of the shots on any of the case and applied no pressure on Barboza or anyone else. Rico had been transferred to Miami months before Bailey's surprise courthouse appearance. Condon was not permitted to have any contact with Barboza. The FBI reported information to the prosecutors and considered the whole matter to be within the authority of the Justice Department, the district attorney and the strike force prosecutors.

But Judge Gertner had no trouble "feeling" the FBI's orchestration of these events, its thwarting of Bailey's efforts to expose the truth. She felt that Hoover, the FBI director, and his minions must have been somewhere behind the scenes, pulling the strings to manipulate the strike force chief, high-ranking Justice Department officials and the district attorney. At one point in her ruling, Judge Gertner even praised the House committee's 2001 investigation, calling it a "stinging rebuke of federal law enforcement officials for tolerating and encouraging false testimony, for taking 'affirmative steps' to ensure that the individuals convicted would not obtain post-conviction relief and would die in prison."

Apparently unaware that many of the committee members were confused about which mobsters actually had participated in the killing, she nonetheless noted that "senior staff close to FBI Director J. Edgar Hoover were in possession of information that could have led them to the conclusion that Barboza was committing perjury and did not disclose it."

With all that is now known, it appears likely that Salvati was not guilty of participating in the Deegan murder. Even Judge Gertner concedes that Salvati was probably included by Barboza for his own reasons. In all likelihood, Salvati was added because Barboza believed Salvati had participated in the robbery and murder of two of his friends who were collecting bail money for Barboza. Salvati claimed that Barboza was upset because Salvati refused to repay $400.

Regardless, none of this had anything to do with the FBI. There is no evidence to support the allegation that everyone in the FBI's "hierarchy" would risk subornation of perjury charges carrying a life penalty to convict a low level hood like Salvati. This is true even if one assumes, as Judge Gertner did, that the FBI just looked the other way to please "their" mob witness.

Early in her ruling, the judge got right to the point: "The conclusions that the plaintiffs have asked me to draw—that government agents suborned perjury, framed four innocent men, conspired to keep them in jail for three decades—are so shocking that I felt obliged to analyze this record with special care ... I have concluded the plaintiffs' allegations are proved." The plaintiffs were convicted of Deegan's murder based on the perjured testimony of Joseph "The Animal" Barboza. The FBI agents 'handling' Barboza, Dennis Condon ('Condon') and H. Paul Rico ('Rico'), and their superiors—all the way up to the FBI director—knew that Barboza would perjure himself. They knew this because Barboza, a killer many times over, had told them so directly and indirectly. Barboza's testimony about the plaintiffs contradicted every shred of evidence in the FBI's possession at the time and the FBI had extraordinary information.

"The FBI knew Barboza's testimony was perjured because they suborned that perjury ... They coddled him, nurtured him, debriefed him, protected him and rewarded him—no matter how much he lied ... When Tameleo, Greco and Limone were sentenced to death, Salvati to life imprisonment, the FBI did not stand silently; they congratulated the agents for a job well done. FBI officials up the line allowed their employees to break laws, violate rules and ruin lives, interrupted only with the occasional burst of applause."

It is useful to examine what Judge Gertner cites as evidence for her brightly colored conclusions, saying that Condon, Rico and the entire FBI hierarchy knew that Barboza would perjure himself in the Deegan murder case because Barboza told them so. The judge's support for this statement rests on Condon's FBI report of an initial March 8, 1967, debriefing of Barboza. At that first meeting, Barboza told Rico and Condon that he would provide information about many or most of the unsolved New England mob murders. At the end of the interview, Condon noted in his report that Barboza told them he did not want to testify against his good friend, Flemmi.

In Judge Gertner's ruling, this put the agents and everyone in their chain of command on notice that Barboza planned to commit perjury. This is because Judge Gertner felt they had to know that Flemmi was in on the Deegan murder, based on reports of other informants and wiretap information. So, they knew Barboza was lying and intended to perjure himself from the very start.

But there is no evidence to substantiate that conclusion. First, as a threshold matter, Barboza's up-front declaration of his intentions to protect Flemmi and the agents' careful documentation of this statement is, if anything, a demonstration of good faith by all of them. Moreover, the record shows that Barboza's comment regarding Flemmi was passed on both to the agents' chain of command and to the strike force prosecutors, including Harrington. When Rico and Condon handed Barboza over to the Suffolk County authorities for the Deegan case, Rico told Doyle, the lead detective, of Barboza's reluctance to incriminate his friend, Flemmi. The FBI had no obligations beyond that. It is clear from the record that the detectives, Zalkind and the defense counsel representing the Deegan murder defendants all knew about Flemmi's reported role in the killing and Barboza's reluctance to incriminate him.

Time and again, the issue of Flemmi's role in the Deegan murder did come up, both in trial preparation by Zalkind, in cross examination by defense counsel at trial and in the defense closing arguments, none of which involved the FBI. In fact, much of the defense case centered on Limone's claim he knew Flemmi wanted to kill Deegan, and this was pointedly brought before the jury in the defense closing, which focused on Flemmi. While the FBI and the Boston police had other informant information pointing to Flemmi's involvement, this was all hearsay of little value in a trial without witnesses. And in that era, the FBI gave up informant reports to no-one, not even federal prosecutors.

Secondly, an initial discussion with someone like Barboza is almost never a comprehensive, detailed interrogation aimed at recording every detail of every crime involving the would-be witness. Much better to firmly plant the hook in the mouth of the cooperator, forego pressing him on less important details—until necessary—and let some line out as the witness becomes accustomed to his change of loyalties. All considered, it made perfect sense for the agents not to press Barboza about Flemmi, and leave that to the local detectives and the district attorney who would, if anyone did, care about Flemmi's role in the Deegan murder. Since Flemmi was unimportant to the feds, it was only logical they would let the local authorities be the "bad guys" on this point, from the perspective of Barboza.

The record also is clear that the federal strike force attorneys and agents cared almost nothing about Flemmi at that point. When U.S. Attorney Paul Markham, who had credited Barboza as being a major player in the successful dismantling by federal authorities of La Cosa Nostra in New England, testified before the House committee on the matter, he confirmed there was no interest in Flemmi. New England LCN Boss Patriarca was the big fish, the target given them by Attorney General Robert Kennedy, and that is where the feds' interest lay.

Judge Gertner's fixation on this point, Barboza's initial declaration about loyalty to his friend, Flemmi, is telling. It betrays either naïveté' concerning legitimate investigative techniques or a wide-eyed focus on her desired outcome—or both. At least some of both is demonstrated by the rest of her analysis: "Barboza's testimony contradicted evidence from an illegal wiretap that had intercepted stunning plans for the Deegan murder before it had taken place, plans that never included the plaintiffs."

The record is clear on this and the statement represents one of the most resilient falsehoods in the entire saga. The Patriarca office "wiretap," authorized at the time by Kennedy but later ruled illegal, produced a treasure trove of organized crime intelligence. It was in place from March 6, 1962, to July 12, 1965, and produced approximately 29,000 hours of recordings. From that raw information, 1,221 summaries were prepared. Just the amount of information and its dissemination was a logistical challenge. As the Justice Department put it in its 2008 appellate brief, "... it would not be particularly surprising to think that amidst this mountain of information, and at a time pre-dating computerized searches, Agents Rico and Condon overlooked this evidence ..."

Five months before the Deegan murder, in a single conversation, Limone was overheard warning Deegan about a murder plot, conflicting, according to Judge Gertner, with Barboza's later statements that Limone in fact solicited the murder. Additionally, just prior to the 1965 murder, Barboza and Flemmi were overheard getting permission from Patriarca for the hit on Deegan. First of all, those experienced in these matters know that criminals' conversations—intercepted or not—are regularly full of lies, misinformation, braggadocio and sometimes the truth. And they often change their minds. Five months in the criminal underworld is almost as long as the same interval in politics. Tomorrow, an LCN member might get an order to kill the same guy considered a loyal friend the day before. And how often is a gang member lured to the site of his death by a close friend with a friendly dinner invitation? This is why courts treat recorded conversations with great care and usually exclude their introduction without a witness to swear to their meaning, subject to cross examination.

It would be a reach to assume that the agents recalled all of the information two and one-half years later, when Barboza was first interviewed by Doyle about the murder. It was not substantially inconsistent with Barboza's story. Certainly, the intercepted information implicated Patriarca directly, but whether to charge him depended on corroboration of Barboza's story independent of the intercepts, which were not themselves admissible in court. Beyond that, the decision to charge Patriarca in Suffolk County or federally as was done was entirely in the hands of the U.S. attorney and the district attorney.

But assume that Limone's intercepted warning, five months before the murder, undermined Barboza's later testimony. It is a huge leap from there to the categorical assumption that Judge Gertner makes. She writes that this intercept proves that Rico and Condon knew that Barboza had to be lying about Limone. In fact, the summary containing the mention of Limone was initialed by Rico nearly two and one-half years prior to Barboza's first interview about the Deegan murder. To conclude that Rico both remembered reading this document and viewed it as conclusive proof that Barboza's first-hand account was a lie, is preposterous.

The other persistent falsehood concerning the FBI's "knowledge" of Barboza's intent to lie is that the somewhat contradictory information from informants gave the agents serious reason to doubt Barboza's statements. First, the informants of varying reliability, reasonably could not have been expected to know about Limone and Tameleo's involvement in procuring and approving the Deegan hit—Limone and Tameleo were leaders of the LCN and never were alleged to be triggermen. Their guilt was in ordering and approving the murder. The fact that some of these informants named Flemmi and others not ultimately prosecuted was interesting, but also not conclusive. This information was all passed to the local authorities responsible for the Deegan murder case, without revealing the sources of the information, as was standard practice.

Any informant information related to the Deegan murder was passed contemporaneously to the local authorities, as was the intelligence from the Patriarca microphone. Typical of the procedure is documented by an FBI headquarters communication catalogued in the congressional report: "3-16-65: Director Hoover instructs the Boston SAC: At the earliest possible time that dissemination can be made with full security to [the Patriarca microphone], you should advise the appropriate authorities of the identities of the possible perpetrators of the murders of ... and [Edward 'Teddy'] Deegan. Advise the Bureau when this has been done."

Note that those in possession of the intercepted communications, as well as the informant information, never considered this information conclusive proof of any "possible perpetrator's" guilt. This was viewed, appropriately, as highly important lead information.

Moreover, all of the same intelligence, including the information pointing to Flemmi's involvement in the murder, made its way into police reports in the possession of the Boston police and prosecutors when the careful trial preparation of Barboza took place in 1967–68. Whether these reports were assembled entirely from independent police informant information or incorporated information obtained from the FBI or some combination is completely beside the point. Those responsible for the Deegan murder prosecution had the information—as did those responsible for representing the defendants.

It is clear from the record that Rico long believed that Flemmi probably was involved in the Deegan murder. Rico repeated his belief in a 1970 formal statement to Suffolk County investigators. So did everyone else involved, including the defense counsel at trial, most particularly defense lawyer Balliro, who knew it for a fact. But beyond relaying this information to the detectives, what else exactly was Rico or any other agent to have done? Neither Rico, nor the FBI, had any role in deciding who was charged with what crime and in what jurisdiction.

When Paul F. Markham, the U.S. attorney in Boston, was questioned by the House committee about whether he was curious at the time as to why Flemmi had not been charged by the local authorities, he said: "I didn't think of it at that time, but I'll tell you why. There is (sic) any number of reasons a prosecutor would leave somebody out of an indictment. (A) He didn't do it; (B) He was going to be a witness; (C) They didn't have a good case against him. Now, all we know is that at some time Flemmi and Barboza, who was a bargain by the way, were down there and requested permission to do it and was given it. Whether they did it or not, I don't know."

To conclude from the foregoing, as Judge Gertner avers, that Rico, Condon and the FBI all knew that Barboza planned to commit perjury at the Deegan murder trial is patently ludicrous—the laying aside of "rules, provisions and standards" as to flatly disavow the rule of law altogether. How else to explain Judge Gertner's $102 million award to those accused in the Deegan killing—including Limone, who went on after his release from prison to become the head of the mob in all of New England.

It makes sense only to those who begin with the premises that the FBI, its agents and its efforts to investigate and prosecute the Mafia in the 60s were thoroughly corrupt and evil. And those assumptions had to include the agents' collective willingness to risk life imprisonment to falsely convict a few unknown mobsters in Massachusetts. There is just no other way to rationalize Judge Gertner's "finding" that "[t]he entire FBI hierarchy was implicated" in suborning Barboza's alleged perjury in the Deegan murder case. Barboza's procured lies, the judge found, were used to "frame" Limone and the others for the Deegan murder as part of the FBI's "program to 'get' La Cosa Nostra."

Judge Gertner's view of the FBI's corrupt plot to "get" the Mafia meant that the mob attorneys' claims had to be true, that former FBI agents Rico and Condon had to have been mendacious, clever tools of Hoover and his minions.

In her ruling, Judge Gertner wrote, "The FBI knew Barboza's testimony was false, that the plaintiffs' convictions had been procured by perjury, that critical exculpatory information had been withheld—but they did not flinch. After all, the killers they protected—Jimmy Flemmi, along with Barboza, and Jimmy's brother, Stephen—were providing valued information in the 'war' against the Italian Mafia, La Cosa Nostra. The pieties the FBI offered to justify their actions are the usual ones: The benefits outweighed the costs. Put otherwise, in terms that are more recently familiar, these four men were 'collateral damage' in the LCN war.

"The FBI, Barboza and Flemmi conspired to suborn Barboza's perjury. The FBI, Barboza and Flemmi conspired to put four innocent men behind bars. The FBI, Barboza and Flemmi conspired to keep them there—thwarting plaintiffs' attempts to win appeals and pardons. The FBI, Barboza and Flemmi conspired to take down La Cosa Nostra—by whatever unlawful means necessary. The FBI, Barboza and Flemmi conspired to keep their web of underworld relationships a secret," Judge Gertner wrote. "On any of these theories, the FBI is liable. In fact, their conspiracy consisted of many acts over many decades, designed to accomplish each of these goals, most importantly to keep their initiatives intact and hidden from public view and scrutiny."

But none of the alleged "many acts over many decades" is documented by the record.

In the same Federal Lawyer article that perpetuates Judge Gertner's "Princess and the Pea" philosophy, she complains that judges, unlike the officials of other government branches, are limited to speaking only "through their decisions." This a curious comment from surely one of a very few—and most famous—judicial bloggers in the country. But she does, it is true, speak through her rulings and in the Deegan case, she had plenty to say, which, according to her stated philosophy of "The Princess and the Pea," may not have been "consistent with formal rules, provisions and standards."

Chapter 27: Full Circle

THE VIOLENT STORM that caused veteran FBI Agent H. Paul Rico's agonizing death while shackled to a gurney in the hospital ward of a county jail in Tulsa gathered slowly at first, propelled by a young detective "consumed and obsessed" by the case of his career. But it gained critical mass when two aging mob killers found themselves facing almost certain death sentences in two states, deciding instead to take a well-trod path to freedom—making allegations of government misconduct.

And as surely as a tornado can lift 20-ton railroad cars from their tracks and drive straw and blades of grass into trees and telephone poles, that storm reached critical mass when its deadly path of deceit and deception found its way to the Boston courtroom of U.S. District Judge Mark L. Wolf. At that point, the Rico story had come full circle to the May 1981 murder of Tulsa multimillionaire businessman Roger Wheeler.

Judge Wolf saw an opportunity to hold an unprecedented, ten-month inquisition into FBI informant practices and the bureau's war on La Cosa Nostra, which quickly became a media and political circus. Rival law enforcement agencies joined the fray, benefiting from the single-minded zeal of a driven, federal prosecutor with at least questionable ethics. The Boston and national media loved the show and could not seem to get enough. It seemed as if everyone with a political or personal axe to grind got in on the act. And Congress could not resist.

Beginning in 2001, House Government Reform Committee Chairman Dan Burton, a former salesman, took over where Judge Wolf left off. The hearings lasted more than two years, producing much heat but little light on the history of the FBI's battle against organized crime in New England. But the publicity and congressional encouragement gave an important push to Tulsa authorities anxious to prove they were up to a big-city organized crime prosecution.

After all the hoopla, the innuendo, the media circus, the hearings and the long-term concerted effort to destroy Rico, one of the FBI's most effective weapons against the mob, first-degree murder charges were filed in October 2003. Tulsa District Attorney Tim Harris charged Rico with conspiracy in the Wheeler murder. It was a dramatic development. Detective Sgt. Mike Huff took his arrest warrant application to a friendly family-court judge and then flew to Miami to make the early morning arrest of the 78-year old retired FBI agent.

The four-page criminal information, filed by the prosecutor alone without presenting the case to a grand jury, is a lengthy, detailed statement. It alleges first degree murder and conspiracy to kill Wheeler, naming Winter Hill mob boss James J. "Whitey" Bulger, mob underboss Stephen "The Rifleman" Flemmi, hitman John Martorano, and two dead defendants— Joseph McDonald and John Callahan, along with Rico. As with so much uncovered in this saga, however, the charge finally filed against Rico, almost 23 years after the Wheeler murder, is revealed to be much less than meets the eye.

The criminal information includes details of overt acts involving the others, but only a single sentence naming Rico: "… on or about May 1981, John Bernard Callahan (Deceased) and H. Paul Rico provided John Vincent Martorano and Joseph Maurice McDonald (Deceased) with the general description, address of both home and work and the make, model and tag number of the vehicle of ROGER WHEELER Sr." The phrasing is careful and while charging documents are not meant to be comprehensive accounts of all the government's evidence, those offered by prosecutors in the Wheeler case offer little in the way of proof for the accused overt act.

There is but a single witness—Martorano, an assassin for the Winter Hill Gang in Boston, who has admitted to 20 gang-related killings and is known to his colleagues as "The Executioner." McDonald had accompanied Martorano on the Wheeler hit and a year later helped Martorano kill

Callahan, but McDonald—a former FBI "Top 10 Most Wanted" fugitive and wheelman in the Wheeler murder—died in 1997. The bullet-ridden body of Callahan, former president of the World Jai Alai Inc., was found stuffed in the trunk of a car at Miami International Airport.

Surprisingly, Martorano told prosecutors that only he and Callahan were present for a supposed exchange of information about Wheeler. He said Callahan gave him information about the Tulsa businessman on a piece of paper the size an envelope. The piece of paper was discarded in 1981. According to Martorano, Callahan told him that the now-missing piece of paper came from Rico.

Martorano testified that prior to the Wheeler murder, he had never had contact with Rico. He testified he did not meet Rico until more than a year after the Tulsa murder and never had any discussions with the FBI agent about any murder. And only Martorano and Flemmi claim that that meeting ever occurred, each placing the alleged session with Rico a year after the Wheeler murder at two different locations in Miami miles apart.

That is the entire factual basis for the single overt act connecting Rico to the Wheeler murder, notwithstanding Harris' claim in the criminal information that "H. Paul Rico provided John Vincent Martorano and Joseph Maurice McDonald (Deceased) with the general description, address of both home and work and the make, model and tag number of the vehicle of ROGER WHEELER Sr."

For that promised tale on the stand, Martorano escaped Oklahoma's death chamber.

Martorano, who personally dispatched Wheeler and many others with a bullet to the face, was allowed by Harris to plead guilty to second degree murder, with a sentence to be served concurrently with any other sentence. This prolific killer is now a free man, free to be interviewed on CBS's 60 Minutes and even, reportedly, to sell his story to a movie producer.

And then there's Flemmi—the state's primary witness, the only person who claims to have discussed the Wheeler murder with Rico. Without Flemmi, and without crediting Flemmi's testimony about Rico's alleged involvement in the Wheeler murder conspiracy, there is no case. It is just that simple.

Any analysis of the validity of his allegations must begin with his general credibility. The record shows that Flemmi lied repeatedly in sworn testimony before Judge Wolf in a separate case in Boston. In fact, the judge found that Flemmi's motive behind his perjury was his attempt to bolster his effort to suppress some evidence in his racketeering case. In that case, Flemmi faced prison—not the death penalty. But leaving aside the documented Flemmi perjuries and the deal to save his life; Flemmi's story is implausible on its face. He claims that in several meetings with Callahan and Bulger in Boston, Callahan told the two he wanted Wheeler murdered to clear the way for the purchase of World Jai Alai Inc. by Callahan and his close friend, Richard Donovan, WJA president. In exchange for the help of Bulger and Flemmi, Callahan promised $50,000 up front and $10,000 per week in skim from parking concessions after the sale went through.

Although Rico was not alleged by Flemmi to be in on the planned purchase for unexplained reasons, Flemmi said Callahan invited him to call Rico in Miami to clear the plans with the retired FBI agent. While it is true that Rico operated Flemmi as an informant in the 1960's, the last time they met was in 1969, prior to Flemmi's flight to avoid separate state murder charges. In 1970, Rico was transferred to Miami. Flemmi returned to Boston in 1974.

It is patently ridiculous to suggest, much less testify under oath, that even if Rico was corrupt, he would accept a telephone call in Miami from someone like Flemmi, whom he had not seen or talked with in 12 years, and would openly discuss a murder conspiracy over the telephone. Any experienced agent, certainly one as street-savvy as Rico, receiving such a call would instantly have pictured Flemmi shackled to a desk in a detective or prosecutor's office with the red "record" light on a tape recorder lit, playing his biggest bargaining chip.

It is not remotely plausible that Rico would do this even if one were to assume he was inclined to conspire in a murder in the first place. Yet it appears that neither Huff nor Harris questioned this obvious concoction.

According to Huff's arrest affidavit, Flemmi said "Donovan had a social relationship" with Wheeler and "that relationship would yield details of Wheeler's description, residence, automobile, office location and personal habits to Rico, who would, in turn, pass the information to Callahan."

It is true that Donovan, as the WJA chief executive, did have a relationship with Wheeler. He had visited Wheeler in Tulsa, stayed in his home, had seen his vehicle and office, and golfed with Wheeler at the Southern Hills Country Club, where the Telex chief would meet his fate. More importantly, Donovan also maintained a close relationship with Callahan, and it is possible or even likely that he was "fronting" for Callahan in negotiating to buy WJA at the time of Wheeler's murder.

But Rico had no such relationship with Wheeler or Callahan, records show, and prior to the former agent's transfer as a prisoner in 2004, the retired FBI agent had never been to Oklahoma. Furthermore, it was Rico who immediately reported information about Callahan's contacts with organized crime figures, leading to Callahan's firing in 1976. So, unlike Donovan, Rico maintained no such relationship with Callahan over the five years preceding the Wheeler murder.

If any information about Wheeler was passed to Callahan and, in turn, to Flemmi, it had to come from Donovan. There was absolutely no need for Rico to be anywhere in the loop. Certainly Donovan, who refused interview requests, never verified any such link. It may be the case that Donovan unwittingly passed the personal information about Wheeler to Callahan, thinking that Callahan would get his "friends" to apply a little "pressure." Donovan was likely as shocked as anyone else when he heard the news that Wheeler had been murdered. In fact, at least one witness reported Donovan's reaction to Wheeler's murder as so strong that he wondered whether Donovan had some very troubling inside information about the crime.

The only reason for Flemmi to include Rico in this story was that he knew the former FBI agent was his key to the door out of the death chamber. Nobody seemed to care about Donovan. Flemmi was easily smart enough to sense that giving up Donovan to the Tulsa authorities bought Flemmi nothing.

Flemmi and Martorano survive in the organized crime world on their wits and, necessarily, developed keen instincts. And while Huff was a well-liked officer in Tulsa, his objectives were likely very apparent to street-wise hoods like Flemmi and Martorano. The two mobsters also had 10 months of hearings in front of Judge Wolf to get a sense of where the interested law enforcement agencies were headed. By the time they talked, both Flemmi and Martorano were no doubt aware that FBI agents, including Rico, were considered the prize in this game. They had a lot of time to come up with a few "facts" to add to their tales. It must have been a little surprising for them to find how little it took to buy their very favorable deals.

As with Martorano's account of the actual murder scene, there was likely much truth told by Flemmi. All good liars tell the truth insofar as possible. In addition to using less memory, this technique provides elements that can be corroborated, though the plausible or verifiable points may be irrelevant to any important issue actually in dispute. This is a common legal trick, a logical fallacy built into more than a bit of what passes for "corroboration" in criminal cases.

Martorano's knowledge of closely held details of the Wheeler murder scene, including the unspent rounds left at the site, are useful to verify that he was there when it happened. That information does nothing to prove that his account of a conversation with someone several days earlier is accurate or that he witnessed anything beyond that scene. Details of discussions involving some real conspirators and the actual murder itself may be completely accurate, justifying a claim that the witness's story has been corroborated, while the little addition in the story is just enough to achieve the desired goal. Here, Huff's goal—making it Flemmi's—was to put Rico in the conspiracy.

Flemmi added a helpful detail, his old informant code-name—"Jack from South Boston." This also has been cited as "corroboration" for Flemmi's story. Such a fact might support the uncontested claim that Flemmi was an FBI informant operated by Rico in the 1960's. It does nothing to verify Flemmi's story that he was able to discuss murder on the telephone with the retired agent in 1981. Flemmi's uncorroborated account of the long distance telephone approval by Rico was thought to be insufficient, so a vague story about a short personal meeting more than a year after the Wheeler murder was added. While Flemmi's "interrogators" and government sponsors were likely not overtly aware that this was a concoction, they had to purposely disregard much of what they learned during their investigation to believe this part of Flemmi's tale.

As Huff's arrest affidavit puts it, "In August, 1982, after Mr. Wheeler was killed by Martorano, Flemmi says he and Martorano met with Defendant Rico at the World Jai Alai fronton in Miami, Florida to discuss the profits they were promised as a result of the Wheeler murder. Flemmi says that Rico told them no money was available because the planned purchase of World Jai Alai did not happen."

The facts show that Callahan was murdered on arrival at Ft. Lauderdale International Airport with two bullets to the head fired by his friend, Martorano, who testified that he fled the area immediately after Callahan's body was found in the trunk of his Cadillac on Aug. 3, 1982, at Miami International.

In 2008, Martorano testified that Flemmi and Bulger, already prime suspects in a bloody, public Boston killing in May 1982, wanted Callahan murdered in Florida specifically because they wanted alibis. If needed, Martorano explained the two mobsters wanted to be able to prove they were nowhere near Florida when Callahan was hit. This, along with Martorano's disappearance following the Callahan murder, make an August 1982 meeting with Rico in Miami a very improbable event. But add to this some of the other sketchy details given by these two witnesses.

While the two have differed in placing the location of this supposed face-to-face with Rico—variously claiming it happened in Dania and Miami—they agree on the purpose and length of the meeting. Flemmi's claim is that the sole purpose of his first personal meeting with Rico since 1969, and federal fugitive Martorano's first and only meeting with the retired FBI agent was to ask one question. As recorded in Flemmi's sworn October 2004 deposition: "… Joe McDonald wanted to know if there was any—if the deal to purchase Jai Alai was still active and so he wanted to hear it from Paul Rico. He wanted Johnny Martorano to hear it from Paul Rico himself. Paul Rico said that there was no deal, it was a dead deal. So that was the end of it."

Interestingly, in the same 2004 deposition, Flemmi specified that he maintained no ongoing relationship with Rico during the former agent's employment by the WJA from 1975 to 1995:

Q. What relationship did either you or Mr. Bulger have to Paul Rico while he was employed by World Jai Alai?

A. I didn't have any relationship with him at the time he was employed.

Flemmi went on to testify that the one and only meeting with Rico in Florida was the supposed meeting in August 1982, and Flemmi said he next saw Rico in Judge Wolf's courtroom in 1998. As told by Flemmi, the sole purpose of this high-risk meeting was to find out if the WJA sale was a "dead deal." In his account, Flemmi introduced the actual shooter, Martorano, to Rico. In other words, Huff and Harris accepted that Flemmi, in the immediate aftermath of the high-profile Callahan murder, would fly to Miami and walk the killer of both Callahan and Wheeler into WJA headquarters to meet Rico. The improbability of this only compounded geometrically when one considers that Martorano, at the time, was a fourteen-year FBI fugitive and, according to both Martorano and Flemmi, this was the first meeting ever between the hit man and Rico. Finally, Huff and Harris had to accept that Rico and his alleged conspirators would choose Rico's place of business, full of security cameras and witnesses, to have this supposed get-together of Flemmi, Martorano and Rico.

The alleged purpose of the meeting, according to Flemmi, was to satisfy the curiosity of McDonald, the Winter Hill gang member, as to whether the deal to buy the WJA was "dead."

When Rico's lawyer, former federal prosecutor William Cagney, first told Rico of this supposed August 1982 meeting, Rico was astonished that Flemmi did not come up with a better story. Rico thought Flemmi would have been smarter to concoct a story that they met at the airport or somewhere else more plausible. When Rico died, Cagney was making plans for a cross-examination of Flemmi and Martorano about the details of the Miami Jai Alai premises, which had undergone substantial renovations between 1982 and the time of Flemmi's telling of his tale.

What remains is that Harris and Huff were so anxious to close the Wheeler case, they believed Flemmi's story that a legendary FBI agent familiar with wiretaps and turncoats would discuss the murder of a major corporate executive over long-distance telephone lines with the life-long mobster. And that Rico would do so after having not laid eyes on his former source for 12 years. They accepted as fact that Rico would literally trust his life to a man who had betrayed his closest friends. Harris and Huff had to then accept Flemmi's claim that, to satisfy the curiosity of McDonald, then a Top Ten FBI fugitive, about the status of the Jai Alai sale, Flemmi was willing to fly personally to Miami to have the first face-to-face meeting with Rico since 1969 and to introduce Martorano, also a fugitive, to Rico for the first time.

Without believing Flemmi's story, there was no case against Rico. Harris certainly understood that, which explains why he was not willing to "pull the trigger" until Flemmi finally told his story and signed his deal with the government just days before Rico was charged in October 2003.

Given that the credibility of Flemmi was absolutely crucial to the Rico prosecution, how much did Flemmi's sponsor, Assistant U.S. Attorney Fred Wyshak, share with Harris on this score. Did Wyshak, as he handed off his star witness for this high-profile murder prosecution of a former FBI agent, fill Harris in about Wyshak's on-the-record characterization of Flemmi as a perjurer. It is unclear if Harris knew or was told that in 2000, Wyshak told the U.S. Court of Appeals that Flemmi, "a lifelong organized criminal," had given "belated, inconsistent and inherently implausible testimony ... concerning events in the distant past" before a federal judge. It is unknown whether Wyshak told Harris that Judge Wolf had issued an opinion saying Flemmi had lied under oath during the hearing and ruling that Flemmi had made patently false allegations of misconduct by some federal officials in his unsuccessful attempt to have his non-capital gambling racketeering indictment dismissed.

Wyshak had an obligation to hand this information over with his witness. He knew that any prosecutor would have an ethical and legal obligation to ensure that any judge hearing Flemmi as a witness had this information. A court would need this information to fairly judge what weight, if any, to give Flemmi's statements in support of, for example, the arrest warrant charging Rico in a murder conspiracy.

Whether Wyshak passed this information to Harris is unknown. Wyshak refused several attempts to interview him.

After weeks of attempts to contact him, Harris responded by saying he was unable to provide any information about the Rico case because to do so might compromise his future prosecution of Bulger in the Wheeler killing. Bulger was arrested in June 2011 in Santa Monica, Calif., after more than 16 years on the run from law enforcement authorities. It is unclear when Harris might get a chance at the former Boston mob boss, who now faces 19 homicides and also is accused of racketeering, conspiracy to commit murder, conspiracy to commit extortion, narcotics distribution, conspiracy to commit money laundering, extortion and laundering illicit mob profits.

Harris protested that he had received many boxes of material but was not specifically familiar with Wyshak's statements about Flemmi's lack of credibility as a witness. There is no indication the Oklahoma judge who signed Rico's arrest warrant was provided with this information.

Certainly Wyshak and Harris would and did argue that they knew any potential jury in the case would know that Flemmi was a hardened criminal with a long rap sheet and that he had cut a deal for his testimony. But the fact that a federal judge found, and the prosecutor now sponsoring this witness had found, that both had gone on record with the conclusion that Flemmi had repeatedly lied under oath within arguably the same case, is another level of impeachment entirely.

The only way for a prosecutor to effectively use a witness with the baggage Flemmi carried is to introduce incriminating recordings with admissions from the mouth of an accused. Few jurors would otherwise believe such a witness, particularly in a murder prosecution. Yet, so anxious and willing was Wyshak to prove the worth of Flemmi, for Harris to validate the pass he gave to the actual Wheeler killer, and for Huff to prove that he was right all along about an FBI conspiracy, they all were willing to look the other way.

When Flemmi finally cracked in October 2003, after years of legal and strategic wrangling, the prosecutors and Huff eagerly listened as Flemmi told his tale. Now, as this "lifelong organized criminal" gave his "belated, inconsistent and inherently implausible testimony ... concerning events in the distant past," they willingly swallowed every bit of it—hook, line and sinker. Rico's fate was sealed at that moment.

One might think there must be much more to this story, a question that prompted an interview of Huff in Tulsa. In most state criminal cases, particularly those that have only progressed to the charging stage, as the Rico case had, the lead detective often is the only person thoroughly familiar with all the evidence. Since Huff had led the Wheeler investigation for over twenty years, he would or should know the details of any "smoking gun" in the prosecution's case.

During a nearly three-hour interview, the only "direct" corroboration offered for Flemmi's tale of the phone-ordered murder-for-hire and later meeting were supposed hotel records in Miami Beach, Fla., in the name of Flemmi's girlfriend and Flemmi's use of his acknowledged informant code name, "Jack from South Boston." There was nothing more.

When one former Tulsa prosecutor was pressed on this, he sought refuge in "grand jury" secrecy rules, and suggested that Huff was constrained by the same obligations. When it was pointed out that Rico was never charged by a grand jury and surely corroborative information obtained outside the grand jury process should exist, the prosecutor quickly ended the interview and refused subsequent calls. And in our lengthy discussion with Huff, he never once mentioned a grand jury, or secrecy rules, or suggested that there was any information he could not reveal.

Instead, Huff tried to suggest that "other" information from informants and other mobsters, fantastic stories of murders and Rico's supposed homosexual trysts with Hoover and his deputy proved that Rico was such an evil guy that he must be guilty of the Wheeler murder conspiracy. And as Huff actually put it, "There is no smoking gun." It was the "whole picture," as Huff suggested, that proved Rico's guilt.

There is other circumstantial "evidence" cited by Huff: That Rico, early on, was named by Donovan as part of a potential group of Jai Alai purchasers. Also, Rico's almost exclusive reliance on the cadre of former FBI agents, many former special agents in charge, and their wives, for security and administrative jobs at the WJA was cited by Huff as yet more evidence of the breadth and depth of the FBI "conspiracy" behind Rico. It far more likely points to Rico's confidence in the legitimacy of their operation and a desire to maintain it.

The lack of evidence to support the repeated allegations of "skimming" perpetuated over the years is discounted by Huff—perhaps just demonstrating the skillful concealment of illegality. The lack of support for this claim from repeated audits by very reputable accounting firms, and careful analysis of any and all records by IRS agents and auditors—were dismissed by Huff as just failures to "ask the right questions." As one Tulsa investigator put it, "sometimes you know what is going on but you can't prove it."

So why, after 22 years, were these charges filed? Huff had been pressing for charges against Rico once Martorano's cooperation had been secured by federal authorities in Boston. Harris refused, in all likelihood because they viewed double hearsay testimony from a contract killer about a missing piece of paper allegedly handed to Martorano by the now-dead Callahan to be insufficient evidence. Harris was persuaded, though, to pull the trigger in late 2003, when Flemmi signed his plea agreement and told his story.

But why was Flemmi's implausible 2003 "addition" to the case enough to persuade Harris? With the backdrop of the years-long controversy in Boston, the hearings before Judge Wolf, the lengthy Congressional investigation and the successful prosecution of Connolly, there was tremendous background pressure on the elected district attorney to demonstrate that the "big case" could be prosecuted in Tulsa. Congressmen had even not so subtly pressured the prosecutors through Huff to prosecute Rico.

And after making extraordinarily favorable deals with Flemmi and the actual killer, Martorano, there was an understandable need to demonstrate the value of these bargains. After all, Harris had freed the man that admitted personally executing Roger Wheeler. The prosecution of the former FBI agent Huff had very publicly identified as the main culprit might just prove these deals worthwhile.

Finally, there was pressure exerted directly through use of the media, which could not get enough of the tales of an FBI agent conspiring with mobsters to commit murder. Some of this pressure was directly applied by Huff in the local media, in a manner sure to get the attention of an elected district attorney. Less than three months before the "special judge" was persuaded to issue a warrant for Rico, the Tulsa World published a front-page expose' of the lenient charging policies of Harris, something very unpopular in a law-and-order state like Oklahoma. The first paragraph of the A-1 feature story, entitled "DA, Law Officers in Feud," laid it out: "A simmering feud between Tulsa County District Attorney Tim Harris and law enforcement agencies has boiled over with allegations that Harris' policies are endangering the public. Police say Harris looks for reasons to reject their cases while complaining about his budget. Harris says his policies are no different from those of past prosecutors."

The newspaper noted that, "Police aren't the only ones complaining … The son of slain Tulsa businessman Roger Wheeler said Harris' office suggested that the family should help pay for the cost of prosecuting the 1981 murder case."

Later on in the article, the Rico case is addressed directly: "Those [cases Harris has declined to prosecute] include a key suspect in one of Tulsa's most notorious murders. In late 2001, Huff presented an affidavit seeking charges against H. Paul Rico and others in the 1981 slaying of Wheeler, who owned the Tulsa-based Telex Corp. Rico, a retired Boston FBI agent, was head of security for World Jai Alai, which Wheeler had bought. Since then, Huff has presented two additional affidavits with new information relating to Wheeler's death, but Harris has not filed charges against Rico. The most recent affidavit is a 28-page document written May 28. It alleges that Rico provided confessed hit man John V. Martorano with details on Wheeler's appearance, whereabouts and a vehicle description."

Not mentioned was exactly how, according to Martorano, Rico allegedly "provided" the Wheeler "details;" how Martorano claimed he got a piece of paper (discarded twenty-two years earlier) with handwriting on it from Callahan (killed by Martorano twenty-one years earlier); that the now-dead Callahan supposedly told Martorano that the now-missing piece of paper came from Rico. Those details may not have been given to the reporter; they certainly did not make the paper.

The pressure to file charges must have become immense when, less than three months later, on October 2, 2003, Harris, an assistant and Mike Huff, flew to Boston to sit down with Flemmi, their prize witness. They were likely in no mood to quibble over details when Flemmi finally told his long-awaited tale. Many investigators have experienced the same rush, eagerly absorbing an anticipated witness's story after a long, difficult investigation. The holes in the narrative become visible sometimes only after cold reflection, discussions with colleagues or review by a critical prosecutor playing "devil's advocate." None of these safeguards had much time to work here. On October 6, 2003, Flemmi finally signed his plea agreement and agreed to testify in Oklahoma. Two days later, Huff was in the office of the friendly family court "special judge," getting the Rico arrest warrant. Harris made preparations for his press conference.

In all likelihood, there never was any critical analysis by prosecutors of Flemmi's story. Once Rico was arrested in Florida, all efforts were focused on holding the aging lawman in jail without bond and bringing him to Tulsa. Rico died there in jail, after the prosecution successfully resisted attempts to have a preliminary hearing on the evidence. The next critical examination of the state's case by prosecutors would not have occurred before preparation for a trial that was never to be. The time for reflection since Rico's death in custody may explain the reluctance of Tulsa prosecutors to speak on the record.

An assessment of the Tulsa case offered by Rico's defense attorney, Garvin Isaac, concluded that "No jury anywhere in the state of Oklahoma would have convicted Paul Rico in this case."

Based on the available evidence, interviews of dozens of people involved in the case and a review of the thousands of pages of court transcripts, no reasonable jury, anywhere, could have found Rico guilty in the Wheeler murder.

So who killed Roger Wheeler and why? Much of what is accepted as fact by even some who have reported on this case for years is simply not true. There is no mystery about who was involved in the killing. Callahan contracted with Boston's Winter Hill Gang to make it happen. Martorano shot Wheeler and McDonald drove the getaway car. Bulger and Flemmi gave their approval for the plan and agreed to help, sending the murder weapon to Oklahoma. For their trouble, Callahan paid $50,000 and may have promised later profits from the WJA, once he got control.

Why Wheeler was killed is a little tougher to answer. What is clear is that the theory of "why" that has persisted for more than 20 years is almost certainly false.

There is no evidence the Winter Hill Gang had anything at all to do with the WJA before Callahan contracted with them to kill Wheeler. Moreover, although law enforcement authorities offered persistent suspicions, there was never any evidence produced that any skimming of profits went on anywhere at the WJA. And when Wheeler bought the company in 1978, Callahan had been gone for two years, fired thanks to Rico's reports of Callahan's socializing with Boston mobsters.

So newspaper claims that Winter Hill was "stealing with both hands from the [Jai Alai] gambling proceeds and they wanted to keep it that way" has no basis in fact. This fundamental misunderstanding is so important because if it is believed—if it is accepted as fact—then it is very difficult to believe that Rico and his group of former FBI agents in Jai Alai security would not have noticed. If Boston mobsters in fact, controlled the WJA "for ten years" how could they have missed it.

In fact, there was no evidence ever presented that there was any skimming at the WJA. The claim was conclusively debunked in 1986, when three law enforcement agencies, including the Connecticut State Police, apologized in writing for acting on false allegations of skimming and paid $100,000 in damages after seizing and scrutinizing Jai Alai records for more than two years.

There is similarly no support for the claim that the WJA was ever infiltrated by the Winter Hill Gang. There is not a shred of evidence that Bulger, Flemmi and the others had anything to do with the company until Callahan asked them to kill Wheeler in 1981. Not even Flemmi has ever said as much. At most, he told investigators that prior to soliciting Winter Hill's help in murdering Wheeler, Callahan had casually mentioned that he might try to get some kind of concession to open a jai alai fronton on an unspecified Indian reservation. Beyond that, Flemmi said, he and Bulger simply knew that Callahan had some previous involvement in the WJA organization, had been fired, and could not obtain gambling licenses in his name.

It is clear that Callahan was the driving force in the murder. He had the connections to Wheeler and reason to kill him; the others wouldn't have even known Wheeler without Callahan. The most likely motives were to get Wheeler out of the way so that Callahan could acquire some interest in the WJA; Callahan's desire to get even with Wheeler after being screwed in a business deal, or some combination of the two.

Callahan and Donovan had been business partners and Callahan brought Donovan into the jai alai business. From what Flemmi told investigators, Callahan expected Donovan to serve as a legitimate "front" for him.

Unlike all of the rest of Rico's associates, Donovan would not agree to be interviewed.

Wheeler was indebted to Callahan, who had been helpful to him. Callahan had assisted in arranging financing for the acquisition of the WJA. Callahan came up with the plan to deduct the value of Wheeler's contract with the jai alai players that saved Wheeler millions in taxes. Callahan was promised 1 percent of the transaction to acquire the WJA or $550,000 for his work. It is unclear if this was ever paid. Wheeler may have made or implied other promises to Callahan. Any broken promise could have led Callahan to strike out at Wheeler.

Callahan had continuing business with the WJA. He was president of the Haywood Wakefield Co. that supplied chairs to the WJA. The chairs were purchased periodically and in three years that Wheeler owned the WJA, the WJA did between $200,000 and $300,000 in business with Callahan's company.

Wheeler was known for being very difficult to deal with in business transactions. He would sometimes appear to agree and at the last minute back out angling for more in the deal. If he reneged on a promise with Callahan, it was unlikely Callahan would look to the courts to be resolve the issue. It is not known if Wheeler promised Callahan something that he failed to deliver or that he reneged on some promise and an angered Callahan simply had his friends kill him.

Callahan paid $50,000 for the murder, certainly enough for the Winter Hill Gang to carry out the assassination with no other benefit promised. The potential of a future share of profits was icing on the cake.

What proved fatal for Rico was the knowledge imparted to two career criminals—Flemmi and Martorano—that their futures were tied to implicating the aging former FBI agent in the murder plot. It may have been difficult, if not impossible, for investigators and prosecutors to interview the two mobsters without conveying information that they wanted Rico, but that is part of a professional investigator's job. Once a street-wise thug like Flemmi or Martorano knows where the interviewer wants to go, and realizes that his own life or freedom depends on going there, perjury can easily be created. This is particularly true in a case where the crime occurred many years in the past, records have been destroyed, and the only other witnesses are dead or missing.

So, Martorano describes meeting Callahan to get a piece of paper with Wheeler's name and address in Oklahoma, claiming that the dead Callahan said the piece of paper, immediately discarded, was provided by Rico. Neither the paper nor Callahan exist to disprove this tale. Flemmi invents two long-distance telephone calls from Boston to Miami, where Rico approves the Wheeler murder. According to Flemmi, Rico told him, sight unseen, that the retired mob-buster was now part of a racketeering enterprise with Callahan, and they wanted Wheeler murdered.

Flemmi and Martorano told substantially true stories of Wheeler's murder, but embellished their accounts just enough to implicate Rico and escape death. In Martorano's case, he bought his freedom. It must have seemed a very reasonable bargain. And it is little wonder that prosecutors and investigators never subjected these two witnesses to polygraph examinations. What is remarkable is that prosecutors were willing to charge anyone with murder based on such evidence, much less a 78-year old law enforcement giant such as Rico.

Dr. Joyce Rico, who visited her father the day he died, said he was happy until the end. He never lost that sense of self; he knew who he was and was comfortable with himself. He said you can give in or you can let it go—he was not going to let them define him.

When confronted with the facts, a senior police official in Tulsa observed that Rico's arrest and death occurred several years ago. He said, "It happened in the past. Why don't you just forget it." Those responsible for what happened to Rico should not be allowed to forget it. Some injustices deserve to be corrected. This is one.

Chapter 28: Responsibility?

OUR INVESTIGATION BEGAN with a casual discussion about the case and a few conversations with agents we respected, who knew and worked with H. Paul Rico. We kept our minds open to the possibility he might be guilty. Early on, we interviewed Connie Rico and some of her children. We liked them and resolved that if it turned out that Rico was guilty, or even if we concluded that it was likely he was guilty, we would walk away from this investigation lest we do harm to some very nice people who had already suffered terribly. As our inquiry began to produce results, we slowly came to the conclusion that he was innocent.

We both had strong faith in our system of justice; after all, we each worked in it for of over 30 years. We expected that in the end, justice would prevail. But as we developed hard facts that showed Rico was innocent of each allegation made against him, it seemed that at every turn another charge appeared that had to be investigated. We examined each, fearing that one would hold up and we would have to walk away. In the end, we never found a single allegation that a fair inquiry of the facts did not dispel. This time, justice had not prevailed.

So who was responsible for the tragedy that happened to Rico?

The media, particularly in Boston, did a miserable job of investigating the facts in the Rico case. Separate allegations involving FBI Agent John J. Connolly Jr. and his supervisor, John Morris, surely were serious and unusual, and merited significant news coverage. And while we don't know of another case where both an FBI agent and his supervisor were corrupted, the media—in looking at the "facts" in the Rico case—was swept away by the Connolly allegations and paid little attention to the possibility that the facts might not be as they were put forward by some very murderous people.

Boston Herald columnist Howie Carr led the charge. He called Rico a "gangster," saying he frequented gay bars and was "one of the most corrupt FBI agents in history." Carr said Rico participated in the Irish Gang War in Boston, murdering various gangsters during the 1960s. He insisted that Rico handled fugitive James J. "Whitey" Bulger as an informant and mentored Connolly into a life of crime.

None of this had any basis in fact. Simple inquiries would have revealed that Rico and Connolly never worked in the same office at the same time; never worked the same cases; that Rico never operated Bulger as an informant; and, in fact, Rico arrested Bulger on bank robbery charges for which he served 15 years in prison. Connolly found his way on his own—he didn't need anyone to introduce him to Bulger, whom he had known since childhood. Carr may have profited from an old adage that says, "Before you call a man a skunk, you should at least sniff the air."

Carr and many of his media colleagues simply accepted the stories told by mobsters and perjurers. The two sources of the most implausible allegations against Rico were Steven "The Rifleman" Flemmi and Frank Salemme. Both were multiple murderers and convicted perjurers, and reporters were happy to believe them without any corroboration.

We particularly focused on news stories saying the Winter Hill Gang had received a $10,000-a-week "skim" from the WJA for over ten years, asking one reporter where she got that information, since like so much else in the Rico case there was not a shred of evidence for it. She had no specific answer, saying only that it was "in testimony somewhere." During our investigation, we were unable to find any credible witness to corroborate the allegation. If the Winter Hill Gang was receiving $10,000 a week, it was making $520,000 a year and $5.2 million over ten years. With such a payoff, there would have been constant chatter by those involved. Yet even Flemmi claims only one conversation with Rico between 1969 when he fled Boston to avoid criminal charges and 1981 when Tulsa multimillionaire Roger Wheeler was killed. Criminals sharing in a $10,000-a-week payoff certainly would have had more than one conversation with an alleged co-conspirator over a 12-year period.

The media report that Rico had committed murders during the Irish Gang Wars is doubtful on its surface. Anyone with an understanding of organized crime would know that a federal agent known by La Cosa Nostra members to have participated in mob killings would be the very first chip offered up when they were charged with a crime. Rico's cooperating witnesses provided testimony in two cases in which Mafia boss Raymond L.S. Patriarca was convicted of murders. If the mob had anything on Rico, that certainly would have been the time to use it. Instead, they were so angered by the arrests they plotted to murder Rico.

Austin McGuigan, who served as Connecticut State's Attorney and was described by his law enforcement colleagues as a "barracuda for publicity," certainly bears some responsibility for his many public comments about "corruption" in jai alai. McGuigan was one of those government officials who, apparently, could never pass up an opportunity to comment. For a period of over 25 years, he was cited many times as an authority on organized crime's involvement in gambling, commenting often on the penetration of World Jai Alai Co. Inc. by "organized crime"—despite never having convicted or even charging anyone at the WJA. It was McGuigan's agency that settled the case involving its search and seizure of World Jai Alai records for $100,000 and letters of apology.

McGuigan certainly contributed to the poisoned public perception that corruption permeated the WJA and, if that was true, it would not be hard to believe that any retired FBI agent working there must also be corrupt. His most revealing comment came in 1999 when *The Courant* newspaper reported that his former witness, Harvey Ziskis, by then a thoroughly discredited "professional gambler," was locked deep inside a Florida prison where he was serving eight years for a greyhound racing scam. Ignoring the fact that Ziskis never provided reliable information about corruption in jai alai, McGuigan was quoted as saying, "I feel bad he can't stay out of trouble … He was on to something with jai alai game-fixing and skimming." Indeed: After 25 years of making allegations, McGuigan and his fellow authorities convicted no one associated with the WJA of anything.

All the news coverage and public comments about jai alai created an image of a corrupt sport dominated by shadowy organized crime figures. That image was held at all levels of society. Before our investigation, we even suspected that the sport was corrupted by organized crime. But our investigation found that the WJA operation was a remarkably honest one. While it would be impossible to prove that no game was ever thrown secretly by a player or players or that nothing was ever stolen from the business, everything that could reasonably be done was done to insure that the games were honest and that thefts did not occur. Audits were performed by a top accounting firm, bets were recorded on a computer that tracked winners and adjusted odds, the State of Florida monitored the betting and money counting, off duty police officers were hired, five former FBI agents worked for the company, every game was recorded on film, a coach observed every game and players were rewarded for winning with cash.

The WJA even ran an undercover operation in which it tested itself by making purchases and then checking to see if the monies were received and recorded. We can't think of much more that the company could have done to ensure a reasonably honest sport. To top it all off, the police and IRS seized the books and records of the WJA and poured over them for more than a year and found no evidence of anything illegal. In the end, the Miami based detectives and the Connecticut authorities wrote letters of apology and paid the WJA $100,000 to settle a lawsuit by Roger Wheeler Jr. In their letters the police and Connecticut authorities admitted that much of the basis for their search warrant was inaccurate or untrue. They also admitted they had no evidence of crime being conducted at the jai alai company.

Republican Reps. Dan Burton of Indiana and Chris Shays of Connecticut targeted Rico when he testified—without the benefit of immunity—before the House Government Reform Committee. The fact that Rico was willing to testify even when his lawyer was against it was one of the things that interested us in the case. Guilty people usually don't testify in Congress without being compelled to do so. Rico's attorney advised him not to testify but he had been on the side of law enforcement all his life and felt a duty to testify.

Burton, the committee chairman, led the way—revealing during lengthy hearings that he was supremely confident that Rico was an evil person, despite showing that he personally was confused by the facts in the case. Burton began talking about Stevie Flemmi when he meant his brother Jimmy, and he didn't understand the difference between an informant who provides information secretly and a cooperating subject who is going to plead guilty to a crime and testify in court. He did not recognize a document contained a report of a microphone recording and thought it to be an informant report. He did not know that Rico was an agent assigned to conduct investigations and was not the squad supervisor, and certainly not the special agent in charge. Still, Burton was confident he knew what was going on.

Shays stated at the outset he was sure that Rico had sent an innocent man to jail and he demanded to know how he felt about it. He ignored Rico's many responses and failed to initiate any real inquiry to get at the facts. He asked repeatedly if Rico felt any remorse. After lengthy questioning, he finally evoked the response he sought when Rico responded by asking if the Congressman wanted tears.

Shays concluded his testimony with comments that Rico had shown "no remorse whatsoever." He said Rico was "cold as can be," adding that the fact a man had spent 30 years in jail was "no big deal. No tears. No regret, and yet you were responsible for that man being in jail for 30 years. You have gotten just like the people you went after. What a legacy." We did not miss the fact that Shays' position probably was influenced by McGuigan, also of Connecticut, who assumed that any agent who worked for the WJA was a crook. McGuigan didn't know what he was talking about and it was apparent that Shays knew less.

Former FBI Agent Dennis Condon, Rico's frequent partner, summed it up best in testimony before the committee. When questioned about Joseph Salvati' s conviction and Barboza's testimony, he strongly responded:

"Now, if you want to analyze things that I didn't do, or should have done, we are talking about 35 years ago; that's your judgment. As I sit here, I know that I did nothing to bring about such a thing. If innocent people were convicted and went away to jail, it's horrendous; and I never, never would have any part of that, or do anything along those lines. Not only because of the people involved, but for self-motivation, too. How could I stand myself, or live my life, knowing that I had done anything to bring about an unfair, an unjust conviction? It wouldn't have been worth it to me; never mind the serious thing of innocent people going to jail."

Unfortunately, Burton and Shays weren't listening.

At the end of Tulsa Police Detective Sgt. Mike Huff's testimony before the committee, Burton made it clear he expected the local authorities to take action against Rico. He told Huff, "Mr. Huff, thank you very much for your diligence over these past 20 some years in pursuing this. Hopefully, it will come to fruition. We are going to continue to try to assist you in getting this case resolved regarding Mr. Rico so we will work with you."

Assistant U.S. Attorney Fred Wyshak in Boston had the serious responsibility of prosecuting Connolly and Morris for corruption. He was regarded as zealous, driven and as a competent prosecutor. He was, however, often overbearing, obnoxious and insulting for no apparent purpose. He helped drive a wedge between the FBI and other law enforcement agencies in Boston and, when it suited his purposes, he allowed inaccuracies to be presented as facts. For example, when he was participating in the Florida prosecution of Connelly and his fellow prosecutor said Rico had mentored Connolly into corruption, Wyshak stood mute. Wyshak must have known clearly that the statement was not true. As we have pointed out, Rico and Connolly never worked together, never shared cases or informants, and did not socialize.

Wyshak's unnecessarily insulting and obnoxious behavior, as reported by numerous other law enforcement officials, contributed to the divisions among Boston law enforcement agencies and made it difficult for good and decent men and women in the FBI to recover from the problems that Connolly and Morris caused.

We applaud Wyshak's drive that resulted in uncovering corruption in the FBI, but we fault him for making the deals he made with two murderous criminals. His two witnesses each murdered 20 people. His primary witness, Steve Flemmi, the only person who claimed to have had a conversation with Rico prior to the Wheeler murder, was cited by Judge Wolf for perjury.

Both would-be witnesses were facing murder convictions in states where people are executed. A capable prosecutor could have made a trade for their lives that would have resulted in their serving life sentences. Flemmi got a deal where he can serve his sentence in a posh federal prison where life can still be enjoyed. Martorano, who murdered over 20 people and admitted shooting Wheeler in the face, is a free man today, even giving interviews to *60 Minutes*.

Good deals for cooperating criminals are often the result of an impatient prosecutor who loses his nerve. The deals with Flemmi and Martorano were too good. It would appear that for all his bluster, Wyshak was not as tough as he would like us to think.

Tulsa District Attorney Tim Harris brought charges in the Rico case based on the testimony of two murderous thugs without any real corroboration. It appears Harris resisted charging a weak case until the pressure became too much for him. But the combination of Congressional encouragement to charge Rico and the local newspaper's criticism that the case hadn't been charged in spite of the fact that Huff had presented the prosecutor with several affidavits, finally wore him down.

A person is presumed innocent until convicted in court. They are not charged, arrested and then punished before being convicted. Rico should have been presumed innocent until, and if, found guilty at trial.

But Harris got mixed up in the order of things. The records show he sought to inflict punishment before there any conviction. He could have had Rico turn himself in but instead had him arrested in a pre-dawn raid. Once in custody, his resistance to a hearing to set bail was not justified. Rico was an old man, a hero FBI agent, no threat to anyone, not a flight risk, and in bad health. There was no reason to keep him in jail before trial unless the goal was to punish him. Does Harris bear responsibility for the veteran agent's untimely death? Consider the prosecutor's intent in opposing a motion to remove the shackles that strapped Rico to his hospital bed. When Rico died, the shackles still in place, Harris said, "We did our part and God took care of the rest."

While Tulsa Police Detective Sgt. Mike Huff was a small city detective well liked by his law enforcement colleagues, he simply did not have the experience and skills necessary to deal with clever big time criminals like Stevie Flemmi and John Martorano. There are, of course, agents and detectives in smaller cities who understand organized crime, informants and cooperating witnesses, but Huff wasn't one of them. Limited by his experiences, he did not understand organized crime or the contributions of an exceptional agent like Rico. Huff was the consummate "small town detective" who didn't relate to big crimes and big cases, someone who did not understand the unique talent it took to recruit criminals as informants.

Huff seemed to believe every rumor and unsubstantiated story that circulated. If FBI Director J. Edgar Hoover was gay, the detective was ready to believe it. He also leaped to the conclusion that Hoover had an illicit gay relationship with Rico. He assumed that because Rico was reputed to have "hung out" with mobsters, he had been corrupted by them. It never occurred to Huff that if you were an FBI agent with a mission to recruit informants you would often go where mobsters can be found. Rico's associations with criminals were neither malevolent nor corrupt. Huff did not understand that if an agent's business is the development of informants, he would often be dealing with criminals. It is true that good and decent folks are not able to provide much information about entrenched and reoccuring criminal activities.

When Huff began to move around in Boston, he fell victim to every sort of rumor and gossip promulgated by officers and agents of the many competing agencies. Huff seemed to believe every tidbit of gossip offered by law enforcement officers who didn't much like the FBI. He came to believe that Rico killed as many as 30 men in the Boston Irish Gang Wars of the 1960s. Yet, somehow, when Rico was so successful prosecuting the leadership of the New England Organized Crime Family that the Mob conspired to kill him, no one used this information against him. It is impossible that Rico participated in gangland murders and Mafia boss Raymond L.S. Patriarca quietly went to prison without mentioning it.

Huff's acceptance of farfetched stories is stunning and discredits his investigative conclusions. Our inquiry could not find a single serious misstep by Rico. We challenged Huff, Harris and others involved in the Rico case to document one instance in which the veteran agent was guilty of serious malfeasance or a criminal act. No one could. The available records and testimony shows that Rico was an honest man who believed in doing the right thing, had the courage to do it and consistently acted correctly from his service in WWII to the end of his life.

Judge Mark Wolf handled the case involving the federal prosecution of Flemmi, his decisions covering 661 pages. The documents reveal that he was looking for more than a simple case against a local mobster. Although largely irrelevant to his ultimate findings, the judge went out of his way to credit one of Flemmi's claims that personally damaged Rico. Based solely on Flemmi's desperate and dubious assertion, Judge Wolf branded Rico a criminal, guilty of "aiding and abetting the unlawful flight of a fugitive." Flemmi testified that in September 1969, Rico tipped off Flemmi and his codefendant, Frank Salemme, that they would soon be indicted for the attempted murder of attorney John Fitzgerald, allowing both to flee.

There is no evidence for this beyond Flemmi and Salemme's claims. Rico denied it under oath. Salemme's account should have alerted any sophisticated person that it was a lie. He described meeting in 1969 with Rico and Condon in which he said Rico tipped them to the indictment. When asked why Rico would trust him to be there, Salemme said "he was an interested party," adding that he (Salemme) was killing "Rico's arch-enemies," the McLaughlins, who were rivals to the Winter Hill Gang. Presumably Rico was grateful and, therefore, happy to commit the crime of tipping off two criminals on an indictment. A corrupt FBI agent who was so indiscrete he would commit a criminal act in front of a known Mafia killer would not last long. But Judge Wolf believed Salemme and Flemmi over Condon and Rico.

Our investigation showed that even though Flemmi was a top echelon criminal informant, Rico was the person most responsible for ensuring that Flemmi was charged with attempted murder. Rico's informants produced the information that Flemmi had committed the Fitzgerald bombing. Rico promptly provided this information and the identity of the principal witness to the appropriate agent whose investigation resulted in the charges against Flemmi and Salemme. But Judge Wolf didn't inquire deeply enough to discover all the facts. Regardless of what the judge ruled, it's obvious from the records and the testimony that Rico was telling the truth and Flemmi and Salemme lied.

Judge Nancy Gertner allowed her bias to influence her decision making, proving that she doesn't much like the FBI and never did. Ostensibly, Judge Gertner ruled that everyone in the FBI from Rico to Hoover conspired to convict four innocent men for a murder they didn't commit. Did she really mean to say that there was no honest agent, field supervisor, special agent in charge, headquarters supervisor, unit chief, section chief, assistant director or director in the chain? She awarded $101 million to four plaintiffs, three of whom, according to the FBI, were La Cosa Nostra made members.

A review of the appeal from the original conviction shows that three of the four plaintiffs in the case before Judge Gertner were guilty. She simply disregarded the inconvenient fact that there was a trial and that Joseph Barboza, the witness she said lied, spent nine days on the stand testifying in front of a jury who believed him. We can't say that Joseph Salvati, the fourth plaintiff, was guilty. It is possible that Barboza lied about his involvement, and we don't know whether he participated in the murder or not. Salvati was regarded by the FBI as a "mob associate" and we learned he was suspected of being the "gun guy" for mobster Henry Tameleo. Whether he was guilty or not, there is no evidence that Rico knew that Barboza may have lied about Salvati or that Rico had any significant role in preparing him for the trial. Barboza was turned over to the local prosecutor and police detectives who prepared him for the trial.

Johnny Martorano, Steve Flemmi and Whitey Bulger were thugs who lied and murdered their way through life. And their lies were nothing until they were empowered by prosecutors, congressmen, detectives, judges and reporters who somehow lost their way.

The public also bears some responsibility for its willingness to believe the most extreme stories without really examining any evidence. Just how many people accept the story that Hoover was a notorious homosexual who sometimes dressed in women's pink dresses? The idea presents a funny picture for some but what is the actual evidence for such a belief? Is it simply that everyone seems to believe it, or that Hoover never married or was known to have had a serious relationship with a woman? We don't know what Hoover's sexuality was, but we have never heard or seen any actual evidence to support the allegations.

The stories about Rico promulgated by reporters who failed to check their facts also have been accepted in large measure by many people without evidence to back them up. Some of the stories should fall of their own weight. Is it possible to believe that an FBI agent conspired to commit as many as 30 murders in the Boston Gang Wars of the 1960s while at the same time maintaining a gay three way relationship with Hoover and his second in command? All this, and it was known to Mafia members who were going to prison as a result of his work, but no one ever mentioned it until over 30 years later?

Was the World Jai Alai Company corrupt? Over the years, Austin McGuigan and others made many comments about corruption in jai alai. But how many arrests and convictions were attained of those associated with the game? What was the evidence that made this so believable? As readers, we must do a better job of evaluating reporting. Before we jump to a conclusion, particularly one that damages a person's reputation, we should wait for facts to emerge.

We held our comments about the FBI's role in this until the end. We spent our lives working for the bureau, and have great respect for our colleagues and the agency's work. If our children or grandchildren were kidnapped, there is no other agency we would want to handle the case. But the FBI of today did not live up to the standards of Rico's FBI of earlier times.

Somehow the FBI's Boston field office overlooked a serious corruption issue in house in which both an agent and his supervisor were corrupted. Corruption is a secret crime and is often hard to detect. But there are checks and procedures that, if employed by supervisors, should reduce the possibility of agents being corrupted. In the FBI organizational structure, the key employee in its field operations is the squad supervisor. It is the supervisor's role to oversee investigations and informants and to ensure that both, particularly important ones, are properly handled. Agent John Kehoe, who was there in the 1950s and 1960s was a terrific supervisor who made sure the Boston office was an effective force in fighting crime. He was assertive, knowledgeable, respected and vigorous in handling his duties.

He knew the cases, informants and the Boston agents who handled them and he made sure they were all going in the right direction.

Kehoe was replaced by John Morris, whose duties as supervisor of the Organized Crime Squad was to oversee and supervise John Connolly's handling of informants. But Morris was no Kehoe. There should have been clues that Connolly might have been too close to his informants. After all, they came from the same neighborhood and had known each other for years. Instead of playing this important role, Morris became corrupted himself, taking money and other gifts from Bulger and Flemmi. He sold himself for a few thousand dollars and a case of wine.

Connolly was convicted in Boston of one count of racketeering, two counts of obstruction of justice and one count of making a false statement to the FBI. He served his federal sentence and is now serving a sentence in Florida following a controversial conviction for the Callahan murder. We don't know the full extent of Connolly's guilt. Some agents we respect say it was extensive and he was a full-fledged member of the Winter Hill Gang. Other also respected agents believe Connolly was unfairly convicted in Florida. From the records and testimony we reviewed, we think it was proven in federal court in Boston that Connolly acted criminally in delivering a bribe to Morris, that he wrote a false letter attempting to influence the judge's decision and that he lied to the FBI about his involvement with Flemmi's defense. How much further Connolly's criminality may have gone is unknown.

Morris, on the other hand, admitted receiving several thousand dollars from Bulger and Flemmi and after a few years becoming so worried they would expose his corruption, he identified them as informants to a newspaper in an effort to get them killed. Causing the death of people, even bad people, is attempted murder. Further, Morris was the boss and had the responsibility to ensure that Connolly, the street agent, didn't get too close to his informants. Instead of fulfilling this important role, he joined with Connolly.

In the end, we were left wondering if Morris had been an effective supervisor, could he have kept Connolly from drifting into corruption? We don't believe an agent is corrupted overnight. Corruption usually happens slowly when a person begins doing little things that are wrong and getting into bigger and bigger acts of corruption as time goes by. A vigorous FBI squad supervisor attentive to the possibility that an agent could get himself into trouble can protect the agent, himself and the FBI. Morris failed himself, Connolly and the FBI.

The system broke down and we think Morris, who held the higher rank, was as responsible as Connolly. Giving a complete pass to Morris for his testimony was wrong. A prosecutor with nerve should have been able to negotiate a plea from Morris in return for his cooperation. Wyshak gave a lot of good deals to a lot of bad people.

The scandal in the Boston FBI involving both an agent and his supervisor energized all the FBI's critics and made it easy to believe rumors and improbable stories about the bureau. If an FBI agent and his supervisor could both be corrupted, it would be easy to believe almost anything else. It was not much of a leap to conclude that Rico, an agent who marched to a different beat, also had been corrupted. Why else would you take the word of a couple of mass murderers desperately trying to escape the death penalty?

But the scandal had one other important consequence for the Rico story that no one seems to have noticed: it paralyzed the FBI. Once it began to play out, more than anything else, the FBI leadership feared doing anything that would appear to be supporting a "corrupt" agent. Notwithstanding Huff's fears that the bureau was interfering with his investigation, it is clear the FBI withdrew from the allegations that Rico was involved and provided no support to the agent lest the bureau be seen as interfering with a local criminal prosecution. After all, Congress, the media, judges and McGuigan all seemed convinced that Rico was guilty.

We believe it is the duty of leaders to support their worthy subordinates even when that is difficult and that Rico was an employee who certainly was worthy of support. Frankly, an honest employee must be defended even if doing so results in a negative impact on the organization—you can't justify allowing an individual to be hurt to protect an agency.

When the allegations against Rico arose, no one knew if they were true but the FBI had an obligation to investigate to find out. Only the FBI had the resources to properly evaluate Rico's work and the allegations about him. The FBI had all his informant reports, they knew exactly how much damage he did to the Mafia and the many criminal enterprises in Boston including the Winter Hill Gang. The bureau's leadership could have done the same job that we did in a fraction of the time it took us but they passed on this important responsibility. Instead, they opened a professional responsibility case and quickly referred it to the local authorities. They got as far away from Rico as they could.

It is inexcusable that the leadership of the FBI failed to fully investigate the entire case pertaining to Rico. If they had carefully and completely pursued the investigation, they would have found what we found, and they could have joined the defense of their agent. But he was long retired and few on-board knew him well, so, fearing a negative public image, they maintained a safe "hands off" posture and they let Rico die shackled to a bed in Tulsa.

A reader might ask what we expect from writing this book. The story is very complicated and there has been so much written that takes a different view, it may be very hard to persuade many that an injustice has been done. After all, judge after judge and reporter after reporter has referred to Rico as a villain.

As we found the facts, we debated how we could correct the gross inaccuracies in the story of Rico that have been accepted by the public. While we investigated and wrote, one judge after another decided cases citing Rico as a rogue agent and a criminal. News reports referring derogatorily to Rico were frequent. Our hearts sank every time another verdict was rendered or news report was published; we knew the mountain we were climbing grew taller with each one. We decided that the only sensible course of action was to just tell the story and let the reader see what we have learned. Public acceptance of the facts we have found is beyond our control. As we wrote, we became comfortable with the idea that all we can do is record what happened and let the truth speak for itself.

This book is not for Judge Wolf or Judge Gertner or Austin McGuigan or Fred Wyshak. They have their version of the story and they must live with the part they have played in it. We doubt they would change their views.

This book is for FBI agents, police officers and citizens who are fair minded and interested in the truth. It is our hope they will see what we saw. And, most importantly, this book is for Connie Rico and her children. They knew the truth about Paul Rico before we started.

Acknowledgments

Joe Wolfinger and Chris Kerr conducted more than 100 interviews to learn what happened in the criminal case against FBI Agent H. Paul Rico, including many with retired agents and current and former detectives, police officers and deputies. They relied heavily on those with first-hand knowledge of Rico and his career, many of whom worked with him during his time with the bureau. Those interviewed included retired Special Agents Bob Mackechney, Ed Clark, Pat McCann, Bob Lawson, Gerald Montanari, Gene Flynn, John Gamel, Bob Hargraves, Tom Lyons, Fran Joyce, Joseph Frechette, Jack Barrett, Brad Benson, John Connolly, Stan Moody, Dick Egan, Al Koehler, Graham "Des" Desvernine, Bill Hagmaier, Jim Darcy, Anthony Amoroso, Tom Baker, Bill Murphy, Tom Diehl, Dave Divan, Jim Ring, Pat Patterson, Jeff Lampinski, Mike Wolfe, Jack Kelly, Gerald D. Coakley, Jim McKenzie, Bill Ervin, Neil Welch, Jim Freeman, Barry Mawn, Ted Foley, Craig Dotlo and Tom Kuker.

Rico's administrative assistant and former FBI secretary Janet Dowd had the best assessment of the likelihood that the veteran agent would murder his boss. She said he knew he had a great job in which he made good money, was furnished a car, had paid trips to Spain to watch jai alai, had his country club membership paid, and had an expense account. "You have all this, and you're going to kill (your boss)?"

As word of the project spread throughout the FBI community, there were unsolicited offers of support—including a $50 check from former Agent Colin Dunningan, whom Wolfinger and Kerr had never met. Told of the check, Connie Rico was quite touched.

Important information for the Rico investigation also came from William Cagney, former career federal prosecutor and Rico's attorney; Roger Wheeler Jr., who took over the primary responsibility for managing WJA after his father was murdered; Senior Judge Edward F. Harrington; and David K. McKown, a former First National Bank of Boston (FNB) official.

The many law enforcement officers, attorneys and prosecutors interviewed included Tulsa Police Detective Sgt. Mike Huff; Barbara Hurst, deputy public defender in Providence, R.I.; Tom Dickinson, former assistant attorney general for the State of Rhode Island; District Attorney Tim Harris in Tulsa, Okla.; Capt. Tom Huckabee and Sgt. Chuck Jordan of the Tulsa County Sheriff's Office; Vin Vespia, chief of police in South Kingston, R.I.; Tommy Griffin, retired Rhode Island state trooper; Bill Charlton, former Brookline, Mass., police officer; John Farrell, retired chief of detectives at the Metro-Dade Police Department; Greg Smith, former Metro-Dade detective; Ed Gonzalez, former Metro-Dade deputy chief and director of the U.S. Marshals Service; Ron Palmer, former chief of police in Tulsa; and Brian Edwards, retired undersheriff at the Tulsa County Sheriff's Office.

Connie Rico and her children—Dr. M. Joyce Rico, Suzanne Rico Brown, John Rico, Christine Rico and Melissa Rico Ferrari—provided valuable information and insight about their family's life.

Assistant U.S. Attorney Fred Wyshak and former Connecticut State's Attorney Austin McGuigan declined requests for interviews.

Wolfinger and Kerr are particularly indebted to those who provided both key information and direction, including Former FBI Acting Director Floyd Clarke, who said there was little chance that Rico had tipped Steven Flemmi and Frank Salemme to their 1969 indictment; Jim Sturgis, retired legal attaché and attorney who reviewed the voluminous federal court records in the Rico case showing that the police who searched the WJA settled the company's lawsuit with apologies and a $100,000 payment; Sean McWeeney, retired chief of the FBI Organized Crime Section, who provided details and analysis of Rico's successful career against organized crime; Rico's FBI partner, Dennis Condon; Alan Trustman, Rico's friend and boss at the WJA and author of the screenplay for The Thomas Crown Affair, who provided background about the WJA and Rico's role; Ken Tomlinson, retired editor in chief at Reader's Digest, who read the original Rico manuscript and offered both criticism and reassurance; Ambassador Fred J. Eckert and Andy Kurins, who provided publishing options; and Marty Taylor, author and friend, who read the first few chapters and provided a critique that redirected the project.

That redirection came in the form of a collaborative rewriting effort by Jerry Seper, a veteran newspaper reporter and editor, who reorganized and refocused the Rico project after reviewing hundreds of documents, interviews and court records that had been collected as a part of the project.

And, of course, the project benefitted immeasurably from the encouragement, evaluation of our drafts and patience of our wives Ginevra, Lisa and Myrna.

The Authors

Joe Wolfinger and Chris Kerr are retired FBI agents who never met H. Paul Rico. They are, however, both experienced and veteran investigators. Both are attorneys.

Kerr enjoyed a 33-year career in the FBI, beginning as a support employee in the busy Los Angeles field office. He worked briefly as an analyst at FBI Headquarters in Washington, D.C., and then was selected as a special agent. He spent 26 years primarily as case agent on organized crime and drug cases in Philadelphia, Washington, D.C., and Tampa, and also served as a Criminal Division agent supervisor at FBI Headquarters. Kerr received many awards and commendations from the FBI and U.S. Attorney's Offices for these investigations, the latest a 2007 award from the U.S. Attorney in Tampa, Florida for his work running a long-term multi-agency organized crime prosecution . He was elected by his peers to three terms on the National Executive Board of the FBI Agents Association, which represents 80 percent of the bureau's agents. He was also elected as national co-chair of the FBI Special Agents Advisory Committee, the bureau's in-house agents advisory group. When Kerr retired, he received his law degree from Stetson University Law School and began a career as a criminal defense lawyer.

Wolfinger's career spanned 30 years and included several major, high-profile investigations and assignments, including his supervision of the counterintelligence squad in Norfolk, Va., that apprehended John Walker, the retired U.S. Navy chief warrant officer and communications specialist convicted of spying for the Soviet Union over a 17 year period in what The New York Times described as the "most damaging Soviet spy ring in history." After graduation from the University of South Carolina Law School, he entered the FBI as a special agent and rose through a variety of positions—serving as a squad supervisor, inspector, special agent in charge and, lastly, as assistant director in charge of the FBI Academy at Quantico, Va. For the past twelve years, Wolfinger has served pro bono as the executive director of the Major County Sheriffs' Association.

Jerry Seper has been a newspaper reporter and editor for more than 30 years and currently is the Investigative Editor at The Washington Times in Washington, D.C. He held a similar position at The Arizona Republic in Phoenix, named to that post after Republic reporter Don Bolles was blown up in his car in a mob assassination. Seper is the winner of numerous writing and reporting awards, including "Newsperson of the Year" in Arizona and the Barnet Nover Award for Best Investigative Reporting by the White House Correspondents Association. He is a U.S. Navy veteran, having served aboard a gunfire support and down pilot rescue destroyer during the Vietnam War. He also served as a police officer in the Los Angeles area.